Pioneers of the Colorado Parks

Pioneers of the Colorado Parks

Richard Barth

The CAXTON PRINTERS, Ltd.
Caldwell, Idaho
1997

Library of Congress Cataloging-in-Publication Data

Barth, Richard C., 1943 –
Pioneers of the Colorado Parks / Richard C. Barth.
p. cm
Includes bibliographical references (p.) and index.
ISBN 0-87004-381-1 (paper)

1. North Park (Colo.) – Biography – Anecdotes. 2. Middle Park (Colo) – Biography – Anecdotes. 3. South Park (Colo.) – Biography – Anecdotes. 4. Frontier and pioneer life – Colorado – North Park – Anecdotes. 5. Frontier and pioneer life – Colorado – Middle Park – Anedcdotes. 6. Frontier and pioneer life – Colorado – South Park – Anecdotes. I. Title.

F782.J3B37 1997
978.8'66 – dc21 97-36878
CIP

Lithographed and bound in the United States of America by
The Caxton Printers, Ltd.
Caldwell, Idaho
162275

Dedication

This book is dedicated to the historical preservation organizations in North, Middle, and South Parks. Without their efforts, much of our past would be lost. Royalties from the sale of this book will be donated to these organizations.

Acknowledgements

For their encouragement and assistance in locating historical materials, I would like to thank Hazel Gresham, North Park historian, Sue Spearing and Jean Miller, Middle Park historians, and Carol Davis and Harold Warren, South Park historians. The staff in the Western History Department of the Denver Public Library was extremely helpful, especially Phil Panum, Randel Metz, and Bruce Hansen. Appreciation is also extended to the library staff at the Colorado Historical Society. I would like to thank Kevin Dwyer at Front Range Community College for his expertise in locating obscure documents and Alice Levine for her thorough edit of the manuscript. Bruce Tilsley deserves recognition for his illustrating ability and patience as I requested changes.

Special appreciation is extended to my wife, Ruth, who was always available to edit chapters and encourage me during this project.

Contents

Maps

Colorado's Parks

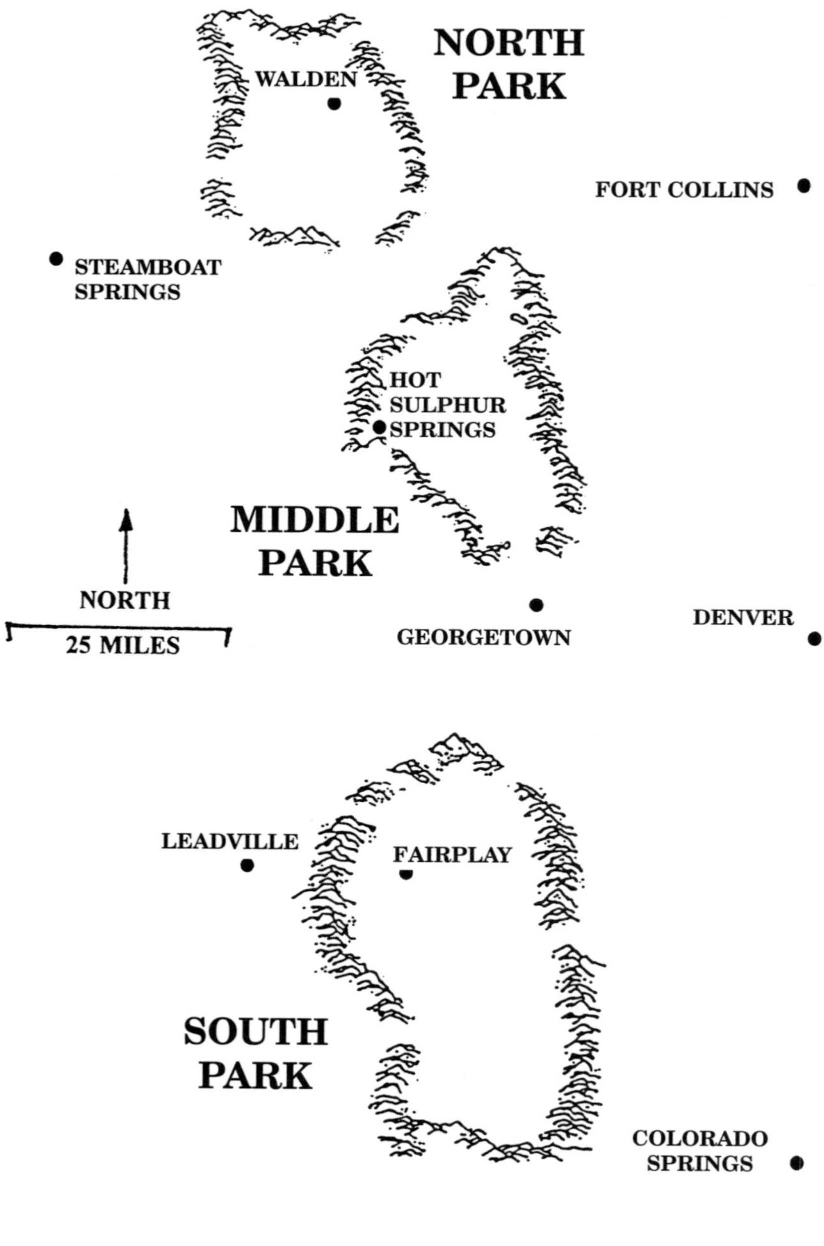

Introduction

The high, extensive mountain meadows of Colorado were termed "Parks" by the early trappers. Three such Parks were designated in Colorado, and each provided the trappers with relief from the dense forest found both above and below these open meadows. Each Park is surrounded by mountains that scour out the precipitation. All three Parks serve as the headwaters for major rivers, are laden with diverse plants and animals, and have geothermal springs.

These Parks have been of interest to a variety of people since the 1850s. One early traveler, Samuel Bowles, was particularly impressed with the Parks when he journeyed throughout the Colorado Rockies in 1868. He wrote a brief summary of each Park:

> The North Park extends up to the northern line of the territory. . . . Through and out of it flow the head waters of the North Platte; its streams are thicker with trout, and its sage brush and buffalo grass and wooded hill-sides offer more deer and wolves and antelopes and bears than are found in the lower and more frequented Parks.
>
> Middle Park lies below, and is separated by a single but high sub-range of the main mountains. This is fifty miles wide by seventy miles long, and as the continental divide sweeps around on its eastern side, all its waters flow into the Colorado of the West and so into the Pacific. The great peaks of the territory lie marshaled around it . . . and snow-topped mountains circle its whole area.
>
> . . . the South Park, which is thirty miles wide and sixty long . . . carries the continental divide on its west, and furnishes the waters of the Arkansas and the

> South Platte. Wide areas of rich prairie open out before the level eye, . . . all the grand panorama of natural beauty that hill and valley, mountain and plain, winter and summer, snow and verdure, trees and rock, water and waste can produce . . . is here spread before the spectator.

As the Parks of Colorado were settled, their human history represented a microcosm of the West – significant events in the history of the western United States also happened in these three Parks, albeit on a smaller scale. Enshrined within each Park are stories of people struggling against the forces of nature and, more often, against each other. This work describes some of these struggles, factual and unembellished, which form our heritage and enlighten our understanding of the present.

North Park

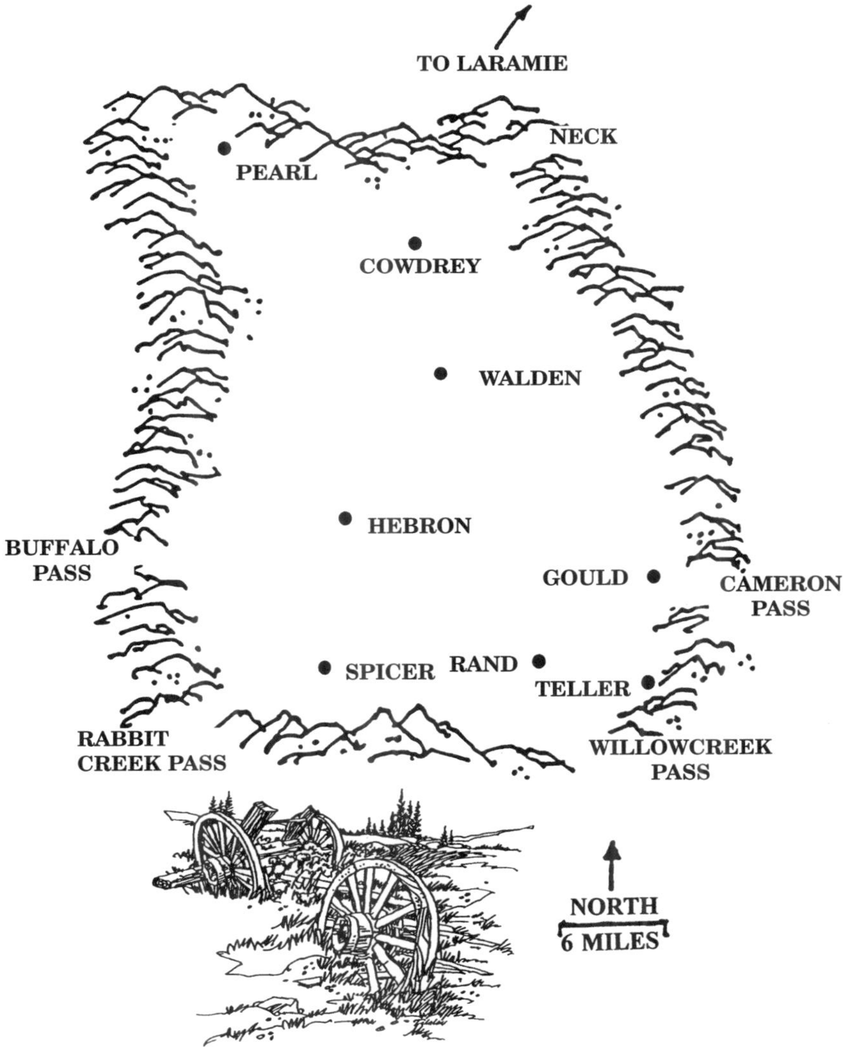
TO LARAMIE
NECK
PEARL
COWDREY
WALDEN
HEBRON
BUFFALO PASS
GOULD
CAMERON PASS
SPICER
RAND
TELLER
RABBIT CREEK PASS
WILLOWCREEK PASS
NORTH
6 MILES

1
Peg-leg Smith

A sharp crack of a rifle was heard, and the smoke curled above a clump of bushes a short distance away. Smith gave a quick exclamation of pain.
San Francisco Bulletin, October 26, 1866

An old trapper like stout, black-eyed, and dark-haired Thomas L. Smith should have known better than to get ambushed in North Park. He was smart enough to leave Taos in the fall of 1827 when the Mexican government seized twenty thousand dollars' worth of beaver pelts from American trappers and killed the man trying to protect them. Smith had saved his furs but only through cunning and bribery. Trappers from the States were not welcome in Mexican territory, which until 1848, extended northward to the Arkansas River in Colorado.

Smith and a party of at least twenty-four trappers left Taos in September 1827 and headed for the high mountain valleys and parks in what later became Colorado. Most of the men in the party claimed French citizenship, but some notable American trappers joined the group. In addition to Smith, Sylvestre Pratte, Ceran St. Vrain, Old Bill Williams, Milton Sublette, and Alexander Branch were among the Americans that left for the mountains.

Although there was severe competition with other groups trapping in the Rocky Mountains that fall, the men managed to accumulate about 300 pounds of furs before they reached North Park. It was late October, and as the weather changed from mild to cold their luck changed from good to bad.

Sylvestre Pratte, captain of the group, became sick. After several days of crude nursing, the trapper died. This unfortunate event threw the men into a quandary. Some wanted to take the catch, go back to Taos, and hope for the best with the Mexican authorities. Others wanted to divide the pelts and supplies so each trapper could go his own way. St. Vrain, now captain, urged the trappers to stick together and finish the expedition. He was immediately supported by Smith and others. So the men decided to stay together, continue their trapping in North Park, and then head southwest for the winter.

Trapping in North Park proved to be good, but the abundant signs of Indians alarmed St. Vrain, who now felt responsible for the men. Since leaving Taos, the trappers had engaged in several skirmishes with Indians, and it looked as if another engagement was imminent.

As was their custom, the men worked in groups of two or three for safety. Trappers spent much of their time in the water, either setting traps or removing the catch. While they worked in the water, their firearms usually lay on the bank – close, but out of immediate reach. A lone trapper could not put up much of a fight against a stalking Indian, so the trappers worked in groups, and one of them always stood watch.

But Smith preferred to trap alone, perhaps convinced that he was too clever to be bushwacked by an Indian. After Smith had brazenly exposed himself to Indian attack, St. Vrain decided it was time for a talk. He followed Smith out to his traps one morning to convince the trapper that the best Indian fighter was one who avoided the most battles.

St. Vrain sat on his horse and urged Smith to pair up with one of the Frenchmen. Smith argued the point as he worked on a trap, then rested his rifle against a tree and prepared to enter the stream. At that moment a shot rang out and a puff of smoke rose from the underbrush. St. Vrain jumped from his horse and flopped on the ground, his rifle cocked and ready to meet the charge. Only there was no charge, just a single shot from a skulking Indian. Smith tried to run for his rifle, but the Indian bullet had found its mark in his leg. The bushwhacked trapper fell to the ground, cursing and writhing.

Moving fast, St. Vrain hoisted Smith onto the horse and returned to camp. A few slugs of whiskey subsided Smith's cursing and allowed St. Vrain to cut away the legging and look at the damage. The bullet had hit Smith just below the knee and had smashed both bones. The bones were "dreadfully shattered and protruded through the flesh."

Hearing the shot, the other trappers quickly returned to camp. They took one look at Smith's leg, then retreated a few steps and talked in low voices. They had seen enough mangled limbs to know that Smith would never use his leg again, even if he managed to survive.

"Cut it off," bellowed Smith when he sat up and saw the damage. But the men did not move. According to a later newspaper account, "none among those rude mountain wanderers had the necessary skill to attempt an amputation, and all shrunk from the sad task of mutilating and torturing him with their bungling surgery." So Smith roared for Basil, the cook, and in no uncertain terms told him to bring the butcher knife. The cook reluctantly brought the knife.

Smith grabbed the knife and cut off several thongs from his buckskin shirt. These he tied together and then wound the leather around his leg just below the knee. With the leg now ligated, and with the courage born of determination and driven by necessity, Smith began cutting off his own leg. His snarls and cursing prodded the other trappers into action. They brought water, horsehair, rags, and, above all, more whiskey. Smith did a good job at slicing the flesh away, but the bones presented a problem. Through clenched teeth and another torrent of cussing, he ordered the men to file teeth into the blade of a knife. When they were done, Smith grabbed the knife and started sawing the bones. But he began to slip into unconsciousness before he finished. Sublette took the knife and completed the job.

Blood gushed from the stump. Smith would soon be as dead as a beaver hat if the flow was not stopped. A red-hot iron was produced to sear the stump. Although he was almost unconscious, the sight of the glowing iron was too much for Smith, and he cursed in protest. He yelled at the men to tie up the arteries with horsehair. The trappers quickly complied, feeling that it did not make much difference what they did at that point. Smith's stump was wrapped in a dirty shirt, and the trapper was covered with a buffalo robe. The men then returned to their work of skinning beaver.

At sunrise the next day, St. Vrain expected to find Smith dead, but much to his surprise the patient was still alive and strong enough to curse him and everyone else in sight. The cold night may have helped the blood coagulate, for the stump was not bleeding. Although the streams around the camp had been trapped out and it was time to move, the men lingered a day to allow Smith to die in peace. Stubborn and uncooperative, Smith refused to die; instead, he grew stronger. The trappers made a stretcher and rigged it in tandem fashion between two somewhat willing horses. St. Vrain then wrapped Smith in more buffalo robes while the men broke camp. The expedition headed west, trapping along the way.

Leaving North Park, they plowed through the dense forests and deepening snow until they reached the Little Snake River. As they were descending the rocky hillside to the river, the horses carrying Smith lost their footing and rolled. Smith was ejected from the tangle and hurtled toward the river. St. Vrain was certain the trapper would be dead when he reached him, but instead he found Smith sitting up to his chin in water and making disparaging remarks about the ancestry of horses. In his red flannel wrapper and a sugar-loaf hat of the same material, the sputtering trapper made a ridiculous picture as they fished him out of the water.

Traveling west and then south, the expedition eventually reached the Green River Valley. The late November weather turned brutal, and the trappers decided to hole up in a Ute village for the winter. It was here that Smith discovered that the two protruding bones in his stump were now loose. Sublette yanked the bones out, using a bullet mold as pincers.

The Utes then took over nursing the trapper. Treatment started with wailing, chanting, and appropriate incantations for a missing leg. Women and children then chewed roots and spit the juice on the stump. This dubious attention continued for several days as the flesh slowly healed. Smith whittled a wooden replacement that resembled a fat broomstick, attached leather straps, and was soon stumping around, almost as good as new. He was renamed Peg-leg Smith by the whites and Wa-ke-to-co, man with one foot, by the Indians.

"The catastrophe did not prevent him following his long-loved passion for wandering among the western wilds," noted a newspaper. He became a trader among the Indians, a prospector who found and lost at least one gold mine, and a respected horse thief who stole five thousand horses from ranchos and missions in Spanish California. Peg-leg Smith found time to become the owner of a trading post along the Oregon Trail and to hire himself out as a "free-lance fighter." Finally, as a "white-haired but robust old man," he became a celebrity.

One of Smith's most important possessions was his peg leg. When he was in a tight spot – a situation that commonly occurred when he was drinking – Smith would quickly unstrap his wooden leg. Wielded by his muscular arms, the versatile leg proved to be a weapon that commanded respect. Leaving a leg behind in North Park had had its advantages.

2
Massacre

After dark last night, a man came . . . from the North Park, who reported that there had been a general massacre of the white miners in there by the Utes.

Daily Sentinel, July 7, 1870

Without a doubt, the Indians of North Park were annoyed. Yet like most Indian problems, the wanton murders likely resulted from pent-up frustration over the erosion of their life style rather than from a planned assault.

About one week before the massacre, a band of about three hundred Cheyennes and Arapahoes crossed the Union Pacific Railroad tracks near Rawlins, Wyoming, and headed south. Shortly after crossing the tracks, the Indians attacked the camp of a horse trader named Purkins. The trader escaped, but his camp was looted.

Lieutenant R. H. Young of Company A, Second United States Cavalry, led a command of thirty-six men in pursuit of the Indians. A day later, thirty miles southeast of Rawlins, the cavalry found the Indians and attacked. The battle lasted for about two hours before the cavalry withdrew to the north and the Indians continued their march to the southeast. Lieutenant

Young thought that several Indians had been killed, yet the battle could not be regarded as a victory for the cavalry.

Meanwhile, a band of Ute Indians entered North Park and set up camp. The Utes were not alone, for a party of miners, led by Jim Baker, established a camp on Independence Mountain. But North Park was Indian territory, and the Utes had no desire to share one of their favorite hunting grounds with white men. A delegation of two Indians, Chief Piah and another named Sohn, rode to the miners' camp and delivered a short, pointed message: Quit the country at once. The deadline, however, was extended to twenty days for two miners, Van Dyke and Shipman.

As the Indians prepared to leave, Van Dyke showed them some gold dust, perhaps to justify the miners' presence and win permission to stay in North Park. Chief Piah liked the yellow sand and wanted to keep it, but Van Dyke said no. When Piah insisted, the miner wisely changed his answer.

Perhaps a week after Chief Piah acquired the small poke of gold, a miner by the name of J. R. Whitehead and at least two companions encountered about seventy Utes fighting a large band of Cheyennes and Arapahoes near Independence Mountain in North Park. It was fortunate the miners met the Utes rather than the Cheyennes and Arapahoes. The Utes professed friendship and, being hard-pressed by their enemies, solicited the help of the miners in fighting the Wyoming Indians. Not fully trusting the apparent friendly intentions of the Utes, the miners claimed that they needed to go back to their camp and get ammunition before they could assist in the battle. The Utes never saw the miners again. "They seemed to be heap scared," later stated Chief Piah.

The editor of the Laramie *Daily Sentinel* apparently agreed with Chief Piah and wrote that the miners' decision was "a very short-sighted and unwise act." Had they joined in the fight, argued the Laramie editor, the miners "would have made it very warm for the Cheyennes," avenged a host of crimes committed by these Indians, and "made fast friends of the Utes."

Friends or not, the miners left the Indians to fight their

own battle in typical Indian fashion. The first day of battle probably involved threats, maneuvering, and a few running battles. The combatants appeared unwilling to commit themselves to a serious fight. During the second day of battle, about fifty head of Arapahoe horses stampeded toward the Ute lines, apparently in search of water. The Utes captured most of the horses, along with their saddles and bridles. Tied to the saddle of one horse was a yellow cloth bag containing a bill of sale to the horse trader Purkins, letters, and other incriminating plunder.

Three Arapahoes pursued the captured stock, one riding a mule and the other two riding horses. As the Indian on the mule was looking back to see if more help was on the way, his mount plowed into a tree and threw him off. Piah shot the Indian. Another Ute, Antelope, darted from the trees and sliced off the scalp. The two Arapahoes on horseback retreated. With the loss of one Indian and a large number of horses, the Arapahoes and Cheyennes abandoned the fight and returned to Wyoming.

The massacre in North Park occurred during the one-week interval between the battle near Rawlins with the cavalry and the Indian battle in North Park. Smarting from their encounter with the cavalry, the Cheyennes and Arapahoes killed miners as they worked their way into North Park. Van Dyke, the miner who had reluctantly given Chief Piah some gold, and his lame companion, Shipman, were later found near Independence Mountain. Shipman was found "shot twice, scalped, two axes driven in his head, and his body mutilated in a manner too horrible and disgusting to mention in print." The Indians killed and mutilated two other miners in the vicinity of Independence Mountain, although some sources put the total number of miners killed at eight rather than four.

For several weeks, there was confusion concerning the perpetrators of the massacre. Initial blame was placed on the Utes, who claimed North Park as part of their hunting grounds. They had camped in the area where the miners were killed and had warned the miners to leave. Regardless of the facts that later emerged, some still blamed the Utes, perhaps as more reason to drive these Indians from the territory.

Under the direction of Territorial Governor McCook, a thorough investigation was conducted. The hostile intent of the Cheyennes and Arapahoes when they entered Colorado, the plunder (including the bill of sale) captured by the Utes, and their route of travel that took them through the miners' camps placed the guilt on the Cheyennes and Arapahoes. On August 9, 1870, the *Rocky Mountain News* put the incident to rest:

> These facts show the Utes are innocent, especially when we take into consideration the various [Ute] statements which in every case are substantiated by the whites. It is indisputable that bands of hostile Cheyennes and Arapahoes were then in the [North] Park, and even without the mass of testimony which now exists to clear the Utes, it would be natural to suppose that the murders were done by Indians which have always been hostile, rather than the Utes, who have always been friendly.

Although the newspaper concluded that "our present and future prosperity as a territory depends upon the friendship and peaceful disposition of the Utes," peace between the two diverse groups was difficult to maintain. Within ten years of the massacre, the Ute Indians were driven from North Park and most of Colorado.

3
The Footrace

The race was pulled off on C Street, the main street of Teller. Sharp had a good part of the stakes in his possession.

J. N. Pettingell, race referee, 1883

Once a month, a loyal contingent of miners from Teller, Gaskill, Lulu, and other mining camps clustered in the southeastern corner of North Park and the northeastern corner of Middle Park congregated in Grand Lake to celebrate and, in the process, to blow most of their month's pay. The monthly celebration was rowdy and centered on booze, brothels, bets, and brawls. During one such gathering in the winter of 1883, the betting portion of the celebration came to the forefront.

The boys from Teller bragged about a miner named Dan Sharp who worked at the Wolverine Mine. During the summer of 1882 Sharp had beaten all takers at a footrace in Teller. The Teller boys had a winner no one could beat.

Their boast was immediately challenged. Harley McCoy, "a character well known in police circles" for wild debauchery and other forms of entertainment, disputed the brag from the North Park boys. McCoy claimed he had a friend in Georgetown named Ewing Montgomery who could outrun a scared jackrabbit with a tailwind. Sharp would not stand a chance against Montgomery, asserted McCoy. Imbibers from Grand Lake enthusiastically supported this contention.

Teller had been challenged, and the boys defended their town with cash. Bets were placed, and soon over one hundred dollars had been committed to the outcome of the race. The contest was scheduled to take place that summer, and in the intervening time, the bets continued to roll in and eventually totaled thousands of dollars, according to Judge J. N. Pettingell, who refereed the race.

During the early 1880s, footraces enjoyed considerable popularity in Colorado, especially in the mountain areas. Easy to arrange, such races provided diversion for an often tedious life. Based on the newspaper coverage, footraces were more common during this period than horse races. Miners, railroad workers, and even cowboys eagerly welcomed the contests.

The town of Teller was no exception to this footrace fever, and after a few contests of their own, the miners from Teller stood ready to challenge the world. After all, they had a first-class runner who guaranteed to put money in their pockets.

Yet McCoy and the Grand Lake contingent were not novices to the sport. Several years earlier, in the fall of 1880, McCoy had run a footrace against David Rockwell in Georgetown that had "excited the entire sporting force of the city." The distance was two hundred yards and the purse one hundred dollars. Rockwell won by ten feet, and "a great many overcoats, and some money, changed hands."

McCoy was again mentioned in the newspaper, this time as a contender in a footrace at Empire. This widely advertised race was held on Saturday, May 20, 1882, and "drew quite a large crowd of spectators from Georgetown and Silver Plume." The race pitted John Roberts of Silver Plume against Harley McCoy of Georgetown; the pot totaled two hundred fifty dollars a side. "The two runners were pretty well matched," claimed the newspaper, "and their respective backers quite enthusiastic in the belief that their man would win." A distance of one hundred twenty-five yards was marked off along the main street in Empire.

At the start of the gun, Roberts darted out in front and maintained a slight lead during most of the race. Both men strained every muscle in a desperate effort to be the first over the finish line. "Being quite evenly matched, they made a close and pretty run to the last, when McCoy jumped ahead, coming out at the finish about eighteen inches in the lead."

While these races were important in establishing the sagacity of McCoy with respect to running, the second race at Empire was equally important. The newspaper made only brief mention of the event: "A second race for one hundred dollars was then run by George Hartman and Ewing Montgomery. Montgomery won by about twenty-five feet." McCoy won his race by only eighteen inches, and he likely concluded that Montgomery won his race not because Hartman was slow, but because Montgomery was incredibly fast.

The Denver newspaper mentioned Montgomery again a few weeks later, noting that the runner would enter another race at the Empire track on June 6. Reports of the outcome have disappeared, but if Montgomery was running up to snuff, he likely won.

Although Montgomery had running credentials, nothing is known about the ability of Sharp other than the faith of his backers in Teller. Both men started training for the race in the winter of 1883.

That summer, the contest took place in Teller. Although past its prime, this isolated mining town had a population of almost thirteen hundred. It boasted a newspaper office, smelting works, sawmills, two physicians, and a two-story hotel with forty rooms and a piano. Most important to the populace were the twenty-seven saloons that never closed and dominated the social life, except when there was a footrace.

The racetrack was along C Street, the main thoroughfare in Teller. Other than the outcome, details of the race have passed into history. Judge Pettingell ruled that Montgomery won the race by seven feet. Yet Sharp was the runner who made the race memorable. For unknown reasons, he had a “good part” of the stakes in his pocket. When Sharp crossed the finish line in second place, he didn't stop running. In fact, he ran right out of town and into the forest. Hidden among the trees were two saddled horses plus an attractive strumpet from the red-light district. Both left North Park in a hurry and never returned.

The men of Teller took their defeat in stride. Between the money absconded by Sharp and that paid to the Grand Lake winners, the sporting fans from Teller had little more than the shirts on their backs.

4
A Pot of Tea

Last Friday evening at supper two of the men, W. L. Keys and Charles Sheldon, got into a dispute about . . . who should pour out the tea.
North Park Miner, August 9, 1883

Laban Keys and Charlie Sheldon drifted into North Park at the start of the mining boom in 1879, but they apparently had no interest in mining. Prior to the tea argument, these men squatted on isolated real estate near Grizzly Creek in the southwestern corner of North Park. A "stray" boy about thirteen years old lived with the pair. The two men were "ranchmen on a small scale, both of them having some horses in the Park." Keys was inclined toward the lazy side, while Sheldon nursed a bad temper. These two traits eventually clashed in deadly fashion.

Neighbors soon moved into the area. Charlie Snyder and his wife, Johanna, arrived in North Park in 1880 and three years later established a ranch along Grizzly Creek. Although Snyder claimed to be a rancher, he apparently had more interest in hay than in the animals that ate it. Hay grew naturally in the broad, flat meadows along Grizzly Creek. Once cut and cured, this high-quality feed could be profitably sold in the proliferating mining towns that dotted North Park.

Snyder's hay fields were ready to cut by late July 1883. Help was mandatory, so Snyder and another area rancher named Frank Robbins decided to assist each other with the harvest. Together they hired additional hands, including Keys, Sheldon, and the stray boy. When haying started, the crew consisted of a dozen men and two women.

Accommodations for the crew on the Snyder ranch left much to be desired. The ranch house was only half finished, so large canvas tents served as the chow room, cookhouse, and bunkhouse. The food was probably good, for Mrs. Snyder and Mrs. Robbins cooked for the crew.

The tea argument occurred on Friday, August 3, as the haying crew was eating supper. The crew sat around a large plank table in the center of the chow tent; presumably, the men watched their manners, for two women sat at the table with them. When Keys attempted to pour water for his tea, the pot registered empty. He asked the stray boy to fill it. Obediently, the boy took the pot and headed for the cookhouse located in an adjacent tent.

The stray did not get far. Sheldon jumped up, took the pot, and declared that he would fill it. Looking at Keys, Sheldon forgot his manners and loudly stated that the boy had enough to do and was not to wait on Keys. Sheldon stormed out of the tent with the teapot in hand, only to return a few minutes later without the damn thing.

Now thoroughly confused, Keys politely asked about the teapot. Sheldon explained that he had left it outside. The tea-thirsty man told Sheldon that he should have filled the pot and brought it back. Sheldon glared at Keys and made a threatening remark. Keys let it slip by, for he was of "very small build" and no match for the "large, powerful" Sheldon.

Keys then left the tent and quickly returned with a teapot filled with hot water. He also held a Winchester rifle in his right hand. The tea man sat down at the table, parked his gun nearby, and poured himself a cup of tea. Perhaps emboldened by the gun, Keys told Sheldon to lay off.

The big man became enraged. Jumping up from the table, he dared Keys to shoot. Sheldon then deliberately turned his back on Keys, offering him an easy target, and slowly walked from the tent. Keys ignored him, but that only made matters worse.

Sheldon returned to the tent a few minutes later with a cocked rifle at his side. He yelled to Keys to come out of the tent and settle the affair like a man. As Keys stood up, Snyder jumped up from the table and approached Sheldon. The rancher grabbed the big man by the arm and told him not to be foolish. After assuring Snyder that he was not crazy, Sheldon started for Keys. Fearing harm as the powerful man advanced, Keys panicked and went for his rifle. "Both reports were at the same time as near as possible," Snyder later testified. "Sheldon's gun was in position first. Keys had to get his gun and cock it."

As the noise of gunfire drifted away, Keys slowly sank down to the dirt floor. Holding his smoking rifle, Sheldon backed out of the tent. He then threw his gun down and ran to the north side of the tent. Snyder followed and found Sheldon standing with his hands around his bloody mouth, trying in vain to talk. Keys was also unable to talk, for he had been shot through the chest and died instantly.

Sheldon, unaware that he had killed Keys, somehow managed to convey to a ranch hand that a doctor was needed for his friend. A messenger set out for Teller. While waiting for the doctor, Sheldon had time to reflect on the foolish tragedy. He decided that hanging around might not be in his best interests, so he headed north on his horse. Later that night he arrived at Trounsell's place and convinced the rancher to take him to Laramie. By the next morning he was conveniently out of the state.

Three weeks later the *North Park Miner* noted that Sheldon was "getting along nicely" in a Laramie hospital. The bullet fired by Keys had entered Sheldon's lower jaw and exited via his neck, just missing the jugular vein. "The shot broke his lower jaw and teeth so that the only way he can receive any nourishment is through a quill," stated the newspaper. Miller, the Laramie sheriff, assured the Colorado authorities that there was no danger of Sheldon being spirited away. The newspaper reported that "Sheldon himself professes a willingness to return to the scene of tragedy, as soon as he is able to travel, and stand his trial."

In November, Sheldon was still "thinking of coming back to North Park," and the citizens were still "anxious to have him brought to trial." However, the surviving records say nothing more about Sheldon. Perhaps he died of his wounds after all, or perhaps the authorities decided that Sheldon acted in self-defense and then quietly closed the case that started over an innocent pot of tea on a lonely ranch in North Park.

5
The Scoundrel

We are again called upon to mourn (?) the departure for greener fields and pastures new of another of the nuisance landmarks of Teller.
North Park Miner, November 8, 1883

The nuisance that left town was John W. Farquhar. The good-natured citizens of Teller deserved credit for not running this scoundrel out of town or, better yet, for not hanging him from the nearest tree. Described as bombastic, self-important, meddlesome, and treacherous, this two-legged plague was tolerated by the miners for three long years.

Farquhar arrived in camp about 1880 and quickly set himself up in business as a dealer in "distilled poison." Operating one of the twenty-seven saloons in Teller, he apparently distinguished himself by the unusually foul nature of his whiskey. The quality of whiskey in mining camps was poor at best. For example, a standard mining camp recipe called for one gallon of raw alcohol, five gallons of water, one pound of red pepper to give the grog a whiz, one pound of old tobacco to add color and flavor, and two pounds of brown sugar. Farquhar may have taken this recipe a step further and added some unknown ingredients that set his whiskey apart from the normal brew.

Despite the lousy whiskey, miners came to Farquhar's saloon. Most regretted their choice. Wanting to establish a reputation as a "bad man from bitter creek," Farquhar picked a fight with a harmless miner named Richards and tried to shoot him. A poorly directed shot was the only thing that saved the unarmed miner. Farquhar was indicted for "assault with deadly weapon with intent to commit great bodily injury." He posted a five hundred-dollar bail bond and was to appear in court in August 1883. Farquhar later dodged his day in court by paying a two hundred and fifty-dollar recognizance bond that postponed his court appearance for another year. By that time he had skipped town.

Farquhar's whiskey business brought in more than one sucker. Horace Gatchel, an old, lonely miner from Germany, sought friendship and comfort from the bottles of tainted alcohol sold by Farquhar. Although he had a promising mining claim, the old man could barely eke out a living. One night, while trying to make yet one more "delusive attempt to revive hope," he sold an interest in his mining claim to Farquhar. When Gatchel recovered from his stupefaction the next day, he examined the note that Farquhar had given him. The old miner found that he had sold his entire mining claim for the promise of a few bottles of whiskey. Farquhar quickly resold Gatchel's claim for one hundred dollars cash. The *North Park Miner* summed up the sorry deal:

> The old man got neither drinks nor money, but we suppose our departed citizen Farquhar felt a satisfaction, not only in having in his possession the one hundred dollars, but in knowing that he had been smart enough to rob a drunken old man.

Although the miners in Teller considered whiskey the staff of life and consumed it accordingly, Farquhar's personality and his particular brand of distilled poison proved too disagreeable for the hardened miners; his saloon business faltered and then failed.

Farquhar soon found another line of business that used his "unlimited amount of cheek, smooth tongue, and continual funeral smile." Remembering how easy it was to cheat Gatchel, he became a mine broker. He used his conniving wiles to convince potential buyers from the East that the Teller mines drooled with rich silver ore and only needed new management and a modest investment in capital equipment to return millions. But to Teller residents wanting to sell, he told a different story. He moaned that eastern investors shied away from North Park mines because of their isolation, difficult mining conditions, and spotty ore. Convincing one group to sell low and another to buy high netted Farquhar a sizeable profit.

At one time during Farquhar's crooked career, he became involved in the Wisconsin and Colorado Mining Company. Instrumental in keeping the company in constant trouble, the scoundrel promised one thing and did another. "He claims to be general superintendent of the company," printed the *North Park Miner*, "and if he is, we wish them success, or a successor to Farquhar, or whatever may best suit them."

Farquhar was eventually successful in finding a friend, probably his only one in North Park. Humpy was his name, and this horse's mean temperament was a perfect match for Farquhar. While Humpy packed the "worthless body of his master" from point to point, his master would pack "more lies, tall-tales, and invent more news than any other man in the county."

Farquhar was particularly adept at inventing political news, and as a "political traitor and shyster" he had no equal. He somehow talked his way into the county Republican convention at Gaskill. There he made a nomination for sheriff, then two days later he went to work with the opposite party to defeat the man he nominated. Commenting on his political activities, the newspaper stated that Farquhar "always presses himself forward, meddles into everything and then goes to the other political party and tells what he has discovered." His betrayal of friends and political alliances created turmoil in a county desperately trying to reestablish trust and political order.

At a later convention Farquhar opposed the nominee for

secretary, "stating that Mr. Towner could not see to record the minutes of the meeting on account of defective eyesight." Farquhar wanted "the minutes kept correctly and accurately," so he nominated someone else who was promptly rejected. The scoundrel then opposed every motion presented at the convention, stating that such procedures were "contrary to Republican principles." When the meeting finally adjourned, all the delegates could talk about was the "cussedness of John W. Farquhar."

The scoundrel's politicking went from bad to worse when, in December of 1882, he arrived in Grand Lake dressed in the latest fashion. "His tight-fitting pants, cutaway coat, fine white vest, shirt of spotless whiteness, and the celluloid collars and cuffs all betokened that something out of the usual course had happened to John Farquhar." The newspaper was correct, for Farquhar had decided to run for U.S. senator. He claimed that Horace Tabor had arranged the matter. Farquhar handed out cards proclaiming his candidacy, but fortunately the heavy winter snows apparently buried his idea of running for Congress. If Farquhar ran for anything, it would likely be for his life. People were sick of his antics, and lynching was considered one of the better solutions.

The *North Park Miner* claimed that it could fill pages with the dastardly deeds of the bad man from bitter creek. Space and deadlines interceded, so the reader had to suffice with two columns on page four. The abbreviated account of the departed nuisance was printed to warn other towns that a visit of the "Asiatic cholera or small pox" would be far better than a visit by John W. Farquhar. Someone listened – perhaps Farquhar himself – for the scourge promptly disappeared from Colorado.

6
Mosquito Meals

We have lost our faith in the animal kingdom, from the humans down to mosquitoes. The cause of it is that we went a fishing the other day.
North Park Miner, July 26, 1883

Charles A. Clark, editor of the *North Park Miner,* a man known only as McKee, and presumably others decided to leave Teller for a few days to enjoy fishing in the Rocky Mountains. Their guide was Warren Gibson, a sensible man who did not like fish and wanted to stay put in Teller. Yet Gibson was the ideal choice, for he knew all about the trails and passes, the mountains, the lakes, and the fish that he caught and ate – but only when desperate for food. And Gibson had to be honest, for the reluctant guide faithfully taught Sunday school in his spare time. Clark had been insistent and persuasive, and Gibson had finally agreed to guide the fishing expedition.

Gibson decided that Lost Lake offered the best fishing in North Park. This name is not definitive in Colorado, for it seems that mountain lakes have a habit of "getting lost." Of the several lost lakes within striking distance of Teller, it is likely that Gibson selected a lake that was lost on the southern slopes of Willow Creek Pass. This lost lake is about twenty miles from

Teller, and the trip would have been easy if Gibson hadn't been the guide.

The expedition apparently ascended Willow Creek Pass without incident and started down the southern flank of the pass. At noon the men stopped by Willow Creek, intending to catch a dinner of fresh fish. An hour later they had bacon, bread, and coffee for dinner. With exception of Gibson, the men hated bacon, for it had become the staff of life in Teller. They had been determined to eat nothing but fresh fish, but Gibson had insisted that bacon was just the thing for frying fish, so the fishermen had packed a slab of the meat.

Leaving the nauseating odor of bacon behind, the party headed east and into the mud, water, dense forest, and fallen timber. Much to the dismay of Clark and the others, Gibson decided to blaze a new trail rather than going along the same route he had traveled before.

The exhausted fishermen finally arrived at Lost Lake late in the afternoon. The small lake was fringed with rocks and surrounded by tall spruce trees that imparted an emerald green color to the clear, deep waters. But the beauty of the lake was lost on the weary travelers. Famished after their exhausting trip, the men from Teller wanted Rocky Mountain trout for supper. They cast their lines into the placid waters of Lost Lake and maneuvered the dry flies with the skill of expert fishermen. An hour later their supper consisted of bacon, bread, and coffee.

After supper, the men divided their time between fishing and swatting mosquitoes. They quit fishing at bedtime but continued the battle with the mosquitoes until sunrise. Clark decided that the mosquitoes served as the guardian angels of Lost Lake and were superbly trained to savagely molest anyone who entertained any thoughts of catching a fish. "They belong to a heretofore unknown tribe," insisted Clark, "and are so far advanced in knowledge that they will lift up the blankets and crawl into bed with you." McKee asserted that they "carry a file under their left wing to sharpen their bill on so as to be able to penetrate an ordinary blanket or the hair and hide of a horse without trouble."

Mosquitoes were quickly forgotten once the sun rose, for the blue sky and glassed surface of Lost Lake beckoned to the fishermen. They insisted that breakfast would feature fresh fish. Several hours later, breakfast consisted of bread and coffee. Clark optimistically decided to save the bacon, for he remembered that Rocky Mountain fish tasted best when fried in bacon grease.

After breakfast Gibson gave the discouraged anglers a pep talk about the large and abundant fish in Lost Lake. The men believed him, for they remembered that he taught Sunday school. With renewed vigor, the men attacked the deep waters once again. Later they concluded that the fish in this lake were well-posted on the Colorado fishing statutes. Clark wrote that they "play on the surface and in the outlet until the first of July, because the law protects them until that time; after that they protect themselves by diving down so deep that our fish lines could not reach them."

Clark was not the only newspaper editor in the area who had trouble fishing in the Rocky Mountains. Bill Nye, described by a competitor as "cadaverous in appearance" and easily mistaken for "last year's broomstick enclosed in gunny sacks," served as editor of the *Laramie Boomerang*. The two editors apparently knew and respected each other, for Nye was frequently mentioned in the *North Park Miner*. During Nye's first and apparently only fishing expedition in the West, he almost caught a "decrepit trout that I had found in a dead pine tree" and his companion caught one by "driving it into a prairie-dog hole." After Nye suppressed a strong desire to kill the companion who had convinced him to go fishing in the first place, the two men told lies about catching trout and shooting elephants in Michigan while they waited for the train to take them home.

Clark undoubtedly empathized with Nye, for both had been misled concerning the great sport of fishing in the Rocky Mountains. Unwilling to give up, Clark and his companions fished all morning on Lost Lake. A few reckless or illiterate fish came to the surface and allowed themselves to be caught, so the men had fish for their noon dinner.

Following dinner, the men packed and started for home. A feeling of satisfaction settled over them, for they had not exterminated the fish in Lost Lake and had provided both entertainment and food for the mosquitoes. That night they camped along Willow Creek, eating bacon and bread, and drinking coffee. The menu was repeated the next morning.

Although they did not catch as many fish as intended, Clark considered the trip an "immense success" from the scientific standpoint. The "nourishing qualities of good bacon" had been thoroughly tested, not to mention the beneficial attributes of supplying human blood for mosquito meals.

7
The Newspaper War

Three weeks ago the editor hereof landed in Teller under the impression that it was just as easy to issue a newspaper here as anywhere. It was a mistake.

Grand County Times, May 12, 1881

The *Grand County Times*, which soon became the *North Park Miner*, had found a home in the booming mining town of Teller. In 1879, silver had been discovered in the southeastern corner of North Park. The rush was on, and by the time the newspaper editor was ready to set up shop, the only place available was a seven-foot-high floorless cabin, with only one small window. Teller itself was not much better. It featured crude accommodations, no brick buildings, and no "mechanical establishments where little deficiencies in machinery can be remedied." But the town now had a newspaper. And the editor, Charles A. Clark, promised that the new newspaper would represent the interests of Teller, North Park, and Middle Park, and "won't have any politics to amount to a row of pins."

Clark was among the stampede of editors, newsmen, and printers who came West with the gold rush and followed the rise and fall of boom towns. The primitive conditions that Clark worked in were typical for "camp papers" and went along with the crude equipment used by most editors. It is safe to assume that the *North Park Miner* was printed by hand from start to finish. After the slow process of typesetting, ink was spread on the type and a sheet of newsprint was moistened with water. Then a lever on the printing press brought the paper and type together, once for each side. The printed sheet was then removed from the press, hung out to dry, and later folded.

The often ragged product that resulted from Clark's efforts was a seven-column paper proclaiming county news on the front page, national and international news on the next two pages, and local news on the back page. News came from telegraphic dispatches (the nearest wire may have been Laramie), from other newspapers (usually without their permission), from travelers (most of whom did not let facts get in the way of a good story), and from the editor's efforts. Advertisements dominated at least three of the seven columns on each page, and everything from shingles to shoes could be bought in Teller.

Clark believed that his *North Park Miner* was indispensable for both Teller and the county. But he soon realized that his newspaper was not the only one in the neighborhood. About twenty miles over a rough mountain pass was the town of Grand Lake and its new newspaper, the *Grand Lake Prospector*. At that time both newspapers represented rowdy mining towns in the same county, both competed for portions of the same journalistic territory, and both claimed they spoke for the county's interests. A war of printed insults ensued, with both newspapers agreeing to disagree on everything of importance.

Editorial warfare reached its height during 1883 when county affairs were at an all-time low. In July, Clark unleashed an arsenal of abuse against the *Prospector* with a front-page statement: "Grand Lake is the only instance on record that we know of where a newspaper has been a detriment to the place." This article went on to criticize the dishonest and selfish manner in which the *Prospector* was serving its subscribers.

Clark's abrasive and derisive editorial dialect did not mince words and in subsequent issues poured additional abuse on its rival. Clark punctuated one front page with the statement that "there was not a word of truth in either of the points" made by the *Prospector* concerning a political candidate. In the same issue Clark hurled another fine insult, stating "The *Prospector* contradicts the truth" when it reported on the state of county affairs. A later article began with the biting statement: "Out of the slush and dirt which we find in the last *Prospector* ..." Printed insults came close to threats when the *North Park Miner* addressed the *Prospector*:

> When you in your mistaken zeal think you are performing a master stroke of cunning in concocting lies and getting up false reports, you may accidently run into a hornet's nest that will amaze you and spoil your circulations.

Obviously, the *Miner* could not think of one good thing to say about the *Prospector*. The Teller newspaper called its rival "contemptible" and accused it of persistently trying to "gall the public"; labeled its reporters "peanut-headed"; insisted it was an honor to be attacked by a newspaper that "advocates the assassination of good citizens"; and called for the *Prospector* to be "censured by the press of the entire state."

It would be wrong to think that the *Prospector* kept quiet about the abuse pouring down from the north. Unfortunately, few issues of this newspaper survived, but those that did hurled insults at its rival. A prime piece of journalism from Grand Lake stated:

> It is cowardly for a newspaper to make low personal attacks on those who have no means of defense. The beautiful boyish blonde who dishes up the slush for the *Miner* should remember this and be a little less abusive in its attacks on the citizens of Teller.

On the front page of a later issue, the *Prospector* commented about the "fiendish journalism" of the *Miner*. "It displays a sort of a ghoulishness of disposition that is not often met within a paper that has honesty and intelligence at its head." The article went on to say that the *Miner* has set up itself as "a social and a political god, and woe be unto him that refuses to worship at the shrine of the brazen calf" located in the newspaper office in Teller. Another issue of the *Prospector* concluded that the "viperish outfit" printing newspapers in Teller might be better suited if it engaged in a "peaceful and honest occupation," such as cattle rustling.

For the most part, the Teller newspaper ignored the insults flowing up from Grand Lake. But the *Miner* could not keep quiet all the time, so in one issue it declared that "if the abuse of the *Grand Lake Prospector* came from a decent newspaper, no matter how unfounded and false its accusations were, we would feel compelled to reply in behalf of the maligned parties." The *Miner*'s tone softened slightly when it later printed:

> The only true statement found in last week's *Prospector* was that Teller is out of whiskey. We acknowledge the fact that there is not a saloon running in Teller, but judging from the appearances of the *Prospector* there must be plenty in Grand Lake, for the type in that newspaper stand on their heads and are fearfully mixed up.

Yet when another newspaper picked on the *Prospector*, Clark called for a temporary truce in the press war and defended his rival. The editor and owner of the *Prospector* had opened a saloon in Grand Lake, presumably to shore up the sagging financial state of the newspaper and to pick up some newsy tidbits from imbibers. The *Miner* criticized the editor of the *Laramie Daily Sentinel* and other "fogies who have grown gray-headed and stoop-shouldered in trying to infuse a spirit of morality and rectitude into the growing generation." This article went on to state that the cause of the criticism against the *Prospector* was most likely the supposition that the "spirit poured out of a bottle is not the proper spirit of the press" and that an editor "cannot compose moral epics and mix fancy drinks successfully at one and the same time." Editor Clark could see no reason, other than outdated tradition, why a saloon could not be run in connection with a newspaper. However, Clark qualified his support by stating that the Grand Lake editor had at last found his natural element, and serving whiskey made best use of his limited talents and abilities.

Perhaps Clark should have followed his rival and opened a saloon in Teller. On August 23, 1883, the *Miner* announced that it had "pressing business" elsewhere and would sell the "entire outfit at a very low figure." The announcement mentioned good circulation, liberal advertising patronage, and a prime location in a thriving mining town. Of course the *Prospector* picked up on this turn of events, and Clark retorted in kind.

> The *Prospector* rises to remark that the proprietors of the *Miner* are in a starving condition. Now that is really unkind of you. Why don't you have charity enough to start a subscription in our behalf? We have been thinking about following your example and start[ing] a saloon in connection with our other business, so as to increase our receipts, knowing that the public sometimes will pay cash for liquor and buy good moral instruction on credit.

But Clark did not start a saloon and found no buyer for the newspaper. The end was announced on November 22, 1883. "With the present number we suspend the publication of the *Miner* for the present. We regret the necessity for so doing, but as we see no prospect of making it pay this winter, have concluded this is the best course for us to adopt."

Its rival expressed sympathy by stating that it was sorry that Clark could not print his "slurring" remarks and "unmanly attacks" against Grand Lake. When someone asked about the *Miner* several months later, the *Prospector* explained that it was quite understandable that few noticed the demise of the newspaper, for "when it sank it scarcely caused a ripple on the slough of journalism which it ornamented." A few years later the *Prospector* also sank.

8
Anything But School

The kids came stringin' in from all directions, like cattle to a roundup bunch ground.
Stephen Payne, on his school days, 1897

Art and Stephen Payne came stringing in from the south; Montie and Park Blevins came in from the west. They made up four of the approximately fifteen reluctant students who attended the new, white-painted clapboard school in Walden.

School opened about the middle of May each year, but many of the students didn't stay long. The older boys were soon needed to irrigate or help with haying, and the older girls were often wanted at home to assist with cooking, cleaning, and washing. Within a month or two, only the young ones remained in school, much to their disgust. Art, Stephen, Montie, and Park ranged in ages from nine to about twelve and formed the more active nucleus of those who stayed in school.

School was a major inconvenience for these four boys, so diversions were the key to their daily survival. Properly handled, almost anything could serve as a diversion, even gophers. Hundreds of these critters inhabited the field surrounding the school. Hurling rocks at gophers was a good diversion, but because they were not skilled in the ancient sport of stoning, it took a large pile of rocks to connect with just one gopher. One of the boys came up with the idea of flushing the gophers from their burrows with water. So at recess the four boys grabbed buckets and started hauling water from the Canadian River that was none too close. After a week of flushings, the mathematician in the group determined that it required six buckets of water to flush just one gopher from its underground refuge. Flushing then lost its appeal and was replaced by the idea of putting the gophers to good use.

This ambitious project required the four boys to trap and brand the gophers, then turn them loose. Each boy would have his own herd of branded critters, just like the men had cattle. While they worked on the details of stock ownership, word leaked out about this budding enterprise. The schoolgirls were horrified, much to the delight of the boys. Unfortunately, the disgusted parents told their sons to pay attention to the teacher and forget the gophers.

But paying attention at school was out of the question. For a time, honing their roping skills replaced gophers as the major diversion. The boys rode horses to school as did most of the other students. The horses, each attached to a long picket rope, grazed the adjacent pasture while the boys were in school. Immediately after school, the four boys ran for their horses, pulled the picket pins, and coiled their ropes. Jumping into their saddles, they galloped off, ropes whirling above their heads and searching for something to snag. Buffalo skulls, an old fence post, or even a bush were targets for their lariats.

The challenge of static targets soon faded, and the boys longed for something mobile. The untamed range cattle that roamed North Park were often a handful for the experienced cowboy and were certainly more than the boys and their horses could handle, even if they were lucky enough to rope one. Then one of the boys discovered milk cows. These mild-mannered beasts were not aggressive and had no interest in sustained exertion. The Leeks had a small herd of milk cows that grazed alongside the beaten track to school. The boys soon found that these cows put up little fuss as Montie or Art repeatedly tried to noose their heads and as Park or Stephen endeavored to snag the hind legs. Best of all, the budding cowboys were sure of getting their ropes off the animals, so there was no risk of losing a valuable lasso.

Although the cows put forth little effort to avoid being roped, any type of exertion decreased milk production. Soon the Leeks realized something was wrong. Their young daughter Mamie was responsible for the cows. Every morning she herded them to the pasture and brought them back home at night. One day after school Montie noosed a milk cow by the horns, and Art swung in behind to heel it. Just as his rope snaked out, Mamie appeared out of nowhere with fire burning in her eyes and a quirt waving menacingly in her hand. Stephen Payne told of the encounter:

> "You kids let our stock alone or I'll lick all of you," Mamie told us. "One at a time, or all four at once. And don't believe I can't do it!"
>
> Park and I had nothing to say; Montie tried to kid Mamie. She wasn't in a mood for kidding and the upshot of the clash was that four ashamed and humiliated boys 'sort of tucked their tails and snuck away,' defeated by one spunky girl. Thereafter the Leek milk cows grazed in peace.

It was difficult for the four boys to pull their thoughts and actions away from cows, especially during the summer of 1897 when the Blevins imported a large herd of Oregon cattle. The herd was pastured on the sagebrush hills near the schoolhouse, and the children watched in fascination as the chuck wagon rolled in and the cowboys set up camp. Each day the punchers cut out about one hundred fifty cattle, herded them into the corral, and rebranded them. The cowboys then drove these cattle to a mountain pasture and returned about noon for dinner.

One day Montie and Park got wind that the cook was to ride into Walden for food. Before the cook left, he would surely make dinner for the cowboys and leave it ready for them. Montie announced all of this at school, then mischievously added that if the cook left before their first recess, they could have a real feed before the cowboys showed up at noon.

Many eyes peered out the windows as recess approached, yet the cook gave no indication of leaving. Finally, just at recess, he saddled a horse and left for town. Fifteen kids boiled out of the schoolhouse, ran across the sage field, crawled under a fence, and descended into the deserted camp. There they found the chuck wagon, old fence timber piled for firewood, a large water barrel, and the cowboys' beds either rolled or scattered about. None of this was of interest, but the Dutch ovens, carefully banked with ashes and coals, and the pots hanging just above the coals grabbed their attention. Montie led the hungry horde to the back of the chuck wagon where they dug out plates and whatever utensils they could find. They popped the lids and found boiled meat with onions and potatoes, baked beans, stewed canned corn; nearby were golden brown biscuits with butter and in the shade a pile of canned tomatoes for dessert. Each kid filled a plate, then sat on the folded beds or on the ground and devoured the food. For weeks thereafter, they expected violent repercussions, but the kids never heard anything about the raid from either the cook or the cowboys.

In terms of repercussions, the goat caper was a different story. On the way to school, the boys passed the Cowdrey Ranch that was home to a small band of Angora goats under the domain of a mean billy goat appropriately named Billy. His meanness was not inborn but likely came from being roped by the Payne and Blevins boys once that spunky girl placed the milk cows off limits. If a boy was on foot, Billy would sneak up and attack from the rear in true goat fashion. Sore butts, skinned faces, and other aches and pains made for a victorious goat and mad boys.

Revenge was in order, and the opportunity came when the Cowdreys left their place for a day. The boys arrived at the ranch just after school. Billy made his usual greeting of wagging his beard, stamping his feet, and glowering at them. The boys reasoned that a simple roping would not be fitting revenge; something more drastic was mandatory. Looking around, they noticed a curbed-up well with a pulley, rope, and bucket. Montie suggested that the bottom of the well was just the place for the ornery goat. Art agreed but then worried that a dirty old goat might spoil the water and make the Cowdreys sick. A compromise was reached: suspend the goat part way down the well.

Montie roped the goat by its horns and dragged him close to the well. Park and Art wrestled Billy down and held him while Stephen tied its legs together. The well rope that hung from a pulley was yanked out and tied around Billy's horns. Then came the hard part of tugging on the rope to get the goat up high enough to clear the well curbing. All four boys pulled; the protesting goat slowly rose, then disappeared down the well. Art tied off the free end of the rope, and all congratulated themselves on hanging the goat.

Intent on their work, they failed to notice that Mr. Cowdrey had returned. With four boys clustered around his well, Cowdrey knew something was up. He walked to the well and asked the kids what in hell was going on. The boys didn't bother to answer, for their hearts were set on reaching their horses before Cowdrey reached them. The boys won the race but lost the battle.

Four boys felt the painful effects of the goat caper for a week and heard about the event for months. Yet they were happy with the ending. Billy was healthy and even more grouchy than ever, and deep inside, the boys were glad that their respected enemy had won another battle.

The next battle the foursome fought resulted in an undisputed loss for all involved. When riding to school one morning, Art and Stephen discovered a skunk under the Canadian River bridge. They considered themselves duty-bound to kill the skunk as no one in North Park had any good feelings for these odorous critters. Once at school they reported the exciting news to Montie and Park. At noon the four boys wolfed down their lunch and, together with the dog named Punch and armed with rocks and sticks, ran for the bridge.

The skunk was housed in a shallow hole in the riverbank. The boys hurled rocks at the striped back, while the skunk retaliated in a manner befitting the species. The dog wanted part of the action and went into the hole after the skunk. He dragged it out onto a small sandbar, and four undaunted boys and one dog eventually won the battle. Thrilled by their victory and one less skunk in North Park, the boys marched back to school. The girls took one sniff and stampeded. The teacher, being made of stiffer stock, refused to be routed and decided that a whipping was in order. She found her switch, but as she approached Montie, her entire face knotted into wrinkles and she gagged. Stephen Payne recorded the conclusion:

> "Go home," she snapped. "All of you, go home. At once."
>
> As we scurried to get our horses, Park remarked with a chuckle, "Skunk killing is one sure way to get out of school. With teacher's permission, too."
>
> "Yeah," Art conceded. "But there's worse things than school. This stink is one of 'em."

9
Grandma Martin

I went over to a neighbor's to visit and stayed all night. My Stars! I never saw so many bedbugs in my life, even in the old railroad house.
Edna Evelyn Martin, August 18, 1880

Once Grandma Martin moved to North Park in 1881 and left the old railroad house behind, bedbugs ceased to be mentioned in her diary. Instead, her journal was filled with personal entries that describe a woman's life in the Rocky Mountains.

Grandma Martin cast a figure that demanded attention. In the style of the day, her dark hair was pulled back severely and tied in a bun. She had a warm face with small eyes, large jowls, and a diminished mouth that descended to a thick neck and sloping shoulders. More important, this buxom woman was large enough to attain geographic significance. In her diary she admits to being weighed on December 22, 1887; she tipped the scales at 235 pounds!

Grandma Martin was probably lighter when she and her husband, William, embarked on their first trip to North Park in June 1880. Leaving from their home in Golden, they passed through Loveland and Fort Collins and then "traveled all day on the range called the Virginia Dale Road." They arrived in

Laramie four days after starting, then headed their wagon southwest for North Park.

Four more days of travel through rain and snow brought them into the Park. Grandma took one look around and declared the Park a "great place for creeks." They continued in a southwesterly direction and eventually arrived in Teller, a booming mining camp of two hundred and fifty homes. "We had dinner in the butcher shop," wrote Grandma, and there she enjoyed the "best apple pie I ever ate." Two weeks later they headed back to Golden, arriving at their home more than a month after leaving.

North Park apparently impressed the Martins, for the diary entry of August 18, 1882, records that they had "arrived in North Park to make our home." They established a ranch east of Walden and were among the first ranchers in North Park. Grandma promptly broke her leg, and it did not completely heal for a year. She was so discouraged during this time that she did not write in her diary. Grandma appeared to be back in stride when the peddler arrived in the fall of 1884.

> **October 11, 1884**. A peddler was here last week, also a sewing machine agent. We bought many things. North Park is becoming civilized fast.

From a woman's perspective, few events assumed more importance than the arrival of the peddler and his stock of goods that a woman desperately needed. There were no dry goods stores in North Park yet, and a trip to the outside world was a big adventure undertaken only once or twice a year. So the peddler filled a void in the lives of ranch women. Cloth, needles, thread, yarn, pots and pans, dishes, and numerous other household items could be purchased from the peddler. The traveling salesman arrived in a high-wheeled wagon in which the bed had been replaced with a jumble of tightly packed drawers, cupboards, and shelves, all built on top of one another and covered with a canvas tarp.

If the peddler had carried spare parts for mowing

machines in his chaos of goods, Grandma Martin could have relaxed during the critical haying season.

> **August 31, 1885**. William broke a piece off of his mowing machine and had to send it to Laramie to be repaired. The piece they returned is too small so don't know what we will do.

Like many ranchers in North Park, the Martins spent most of their time fencing, irrigating, and harvesting hay crops that sustained their stock when snow buried the grass. The disastrous winter and spring of 1884 had taught ranchers that putting up hay was essential if they expected their stock to survive the frequent hard winters of North Park. The stock owners emphasized the importance of hay by renaming the seasons "before haying," "haying," "after haying," and winter.

Because of the central role of hay in a rancher's life, any delay in its harvest was a serious matter and usually resulted in a loss due to spoilage. The Martins could not afford any more delays, and apparently William either found some way to fix his mowing machine or he sharpened the scythes and cut the grass by hand. Grandma Martin makes no further mention of haying in her diary, so it is a safe assumption that the vital crop was harvested without further incident.

Although the haying season in North Park focused on the temporal aspects of ranch life, Grandma Martin did not ignore the spiritual side of human existence.

> **July 29, 1888**. Oh Joy! I have been to hear preaching today in Walden; the first I have heard since I came to North Park. The preacher's name is Bainton.

Henry W. Bainton, a Presbyterian, was the first Protestant minister to preach in North Park. He arrived riding a high-wheeled bicycle. As he tied up in front of the post office and disappeared into the nearby school, one of the loitering cowboys, Lafever, threw out a challenge to his companions.

"I'll bet no one in this bunch can ride that horse."

"I'll bet I can," confidently stated Dwinell, another cowboy.

"Try it," dared Lafever.

Then thinking, Dwinell added, "He might not like it."

"Go ahead," said Lafever, "we'll stand by you."

Just as Dwinell was about to climb onto the iron horse, Bainton emerged from the school. "There goes one of those cowboys on my wheel," thought the preacher. "He will sure smash it up and I am a long ways from repairs." But the preacher said nothing and enjoyed a good laugh as the cowboy rode the bicycle with surprising skill.

Bainton was an itinerant preacher who rode all over the rural parts of Wyoming and Colorado on his "wheel." Enjoying his calling and "always full of jokes, wit, and fun," he made Walden a regular stop. Reverend Bainton returned in September of 1888 to preach again, and Grandma Martin was disappointed that few people made it to the meeting. "I think it is just awful that the people won't go to church when they do get a chance," wrote Grandma Martin.

While Grandma Martin lamented missed spiritual opportunities, ranchers often lamented missed opportunities to move their cattle out of North Park and into a milder climate for wintering.

> **March 23, 1890**. A great many people have tried to get their cattle out, but have left as many dead by the roadside as they got out.

Winters were tricky for North Park ranchers. It was a running battle to stretch the hay crop until the snow melted and green grass was available. When a rancher miscalculated, the only means of saving his cattle often consisted of driving the critters along one of the snow trails that headed out of the Park and north into Wyoming. Once on the Laramie Plains, the wind exposed patches of sagebrush and grass that could sustain half-starved cattle.

Snow trails became part of the winter landscape of North

Park. During the early part of winter, sleds and horses' hooves packed the snow solid. Wind quickly filled in the paths with more snow that in turn was packed down. The snow trails slowly built up and became higher than the soft, loose snow on either side. Falling off the trail could be serious, for it meant floundering around in the deep snow until man or beast could scramble back onto the packed snow. Cattle possessed little skill at extricating themselves once they fell off the trail, so they had the right-of-way. Although this privilege helped, many still fell off the snow trail, struggled in the soft snow, and soon died. By the time spring arrived, the roadside was littered with dead cattle.

As Grandma Martin sadly found out a year later, death was not limited to the livestock in North Park.

> **July 8, 1891**. My dear husband, William Martin, died today after being sick eleven weeks, from after effects of grippe.

In the summer of 1891 the grippe hit North Park; William was the first victim of this viral form of influenza. The high fever that accompanied this illness often weakened the patient and invited deadly secondary infections. Following the death of Grandma Martin's beloved husband of twenty-five years, the epidemic intensified, and by the following January, Grandma noted in her diary that "everybody around here is sick with the grippe, and there have been many deaths."

Although death brought sorrow, Grandma was determined not to spend the rest of her life in mourning. So she picked up her knitting needles and headed for the neighbors.

> **February 4, 1894.** I have regularly knit a stocking a day ever since I have been here. Expect to finish this week – twelve pairs of stockings and twenty-five pairs of mittens.

Once the lonely winter set in, Grandma Martin enjoyed

traveling to friends and neighbors to catch up on local happenings and to break the now lonely ranch life. Trips lasted several weeks to a month or more. Never idle, Grandma kept busy on these trips by knitting. She was one of the fastest knitters in North Park, and one stocking a day represented nothing unusual. Perhaps regretting that she was never able to bear children, Grandma Martin particularly enjoyed knitting small mittens.

But like many women, Grandma Martin was interested in more than knitting; she enjoyed politics and wanted to vote.

> **July 8, 1896**. Yesterday they were electing candidates to go to Fort Collins and I voted for the first time and I am sixty-three.

Colorado was among the first states to give women the right to vote. The women had fought hard, for men believed that allowing women to vote might destroy the delicate nature of womanhood and expose innocent and virtuous women to a world where men fought for fortune and fame. After decades of work, an 1893 referendum granted voting rights to women.

Grandma Martin's first opportunity to vote came three years later. The election apparently involved selecting delegates for a party convention in Fort Collins. Grandma was proud to vote and most likely took her new civic responsibilities quite seriously.

Civic responsibility also extended into other areas, such as caring for Mr. Kelly.

> **April 17, 1898**. Last week some of the people thought they would go up to see if Crazy Kelly in Kelly's Canyon was all right and found his body almost devoured by rats.

Kelly was an Irishman who once worked as an Army scout. Although well-educated, he became a hermit shortly after his arrival in North Park in the late 1870s. He built a shack in an isolated area that bears his name, Kelly Canyon. Kelly claimed he saw visions of heaven and soon became known as Crazy Kelly. As he grew older, the number of visions increased, and his ability to take care of himself decreased. People in North Park occasionally took food to him, and Grandma Martin probably knitted stockings for the old man. In the fall of 1897, Dave Sudduth had brought the hermit some groceries to tide him over until spring. When Sudduth returned in April, Crazy Kelly was dead and the groceries unopened.

Grandma Martin's concern ranged from Kelly to cowboys. An entry in her diary demonstrated that her caring nature extended to everyone.

> **July 5, 1909**. I am over at Norell's making bunkhouse quilts for the haying season.

This notation was among the last entries in Grandma Martin's diary, and the comment reflected her character. The events most often mentioned in her diary spoke of helping others. In the summer of 1909 she was again helping neighbors, and this time she put aside her knitting needles and made quilts for the bunkhouse crew. Kind and loving, Grandma Martin was not the type to stay at home and sit around. She wanted to help, even at the age of seventy-six.

10
Winter

The past week has been a hard one on our ranchers. It has been almost one continual storm of wind and snow.

North Park Union, January 27, 1899

Stephen Payne was well aware of the weather as he snuggled deeper into his warm bed. He remembered with a shiver that winter had arrived in early October when snow and cold hit North Park. The lousy weather continued into the middle of January when the blizzards arrived. Now the eleven-year-old boy faced the dreaded task of leaving his bed to light the fires.

Stephen and his brother, Art, older by two years, held down their North Park ranch while their father visited their sisters and relatives in the East. The boys' mother had died several years earlier, and after one of the girls had died of the whooping cough, their father realized that he could not properly take care of his remaining two young daughters. He reluctantly sent them East to live with relatives.

His father's absence did nothing to help Stephen get out of bed on this cold morning. His brother was awake and loudly reminded him that it was his turn to light the cookstove and fireplace. Both were nearby. As soon as their father had left, the boys pulled their beds into the living room where it was occasionally warm, and they agreed to take turns lighting the morning fires.

Knowing that he could no longer delay the dreaded task, Stephen took a deep breath, clamped his teeth together, and jumped out of bed. The cold immediately penetrated his nightclothes as he ran to the kitchen, fumbled for the matches, and after several unsuccessful tries, lit the wood shavings placed in the stove the night before. Stephen next threw an armload of kindling into the fireplace and soon the second fire was blazing. Another winter day had started.

The boys dressed in front of the smoky fireplace that ate wood faster than a hungry horse ate oats. Bundled in sweaters, heavy coats, overshoes, hats, and mittens, both boys took lighted lanterns and pails and plunged into the below-zero darkness. The family cats left their warm beds under the cookstove and followed.

The four milk cows in the small barn kept the place somewhat warm; Stephen and Art forgot the biting cold as they stripped the cows of milk. Neither boy was skilled at milking, and it took them more than an hour to complete the job. Meanwhile, the impatient cats loudly demanded, and eventually received, a pan of warm milk. Art left with the cats and two pails of milk while Stephen stayed to muck out the barn and feed the milk cows. When he finished, he fought the snowdrifts to the horse barn where the saddle horses waited to be fed and for their barn to be cleaned.

These early morning chores exhausted Stephen, but he knew that Art would have a good breakfast for them. Necessity made a passable cook out of Art, and breakfast during their father's absence typically consisted of pancakes with butter and corn syrup, oatmeal with cream, slices of fried beef or pork, and stewed fruit, usually apples.

Breakfast over, one of the boys swept the house while the other skimmed cream from the milk pails. The cream went into a big crock and the skim milk was poured into pans on the stove so it would be warm for the calves and pigs. Then one boy washed the dishes and the other dried. Dreading the outdoor cold, Stephen habitually dawdled over the house chores. Yet the time finally came to return outside to feed the chickens, pigs, cattle, and calves; to open water holes in the ice-bound creek and to bring in firewood.

The calves and their mothers spent most of their time in a tight shed that was usually warm enough for a newborn calf to survive. But if there was any doubt that a calf could not get up on its feet soon after being born, special treatment was needed. Art and Stephen carried these “hospital cases” into the house, put them on gunnysacks by the fireplace, and dried the newborn calves with another sack. Then the calves were fed warm milk from a bottle and nursed along until ready to rejoin their anxious mothers.

After taking care of the new calves, the boys shifted their attention to the main herd of dry cows, young heifers, and steers. These cattle wintered in a large pasture where thick willows along the river provided good shelter. The stacks of hay looked like giant mushrooms to the boys as they drove their hayrack sled to the nearest stack. Part of the hay was loose and could be easily forked from the stack with a pitchfork. But most of it had to be cut out. The snow that had fallen and melted during the fall had filled the hay with water that was now frozen. Just as bad was the wind-driven snow that had penetrated deep into the hay. This portion of the haystack had to be cut out with a hay knife and then chopped. The half-starved, hollow flanked cattle milled around, waiting to attack the hay. By late morning the cattle had been fed and it was time for dinner.

Art and Stephen prepared their noon meal as quickly as possible, often eating leftovers from the morning or the night before. Dishes were left unwashed as they hurried back to their work. Once outside, the boys cut holes in the river for the cattle. These creatures had yet to learn that eating snow would provide water, and they could die of thirst standing knee-deep in wet snow.

Collecting firewood was the last outside chore of the day and probably the worst. Winter had arrived before they could go to the adjacent mountains for wood, so they now burned old fence posts that had been replaced with new ones. They hitched up the hayrack sled and followed the fence line to their northern pasture. On the way they stopped to check on the horse herd. At first all they could see were dark, motionless humps against the white snow. Their concern turned to laughter when they drew abreast of the horse pasture. Heads, front legs, and shoulders were out of sight in the deep snow; only their tails, hind legs, and hips stuck out of the holes they had dug in the snow to get to the grass. Once the ostrich-like horses realized someone was coming, they scrambled out of their snow pits. The Payne horses were shaggy but in good shape and looking for a handout.

The boys dug out a load of old fence posts and headed back to the house. There they used a dull crosscut saw and a beaten-out old axe to cut and split the wood. It was dark by the time they finished.

Supper consisted of boiled beef or pork, beans, spuds, dried fruit, and cornmeal mush. On rare occasions there was baked bread. Usually the boys found it impossible to keep the dough warm enough for the yeast to act, so the pigs often ate the rock-like bread that defied human teeth.

Two bone-weary boys were ready for bed, but work remained. Dishes had to be washed and food prepared for the next day. Sooty lantern chimneys needed to be cleaned and the wicks trimmed. Cream must be churned into butter, clothes washed, and kindling set aside for the next day.

In bed at last, the boys found sleep was slow in coming. Both suffered from chilblain that came with the cold of winter. Neither salves nor kerosene nor turpentine did any good for their red, swollen, and itchy feet. Then there was the agony of a snow-blistered face that included burned and peeling cheeks, sore and swollen lips, and a nose so tender it was torture to blow it. They tried vaseline, but that was a mistake. It fried on their faces and had to be peeled off in great patches of goo and skin. Growing a beard would have helped, but only Art could manage some ineffective fuzz on his chin. So they suffered, especially at night.

The novelty of holding down the ranch had worn off, and the boys longed for their father to return. Eventually, the day came when their father stepped off the inbound stage. After he had a chance to look around and see the stock, Stephen remembered him saying, "You've done a good job. I've reason to be mighty proud of you kids!"

With three of them now doing the chores, the boys had time for long-delayed projects. First on the list was to break the house cats to do their share of the work. They decided that if the cats could be broken to a harness, they could pull a small sled around and help with the chores. Art made collars out of cloth torn from worn-out overalls. To the collars he attached tugs of the same material. Stephen decided that an iron fire truck – complete with ladders, driver, and tongue but lacking horses – would be the ideal vehicle for breaking the cats.

After a week of work, everything was ready for a trial run. Then they waited another week for their dad to leave them alone in the house. As soon as the coast was clear, the boys used a broom to dislodge one cat at a time from its warm bed beneath the stove. Stephen held each cat while Art slipped a collar on and fastened the tugs. When all was ready, they turned the cats loose. Stephen Payne described what happened next:

> Rattle and bang went the iron vehicle! "Wrouw! Spit! Grrr!" of the cats as they scooted out of the living room, across the kitchen and under the stove. Here occurred a calamity as they and the harness and the truck tangled up around one of the stove's legs, resulting in a yowling, snarling, scratching and biting mess of fuzzy-tailed cats which we dared not try to untangle.
>
> Cats, for their size, are very strong. Tugging and yanking, they pulled the stove leg loose and tipped the stove halfway over! This disconnected the stove pipe. Down it crashed, its joints breaking apart and sending thick black soot cascading all over the room. To worsen

matters still more, there was a fire in the stove from which wood smoke immediately began to fill the kitchen.

The kitchen was a mess and getting worse by the second. Their dad would raise the roof when he came back, and all their hard work when he was back East would be forgotten. Stephen ran for the door and opened it to let the smoke out. Somehow the cats got untangled and headed for the open door, fire truck and all. Next was the stove. Art was so panicked that he was able to lift the stove by himself and hold it while Stephen put the leg in place. Then, choking on the black smoke, they finally got the stovepipe jointed and reassembled.

Casting anxious glances to see if their dad was returning from chores, they went to work with brooms and rags to remove the soot that was everywhere. They only managed to smudge and smear the soot. Stephen then grabbed a copper boiler, filled it with snow, and placed it on the stove. But they were too impatient to wait for it to melt, so they used the snow itself for scrubbing. It worked well, and soon the kitchen had the most thorough cleaning in years.

Their father finally returned, took a sharp look at the kitchen and at two tired and uneasy boys. What happened next is best told by Stephen Payne:

> "Boys," their father said, "this is the nicest surprise you could have given me. Glad to see you've got enough gumption to clean the house without being told."
>
> "Oh, we do lots of things without being told," Art said enigmatically, and we grinned at each other.

11
Woollies

The fight for pasturage is an old, old story in that section [North Park], but it has never before reached such serious proportions. Heretofore the settlers have contented themselves with driving sheep over bluffs or shooting a few of the leaders now and then.

Denver Times, October 25, 1900

Conflict between cattle and sheep interests in North Park and in other parts of Colorado was inevitable. A cowboy had little in common with a sheepherder, yet both wanted to use the same vast, open stretches of real estate.

One source of conflict resided in the personalities of the cowboys and the sheepherders. High-spirited, proud, and mostly young, cowboys considered themselves masters of the range. More at home on a horse than on foot, these men adeptly handled dangerous, ornery critters capable of inflicting injury and death. Athletic, impulsive, aggressive, and always ready for a fight with a cow, horse, or man, they reinforced their rakehell image every time they entered a town. Although poorly paid and unemployed during the winter, most cowboys found enough money to regularly upgrade their dramatic, but useful, clothing and gear.

Sheepherders were a different breed altogether. Often Mexican or Basque, these older, solitary men watched over small, timid animals that threatened no one. They found nothing to fight, other than hungry coyotes with appetites for fresh mutton. Sheepherders enjoyed a slow, peaceful life with few visits to town. Dress was unimportant, acts of bravado unnecessary, and horses used only occasionally. Employed throughout the year, they commanded a higher salary than cowboys. Finally, sheepherders made their beds with square blankets while cowboys insisted on using the rectangular ones.

Although the differences in personalities alone spelled trouble, the argument over grazing rights added a deadly element to the conflict. North Park and the rest of northern Colorado were cattle country and had been since the 1870s. With exception of a few hard winters, cattle flourished in the rolling, grass-covered hills. That changed in the 1890s when a succession of dry years dramatically reduced the forage. To make matters worse, sheep moved into the area during this time. "It is hardly to be wondered at, then, that cattlemen are aroused almost to the fighting point by what they consider the determination of the sheepmen to take what little is left," commented the *Denver Times*.

The fighting point was soon reached in North Park, for sheep could not be kept out of the vast areas of public land claimed by the cattlemen. Many ranchers in southern Wyoming converted from cattle to sheep in the late 1880s when the demand for wool and mutton increased dramatically. Sheep operations required less capital investment than cattle, and a stiff tariff on imported wool virtually guaranteed good profits. It was simply a matter of time before the Wyoming herds made their appearance in North Park.

That time came during the fall of 1900 when sheepherders employed by Wyoming Senator Francis Warren moved a large herd of sheep across the border and into North Park. Warren, considered to be the greatest shepherd since Abraham, listed among the assets of the Warren Live Stock Company nearly one hundred thousand sheep. Now some of these sheep resided in Colorado, and the cattlemen were not about to stand by and watch a bunch of bleating woollies strip their ranges when, in their opinion, God obviously intended the grass to be eaten by cattle and horses. Warren's sheep "are so crowding and devastating the range that they [the cattlemen] cannot get pasture for their cattle and horses," claimed a newspaper.

Unrestrained by the law and "driven to desperation by the encroachment of Warren's sheepherding outfits," cattlemen of North Park turned to violence to rid the range of the unwanted intruders. They used "the gun and club on the sheep king's property with such effect that hundreds of dead sheep lie about on the scene of the struggle."

The North Park struggle followed the traditional pattern for a western range war: Attack only when victory is certain and maximize the killing. So in the fall of 1900, a large group of masked men attacked Warren's sheep camp at night, apparently catching the sheepherders asleep. "Warren's army of shepherds attempted to interfere," stated the *Denver Times*, "and a fierce fight began, ending in the flight of the herders." The "army of shepherds" probably amounted to just a few outnumbered men who wisely retreated. The masked men then grabbed clubs, perhaps using spokes broken from the wheels of the sheepherders' wagon, and started after the abandoned sheep. They drove the "hoofed locusts" into a woven wire fence across a gulch and within a few hours' time, clubbed to death over four hundred sheep.

As soon as the raiders had left, the sheepmen returned to their camp and picked up the pieces. But these men stood their ground and refused to move their flocks back into Wyoming. The raiders returned a second time and killed another seventy sheep; still the stubborn herders refused to leave. Instead, they called the sheriff, who poked around a bit before concluding that he could not identify any of the attackers. The law was impotent, and the war continued.

Although outnumbered and at a distinct disadvantage during this war-on-the-hoof, mutton punchers retaliated. They stampeded cattle and took potshots at cow punchers. One North Park cattleman, Scott Decker, rode into an ambush and had his horse shot from under him; sheepmen were blamed.

Similar skirmishes occurred along the entire length of the Colorado-Wyoming border. Large herds of sheep, often ten thousand to forty thousand in a single herd, were driven down from Wyoming to graze the Colorado grass. Irate ranchers claimed that the sheep dined in Colorado all summer and then left for Wyoming when the plate was empty. Ranchers north of Steamboat Springs complained that "sheep eat very close, so close, in fact, that they devour every blade of grass about." It is a fact, stated the cattle ranchers, "that dozens of small farmers are unable to keep a family cow on their range because sheep eat up to their very doors."

Siding with the cattle interests, the *Craig Courier* claimed that the border country was settled by cattlemen, and because cattle and sheep cannot live on the same range, the "stockmen are certainly justified in their efforts to exclude the sheep." During almost fifteen years of open warfare to drive sheep out of northern Colorado, more than twelve thousand woollies died at the hands of angry cattlemen. Cattle and horses were killed; barns, homes, and wagons were burned; and human participants on both sides were shot and some were killed. This nasty war without a winner "finally stirred up the stockmen to the fact that their only salvation lay in ownership of their grazing lands," concluded the *Denver Times*.

In 1901, Colorado sheepmen and cattlemen bought over twenty thousand acres of rangeland and leased other areas that could not be bought. The federal government belatedly entered the picture and in 1905 began charging ranchers a fee for every animal grazing federal lands and enforcing a system of grazing permits. This combination of land ownership and federal management finally won the war.

At the height of the range conflict in North Park, the local newspaper, the *North Park Union*, failed to recognize the problem. The untimely demise of a few hundred woollies in cattle country was nothing to write about, especially when the sheep belonged to a rich Wyoming rancher. Besides, a poultry poacher was on the prowl. "There are good reasons for believing there is a chicken thief in town, and he isn't a coon either," declared the Walden newspaper. "He had better keep sly or he'll get into trouble." Although unwritten, the same advice applied to sheepmen.

12
Rattlesnake Jack

After the first day of January, 1900, and until further notice, the North Park Stock Growers Association hereby offers a bounty of thirty dollars on each grey wolf and fifty cents on each coyote killed in North Park.

North Park Union, January 5, 1900

Grey wolves, looking for an easy dinner of fresh beef, invaded North Park. No one had actually seen a wolf, but a sharp increase in maimed cattle pointed toward wolves. Conclusive proof rested with the would-be victims. Wolves bring down their prey by attacking from behind, aiming to hamstring the victim. If their aim is off, the intended victim often escapes. During the late fall of 1899, North Park ranchers found injured cattle with teeth marks along their legs and tails where a wolf had missed its grab. Wolves had arrived for the winter.

A meeting of the North Park Stock Growers Association was called and a bounty set at thirty dollars per wolf. James Marr, Association secretary, stated that the bounty offered was "double the bounty of any state, county or association that I know of, and fully the amount offered by the Russian Empire for the destruction of the same species." How the Russians were involved is not known, but the local newspaper wanted a piece of the action. The *North Park Union* offered a year's subscription to the first person who killed a wolf in the Park.

A month later, S. J. Casteel shot a large grey wolf and claimed both the bounty and the year's subscription. The local newspaper made no other mention of wolf bounties being paid that winter, so perhaps it was a one-wolf winter. Yet the Stock Association seemed happy and voted to discontinue the bounty as of April 1, 1900. Regret soon followed this decision.

A beef-eating pack of wolves entered North Park a few years later and in short order consumed forty-eight cattle and three horses. Members of the Stock Association met and quickly set a bounty of seventy-five dollars for each wolf killed in the Park. But money alone would not solve the problem, so an urgent summons went out for Rattlesnake Jack.

S. A. McIntyre was a "well educated and scholarly" man who traveled with a circus as a snake charmer. He boasted that he was the only living man who handled rattlesnakes with their fangs intact. "All the other rattlesnake charmers pulled the fangs before they touched them," claimed McIntyre. He soon became known as Rattlesnake Jack.

He apparently left the circus during the 1880s, came West, and took up trapping in Wyoming and Colorado. Through trial and error he learned what it took to catch wolves, and in one year Rattlesnake Jack trapped ninety-eight wolves and five hundred coyotes. Stockmen paid him over sixteen hundred dollars in bounties during 1903. Without a doubt, Rattlesnake Jack was the best wolfer in the West.

The famed wolfer was in no hurry to travel to North Park, and it was well into January before he arrived. Rattlesnake Jack pulled into the Payne ranch with a team, a rig loaded with equipment, two pet rattlesnakes in a glass box, three mongrel dogs, and his son, Little Rattle.

The senior Rattle was a heavyset man past middle age with "a meaty face and strange, bloodshot, wild animal eyes," according to Stephen Payne. Payne added:

> He had sort of scattered whiskers of a nondescript color, neither gray nor brown nor white. Layers of dirt caked on his skin gave his face an odd color and probably influenced the color of his beard and mustache.

Others described the eccentric wolfer as a "dirty, evil-looking, wizened-up fellow who wore a feather-decorated fur cap the year around." Yet this unkempt appearance was nothing compared to his smell. "Any normal human could smell Rattlesnake Jack a full quarter mile away," said Payne. Little Rattle, in his late twenties, was not yet as unwashed and loud smelling as his father. He was, however, misnamed, for the husky six-footer occupied as much space as Jack.

Dealings with Rattlesnake Jack and his son had to be conducted outside where fresh air and, it was hoped, a brisk wind would dilute the noxious stench. So when they arrived at the Payne place around dinnertime and commented on the good-smelling food, Jack Payne didn't invite them in. Instead he suggested that the wolfers set up camp at an abandoned ranch several miles downwind. Besides, Rattlesnake Jack's favorite dishes consisted of fried rattlesnake, stewed muskrat, and fried skunk, and Jack Payne was probably cooking beef.

Within a few days of their arrival, Rattlesnake Jack came in with his first wolf and claimed the bounty. Perhaps it was at this time Rattlesnake decided to visit the pool hall in Walden for an evening of entertainment. He brought his pet snakes with him, and as soon as he arrived he released them. Both rattlesnakes took off across the floor and pandemonium broke out. He had the pool hall to himself.

Yet Rattlesnake Jack was dead serious when it came to wolves. His secret resided in scents – the lack of some scents and the overpowering presence of others. Any trace of human scent must be eliminated from the trap, so Rattlesnake Jack never used soap on himself or his traps. He claimed that a wolf could pick up the scent of soap faster and from farther away than any other scent. "Them fools as use soap'll never catch nothin'," snorted the trapper to Stephen Payne.

Rattlesnake Jack's success rested with a villainous aroma that was potent enough to pull in wolves from miles around. The scent was so famous that it was mentioned in Rattlesnake Jack's obituary. The notice stated that "with Rattlesnake Jack perished a secret formula for the concoction of wolf bait, which it is claimed never failed to lure the animals into the trap."

The basic ingredient for a wolf scent was rotted meat. One Wyoming recipe called for placing half a pound of raw beef or venison in a crock and allowing it to decay in a warm place for about six weeks. Once the odor had become as offensive as possible, a quart of sperm oil was added (some thought prairie dog oil was better). Half an ounce of assafoetida and one ounce of beaver castor was mixed with the meat and oil. To increase the mixture's attractive powers, a healthy slug of skunk "perfume" was added. Other ingredients found their way into this basic recipe: mice, fish, musk, female wolf urine, oil of rhodium, and undisclosed ingredients were added by wolfers. When the mixture was complete, trappers stored the reeking concoction in a glass bottle. A few drops of the scent applied to a stick or bone strategically placed between two traps usually snagged a wolf.

Rattlesnake Jack believed in the liberal use of scent, and everything he owned eventually became saturated with a reeking stench that offended the nostrils of everything except a wolf. And, of course, soap and bathing were out of the question for this bizarre wolfer.

Within a few months Rattlesnake Jack and Little Rattle had trapped about six wolves and dozens of coyotes. Although they had reduced the predator menace in North Park, not everyone was happy. The editor of the *North Park News* wanted a bounty on predatory burros. "It is impossible for a ranchman to drive into town and leave his sleigh if there is anything eatable in it without the sleigh being surrounded by a herd of burros who eat everything in sight from overshoes and whips to spring seats and whiffletrees." Brooms, clothes on the line, and "stove wood when it is nicely split" represented other items on the burros' menu.

Rattlesnake Jack wasn't interested in trapping burros. He

was a wolfer, and after collecting his bounties from the Stock Association he stayed in the area, working as a professional trapper for the government. Then, in the winter of 1911, the following notice was published in the newspaper:

> WALDEN, Colo., Feb. 27. – S. A. McIntyre, hunter and trapper and better known throughout the mountainous district of Wyoming and Colorado as "Rattlesnake Jack," ended his life about 8 o'clock Saturday night by shooting. For twenty-five years he had lived in the mountains . . . and earned the reputation of being the best trapper in the Rockies.

13
Lead with the Mail

When Price drew off his right mitten, King, who was driving the stage, handed the lines to young Howell and took hold of his gun.
North Park Union, March 29, 1901

Norv King had good reason to grab his Winchester. John Price, a North Park rancher living in the "neck" of the Park, had a grudge against stage drivers who carried the mail. "Price seems to have had a mania for terrorizing stage drivers," printed the Laramie *Boomerang*, "and is said to have threatened the lives of four of the company's men from time to time."

The newspaper added that "John Price moved into the Park about twenty years ago and married eight years ago, but had no children." Originally from Kentucky, Price was perhaps forty years old when King reached for his gun. Norv King, a quiet, conscientious driver for the Laramie and North Park Stage Company, was twenty-four years old and both the son and son-in-law of prominent North Park ranchers.

Price was incensed that stage drivers charged a delivery fee for mail. He demanded that his letters and packages be carried free of charge from the post office to his ranch. But the stage company did not provide free delivery service. He offered ten and later twenty-five cents per month for the service, but the company stood firm at its rate of fifty cents.

At one point during this long-running dispute, stage driver Sid Lawrence had to knock Price off the stage when the ranchman became violent over delivery rates. King was likewise the subject of his wrath. Earlier in 1901, Price, "without any provocation whatever and without warning," jumped on the stage, seized King by the collar and threatened him with a knife.

That was enough for King. He wrote to the stage company, stating his intention to quit and recommending a replacement. However, after a few days off, King reconsidered and decided to return to his job. Worried about his son, King's father wrote to the company's agent requesting that "some protection be afforded his son." The company responded by notifying the postal inspector about Price's violent nature. That only made matters worse.

King had just resumed his duties when Price, riding a horse, met the stage in the neck of the Park. On that day King had only one passenger, a young man named Jimmie Howell, who was riding outside. Price came to within fifty feet of the stage before he stopped and dismounted, putting his horse between himself and the stage. Suspecting trouble, King stopped the stage and moved to the far side of the driver's seat, putting a few more inches between himself and Price. The rancher yanked off his right mitten and threw his hand into his overcoat pocket as if to pull a gun. "At about this instant (and on that point the evidence was not clear), Price said, 'What in hell is the matter with you now?' or some such remark, as near as the witness could remember it," according to the account in the North Park Union.

King threw the reins to Howell, grabbed his Winchester, and fired. The hasty shot found its mark and plowed through Price's head. At the sound of the gun, Price's horse "whirled about and started back home on the gallop."

Without dismounting or taking a second look at Price, King immediately took the lines and drove on. At the end of his run he told his story to Sid Lawrence and then returned to Walden to surrender to the authorities. The only authority King could find was the town treasurer, Clarence Mosman.

Undertaker Manly Capron and Justice of the Peace W. D. Beckwith were dispatched to the scene. There they found Price's wife, Lizzie, by the side of her dead husband. Alerted by the return of the riderless horse and informed by a surveyor that her husband had been shot, she had run to the scene and stood vigil over her husband. Capron and Beckwith conducted an investigation and hauled the body to Walden.

Larimer County Deputy Sheriff Clampitt and County Coroner Gough arrived in Walden on Thursday, the day after the shooting. On Saturday an inquest was held in city hall over the body of John Price. Jimmie Howell provided most of the testimony, for he was the only witness to the shooting. But he was unable to provide any explanation as to why Price had met the stage and dismounted. Perhaps Price had wanted to talk about why he had been reported to the post office inspector. It was possible that Price had finally agreed to the fifty-cent monthly charge for mail delivery. Or perhaps the rancher was out to provoke more trouble.

Testimony given by Undertaker Capron suggests that Price's intentions were peaceful. Capron found that the only weapon carried by Price was a small, two-bladed knife in his right pants pocket.

Although King had killed an unarmed man who may not have been looking for trouble on that fateful day, many felt that "someone had to kill Price and that King was the unfortunate man chosen by destiny to do it." Stage drivers considered Price a dangerous man who was "extremely quarrelsome and of an ugly disposition." He was possessed by violent moods that "came often as the changes of the moon." Some considered the rancher a "would-be bad man who, when it came to a showdown, had very little sand."

The coroner's jury deliberated for only a short time before coming to the verdict that "John Price came to his death at the hands of N. S. King, by a Winchester 45-70 rifle, on the 20th day of March, 1901, without felonious intent."

Price's funeral was held on March 23 at the Methodist church in Walden. "The weather was raw and the wind was cold," noted the *North Park Union.* Attendance was fair, Reverend Wilson delivered an appropriate address, and a few friends sang songs. Before the mourners left the church, the coffin was opened and the lone family member, the widow Lizzie Price, went to her husband and "in a voice smothered in emotion said, 'Good bye, John, good bye,' and turned sorrowfully away."

Although the Prices had lived in North Park for many years, John had never allowed his wife to visit Walden. Following his death, Lizzie remained at the ranch only a short time before moving to Walden where she worked in a restaurant. Lizzie later married George Clark, and they moved back to her ranch in the neck of the Park. The couple soon opened a road ranch where North Parkers stopped on their way to and from Laramie. Lizzie and George quickly established a reputation as "wonderful people, beloved by all travellers."

14
Willow Creek Pass

There we were [on Willow Creek Pass], my mother and I, in an open sled and with nothing to eat but frozen food since morning.

Elizabeth Quinn, winter survivor, 1906

Although Willow Creek Pass had been used for centuries by the Indians, settlers did not realize the potential of this trail until the mining boom in the 1880s. During the summer of 1883 the *North Park Miner* reported that settlers "were astonished to find that there was a pass in the ranges as low and of as easy grade" as Willow Creek Pass.

The trail started from Illinois Creek in North Park, followed a gradual ascent to an elevation of 9,750 feet, and then descended along Willow Creek on the south side. It meandered through open timber and meadows, and "there would be no great snowdrifts or danger of snow slides as is now the case in the winter on the trails between North and Middle Parks." The newspaper concluded that it would not be difficult to build a wagon road or railroad over the pass.

Years passed before North Parkers finally hacked a road through the spruce forests and over the pass. Then in 1905 the railroad reached Middle Park, and another railroad started to connect Laramie and North Park. A party of surveyors located a grade over Willow Creek Pass, and it appeared a matter of destiny that the two Parks would soon be connected by rail.

Not wanting to wait for the railroad, Harford Loucks of Walden established a four-horse stage line, via Willow Creek Pass, between North and Middle Parks. David and Lydia Gresham took an immediate interest in the new enterprise. A few years earlier they had owned a North Park road ranch at Cowdrey and later ran a boardinghouse at one of the North Park mines. With the opening of Willow Creek Pass, they decided to build a road ranch at the top to serve the stage traffic going to and from the railhead in Middle Park. During the late spring of 1905, the Greshams and their young daughter, Elizabeth, hauled their belongings up the pass and there built a large log house, barn, and various outbuildings.

The canvas-sided stage arrived at the summit of the pass every day around noon. While Dave hitched fresh horses to the stage, Lydia served dinner to the passengers and driver. Business boomed for the Greshams, thanks to excellent cooking, friendly proprietors, and good accommodations.

As cold weather approached, the Greshams decided to spend the winter on Willow Creek Pass. Although snow would soon close the road to all travel, they had stocked in a supply of staples. Their cows, chickens, and turkeys would provide additional food. Dave hauled in piles of firewood, chinked the cabin walls, and made a snug home for his family.

The family did not worry as the snow piled up and isolated them from the outside world. Their plan would have worked if Lydia had not been expecting a baby in the spring. As the pregnancy advanced, her health slowly changed from good to uncertain. They began to worry. Lydia might need medical help, and help was out of the question during the winter on Willow Creek Pass. They decided to go to Walden.

The snow varied from five to twenty feet deep, and traveling was not going to be easy. On February 9, 1906, Dave Gresham hitched up the team and worked all day to break a trail down the north side of Willow Creek Pass. The next morning the family loaded their open sled with food, blankets, clothing, and household items. Their fifty chickens and five turkeys occupied wooden cages that were strapped to the sled and covered with blankets. Two calves, not yet big enough to push through the snow, found spots in the sled. That left three cows and five horses to follow behind.

Dave, Lydia, and Elizabeth climbed on the sled, and the horses started toward Walden. They quickly found that windblown snow had completely covered the trail Dave made the previous day. By the time they struggled around the first bend in the road from the house, the Greshams concluded that they would never make Walden with their heavy load. Dave sadly unloaded the chickens, turkeys, and calves, hoping they would go back to the barn and perhaps find enough food to survive.

The lightened sled traveled better, but progress was slow. Elizabeth remembered her father "unhitching the team and breaking road a little way and then coming back to the sled and hitching up again and pulling as far as he could, then breaking road again." By nightfall they had traveled less than one mile from their house. Dave made a crude camp by cutting down trees and using the bows to form a shelter over the sled. He built a large fire and cooked supper; then the family settled down for a cold night. Lydia and Elizabeth slept in the sled while Dave tried to keep the fire burning.

Conditions were not better the next day, and they made only four miles through the deep snow. With horses too exhausted to pull the sled farther, they were forced to stop just two miles short of Sol Nixon's sawmill where food and shelter would be available for the weary travelers. The family was stranded, and with no hay for the horses, Dave feared that the exhausted animals would not make it through the night. So he left Lydia and Elizabeth in the sled, promising to plow ahead with the horses and get help.

As daylight faded, mother and daughter huddled in the sled. They were unable to make a fire and had nothing to eat but frozen food. Sick from the cold and fearful of attack by mountain lions that prowled the area, they spent a long, terrifying night. Elizabeth later recalled that they had "no idea how long we would have to stay there alone, how long it would take Father to get through or if he could get through at all."

Dave and the horses did finally arrive at the sawmill. But all were too exhausted to return to the sled that night, so Nixon left his warm cabin and headed for the stranded mother and daughter. In the early morning hours, Sol Nixon found the sled. Lydia and Elizabeth had weathered the night without serious harm, but Nixon had not fared well. Bucking the deep snow had been too much for him, and his heart "developed a terrible spell." Lydia thought he would die, but after a few hours of rest, Nixon felt better. He built a fire, mixed a flour dough, and cooked bread on a snow shovel. Lydia and Elizabeth had never tasted bread as good as the hot and crusty snow shovel loaves cooked by Nixon.

The stranded travelers still had no way of getting out, and Nixon was in no condition to hike back to his sawmill. Again they waited. In the early afternoon of February 12, a rescue party arrived. Two men came first, then a woman on horseback to break the trail. Dave followed with the team. That night they safely rested at Nixon's place.

The next day Dave decided to go back for the livestock that he had left behind. It had been a calm night, so the trail made the previous day remained open. Dave found his stock in the barn, but coyotes had killed two of the turkeys and about half of the chickens. He gathered the remaining stock and hauled them down the pass.

Two days later the family arrived in Walden, never to return to Willow Creek Pass. The premonitions about a troubled pregnancy came to pass, for several months later the baby was born dead.

The road ranch on Willow Creek Pass slowly rotted away and steel rails never replaced the road. By the time the railroad reached Walden in 1911, there was insufficient commerce between the two Parks to warrant a rail connection.

15
Rustler Arvean

Arvean was charged with cattle stealing. In North Park cattle stealing was a more heinous crime than murder.

Fancher Sarchet, defense attorney, 1926

Attorney Fancher Sarchet's first trip to North Park had nothing to do with rustlers and everything to do with hunting and fishing. It was the summer of 1914 when North Park was still sparsely settled cattle country.

Sarchet loaded a wagon with tents, bedding, food, and other supplies and sent it from Fort Collins two days ahead of his own departure. The attorney followed in an automobile, and the two parties met along the Platte River in North Park. The hunting and fishing were excellent, and soon the men had crocks of salted trout and preserved sage hens that would last until winter.

One afternoon during this hunting trip, Sarchet drove into Walden for supplies. He described Walden as "wild and western" with several saloons and a great circular water trough in the middle of town. While in town Sarchet met Elmer Mallon, a county commissioner, and Harry Green, former mayor of Walden. Mallon and Green were best of friends; where one went, the other followed. These two ranchers invited Sarchet to join them for a few drinks. When Green decided to move from one bar to another, Mallon followed. As Green walked past the watering trough, he idly swirled his hand in the water and for some unknown reason, walked around the trough. When Mallon followed, Green thought he was following him. Each one thought the other was going some place, so around and around they went. Sarchet stood on the sidelines, convulsed with laughter as he watched the tipsy ranchers walking around in circles. No self-respecting attorney would circle a watering trough, so Sarchet thought he had one up on the North Park ranchers. Twelve years later the tables turned.

In 1926 Sarchet was hired to defend Arvean Marsh, a young man of about twenty-seven who had started as a ranch hand in North Park when he was eighteen and now had a small cattle herd of his own in the south end of the Park. His cattle herd was peculiar in that he owned a large number of calves in comparison to the small number of cows. To make matters worse, most of the calves were unbranded. While riding the range, he had a habit of finding "orphaned" calves, especially on his neighbors' lands. At night the "homeless" youngsters were placed in his barn for safekeeping.

During the late afternoon of May 24, Arvean's neighbor, Frank Kendall, found one of his cows about a mile from Arvean's barn. Her bag was full, and she was frantically looking for her calf. Kendall and a ranch hand searched until well after dark to find the calf but had no luck. Around midnight the two men drove the cow to the Marsh barn, opened the door, and soon had mother and offspring reunited. As attorney Sarchet later put it, "They rushed into each other's arms." Kendall promptly filed charges, and the case of the *People v. Arvean Marsh* was born.

Sarchet arrived in Walden the day before the trial to check things out. A trip around the bars revealed the disturbing fact that every man on the jury panel was a member of the North Park Stock Growers Association. The future looked short and bleak for Arvean until Sarchet started asking questions about Kendall, who was known throughout the Park as a rancher who had a long rope and a quick iron. With one suspected rustler pointing the finger at another, Sarchet had hope for his client.

Attorney Sarchet arrived at the Jackson County courthouse early the next morning. The small courthouse was an attractive building constructed of native stone and located on a slight rise that commanded an enticing view of North Park. In contrast to the small offices that contained a deluge of government officials crowded into every nook and corner of the building, the courtroom was spacious. Windows occupied two walls of the courtroom, and rows of high-backed oak chairs accommodated spectators. A railed-off portion at the front of the room had seats for the jury and a judicial stand, witness box, and other courtroom fixtures. The jury panel soon filled most of the spectator seats. With Judge Smith presiding, a jury of twelve North Park ranchers was quickly selected.

Kendall took the stand and retold the events of May 24. His convincing story was corroborated by his ranch hand. Arvean was doomed. There is no better proof of parenthood than a mother nursing her offspring. With a sinking feeling Sarchet cross-examined Kendall, but to no one's surprise, the rancher stuck to his story.

Arvean was called to the stand by Sarchet. The young rancher told the jury a compelling story about how he had found this motherless calf wandering around near his ranch. His concern and work saved the calf from certain death. Sarchet suspected that no one bought the story, but when rustler versus rustler, the outcome is difficult to predict.

The trial was complete, except for the closing argument on behalf of the defendant. Closing arguments were Sarchet's strong point; his crypt, caustic, and pointed style might yet win the day for his client, especially if he could shift the blame onto Kendall. He faced the jury, looked each member in the eye, and according to his memoirs, stated: "Gentlemen, [Kendall] drove the wet cow to the Marsh barn at mid-night, grafted one of Arvean's calves to the cow, and left with both cow and calf."

This telling argument had a profound effect on the jury, and Sarchet may have smiled to himself; accusing Kendall of stealing the calf was a brilliant move. In the now quiet courtroom, the defense attorney was undoubtedly pleased to see Jay Monroe, foreman of the jury, slump forward and put his face in his hands. But Monroe was not overcome with emotion; he was just trying to hide his snickering. It didn't work. Another juror in the back row let out a loud guffaw. With this, the entire courtroom exploded into peals of laughter.

Judge Smith gave up the idea of calling for order and instead snarled through the side of his mouth, "Court adjourned!" Then the judge, district attorney, and Sarchet hastily retreated to the judge's chambers where they looked dumbly at each other. The consensus was that something Sarchet said caused the torrent of laughter, but they were at a loss as to the reason until the clerk arrived.

The clerk patiently explained that the process of grafting a calf to a cow was a complicated and difficult procedure that took a week or more. Cows were very fussy about which calf drank at the spigot, and ranchers often had to tie up the cow, head and feet, until she accepted the foreign calf. This grafting process commonly failed, and the calf had to be fed from a bottle if it was to live.

Certain that his client's goose was cooked, Sarchet recommended that the trial be concluded. The judge concurred, returned to the courtroom, announced to the still-snickering jury that there would be no further argument, and sent the jurymen to their room to reach a verdict.

Sarchet left the courtroom and walked up the main street of Walden. He likely wanted to regain some measure of composure before facing Arvean once the jury reached its verdict. His solace was short-lived. Charley Murphy, a successful young rancher who had attended the trial, spotted Sarchet and called him over. The attorney remembered the conversation:

> Sarchet, the fishing is good out at the ranch, and I would like to have you come out and spend a month with me. There will be a nice place for you to bunk, the meals are good, and I might even pay you five dollars a

> day during your stay. Oh yes, there is a little chore I would like to have you do while you are with me, one you can do in between fishing, eating, and sleeping. I have about five hundred calves out there I would like to have you graft.

Sarchet joined in the laughter this time. Before he could respond to Murphy's offer, the sheriff arrived and informed him that the jury was ready with its verdict. With a sinking feeling, the attorney entered the courtroom and faced his client. The clerk then read, "We, the jury, find Arvean Marsh not guilty."

Right or wrong, the grafting worked!

Middle Park

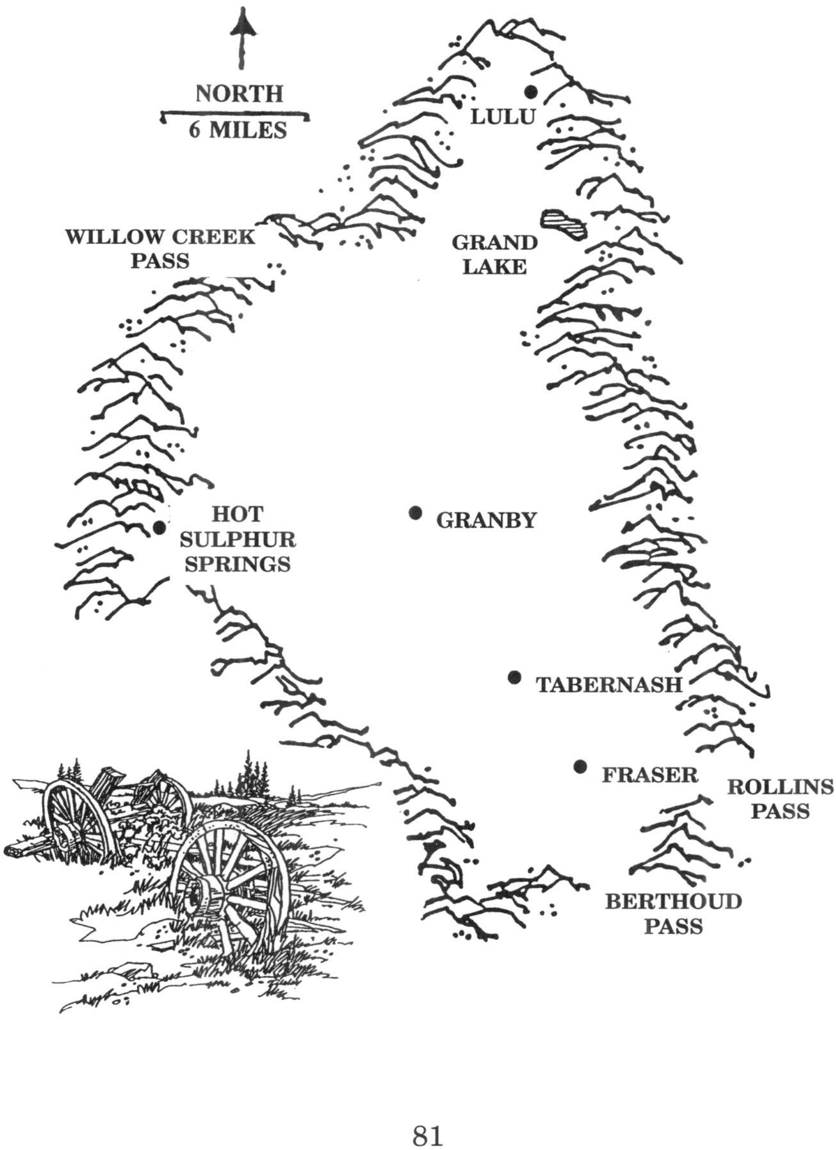
NORTH
6 MILES
LULU
WILLOW CREEK
PASS
GRAND
LAKE
HOT
SULPHUR
SPRINGS
GRANBY
TABERNASH
FRASER
ROLLINS
PASS
BERTHOUD
PASS

16
Standing Bear

The principal tribes inhabiting this section of the country [Middle Park] were the Utes, Arapahoes, and Cheyennes, and between the former, who were the mountain Indians, and the latter tribes, who pitched their tepees on the plains, was waged a perpetual warfare.

Rocky Mountain News, July 9, 1883

Many Indian legends tell of this perpetual warfare for control of the prized hunting rights in Middle Park. One of the favorite legends about the struggle centers on Standing Bear, a young Ute anxious to be recognized as a man. Lending credibility to the story is the fact that the Indian fort that plays an important part in the legend can still be found above a rocky cliff near Granby.

The story began on a summer's day as Standing Bear hunted along Willow Creek in the central portion of Middle Park. The sun had yet to creep over the eastern mountains, but in the predawn light Standing Bear saw a small herd of elk peacefully grazing in a meadow several miles away. As he was about to start toward them, the elk suddenly threw their heads up and stared at the timber that fringed Willow Creek. They momentarily stood motionless, then abruptly wheeled and bolted into the forest.

Standing Bear soon discovered what had startled the elk. A band of about forty Indians, half hidden by the trees, cautiously picked their way down Willow Creek. Their dress identified them as Arapahoes and Cheyennes. These Indians had most likely come from the Laramie plains, down through North Park, and then into Middle Park. The absence of children, women, dogs, lodge poles, and skins marked the group as a war party.

The young Indian turned his horse and raced for the confluence of what was later known as the Colorado and Fraser Rivers where his tribe was camped. His people, who had been hunting the abundant game of Middle Park, now roasted meat over smoky fires and fleshed stretched hides. Their enemies would surely see the smoke.

His horse lathered, Standing Bear burst into the camp and sounded the alarm. The Indians immediately broke camp and headed eastward where a series of hills and bluffs offered some protection.

The Utes had good reason to flee from the Arapahoes and their allies, the Cheyennes. With women and children in tow, the Utes had to protect their families first, thus reducing their response to strictly defensive measures. Yet they ached to revenge at least one legendary encounter with their enemies.

Years ago, the Utes had camped along the shores of Grand Lake. While the men hunted one day, a war party of Arapahoes found the camp. Facing an almost hopeless situation, the women quickly made a raft using logs lashed together with rawhide strips. The women then grabbed their children and paddled into the middle of Grand Lake where they sadly watched their enemies loot the camp. But the safety of the raft did not last. Gusty winds suddenly raked the lake, churning the once placid water and capsizing the crowded raft. According to the legend, all but a few drowned in the deep, frigid waters. From that time forward, the Utes regarded the lake as a dwelling place for departed souls. They avoided the haunted place, which they named Spirit Lake. And the Arapahoes became perpetual enemies.

Now the Arapahoes and their Cheyenne allies had again caught the Utes in a difficult spot. The fleeing Indians quickly reached the crest of a ridge near the Fraser River. The east side of the ridge abruptly ended in a rocky bluff about thirty feet high. Timber fringed the west and south sides of the ridge, leaving an open north side that descended to the grasslands below. Fallen logs and loose rocks were quickly thrown together to form a breastwork several feet high on three sides of their position. There was no reason to fortify the east end, for the Utes could easily stop anyone from climbing the cliff.

The small, triangular-shaped fort had no room for horses, so they were released. Perhaps the enemy would take the horses and consider that victory enough. Utes prided themselves on their ability to steal horses, and they could easily replenish any lost stock.

The Utes prepared for a battle they hoped to avoid. Women and children took shelter in the rock crevices that extended from the cliff inward. Men took positions along the breastworks. Secure in their mountain fortress, the Utes waited for the attack. Although the Ute culture regarded war as a nuisance to be avoided, they were considered among the bravest and most fearsome fighters when war was the only option. When the Cheyennes and Arapahoes ignored the loose horses and advanced toward the stone fort, the Utes realized that fighting was the only way out.

The enemy cautiously approached the fort, trying to determine the strength and position of the Utes before attacking. Much to the dismay of the Cheyennes and Arapahoes, the attack would have to be made without their horses. Dense timber, boulder-strewn ground, the entrenched position of the Utes, and a lack of maneuvering room forced them to approach on foot.

Legend claims that Standing Bear was the first to spill enemy blood. When he caught a glimpse of an Arapahoe running from tree to tree, Standing Bear patiently waited for the warrior to make another move. When he did, the young Indian sent an arrow into his chest. With the scream of the fallen warrior, a torrent of arrows hit the breastworks and the battle was on.

Although the Utes were greatly outnumbered, they were aided by their excellent defensive position and by possession of the only gun on either side. The proud owner of the old flintlock had plenty of gun powder but had used up his meager supply of lead while hunting elk. Fortunately, the rocky ground yielded abundant small pebbles that were packed into the barrel after a large charge of powder. Although its deadly blast did not extend far, it was put to good use by simply firing it in the direction of the enemy. It made a thunderous roar that unnerved the attackers.

The battle raged throughout the hot day, with no side gaining the advantage and with few casualties. The Utes knew that they would eventually be driven from their fort, either by the sheer force of numbers or by the lack of water. Their only hope was to send a messenger to the hot springs, a distance of about fifteen miles. The Indians considered the hot springs sacred, and large groups of Utes typically camped in the vicinity of the springs during the summer. Without hesitation, Standing Bear volunteered for the mission.

Late that night, men silently lowered the young Indian down the cliff. He slowly made his way around the sentries and into the timber where he hoped to find one of the abandoned horses. Otherwise, Standing Bear would be forced to steal a horse from the enemy's herd, a risky task that would eat up precious time. The gods blessed the young warrior that night, for he soon found two of his horses grazing in a small meadow.

As he was about to mount, a Cheyenne stepped out of the forest. Mistaking the Ute for one of his own tribe, the enemy approached and asked if there were any more horses around. Standing Bear mumbled a reply that brought the Cheyenne closer. Once the enemy was within striking distance, the young warrior grabbed him by the throat and drove his knife into the Cheyenne's chest. He died without uttering a sound.

Standing Bear quickly mounted one horse and pushed the other one ahead of him. By a circuitous route, he cautiously worked his way around the enemy camp. Once beyond hearing distance of the enemy, he raced his horse for the hot springs. When his horse began to tire, he changed to the fresh horse.

The Ute camp at the hot springs was larger than usual that year, and the warriors were more than eager to join the fight. Standing Bear guided almost one hundred men to the rock fort. They arrived shortly after the attack had been renewed at dawn.

The hot springs reinforcements immediately joined the fight. Surprised by the attack from the rear, the Cheyennes and Arapahoes ran for their horses, but less than half their number remained standing to escape to the plains. The rest lay dead on the ground.

Although war honors were not a part of the Ute culture, his tribe recognized Standing Bear as the hero of the stone fort battle. Now considered a man, he received the honors befitting one of high stature. Years later, Standing Bear became a tribal chief. At least that's what the legend claims.

17
Expeditions

Before we passed the Kansas, we came upon an encampment that attracted attention. It turned out to be a grand hunting company for the plains. Sir George Gore, an English Baronet, had taken it into his head that it will be fine sport to hunt buffalo, &c, on our great western plains. So he packed up his trunks.

Daily Ohio State Journal, June 20, 1854

Sir George Gore packed more than trunks for his grand hunt. His retinue consisted of forty servants and assistants, one hundred and twelve horses, twelve yoke of oxen, three milk cows, fourteen hunting dogs, six wagons, and twenty-one carts. The wagons and carts carried guns of every caliber, tables, rugs, a linen tent, vintage wine, a brass bedstead, and even a bathtub. Gore did not travel lightly, and he did not forgo any creature comforts befitting a young man of immense wealth.

Jim Bridger, however, traveled light. He had no use for a rug or bathtub, and one reliable gun was all he needed. Now fifty years old, Bridger was described as "tall and spare, but erect, active and energetic." His abundant brown hair flowed around sharp gray eyes that reflected his friendly and hospitable nature. As a scout, trapper, and guide, he was "respected and trusted by white men and Indians alike."

In the early 1850s, Bridger's agreeable nature was put to the test by the Mormons. For more than ten years, Bridger operated what amounted to a truck stop along the Oregon Trail. From his fort in western Wyoming he repaired wagons, sold supplies, traded horses, and gave advice to travelers along the Oregon Trail. Bridger also sold guns to the neighboring Indians whom he considered valued friends. However, the neighboring Mormons took a dim view of Bridger's arming the Indians, and this disagreement finally drove Bridger from his fort.

So in the fall of 1854 Bridger abandoned his Wyoming fort and headed east, while Gore blasted his way west. The two met in Fort Laramie where they sized up each other and liked what they saw. Restless from years at his fort, Bridger realized that the enthusiastic, likeable Gore would provide the excuse he needed to wander in the western mountains. In turn, Gore respected Bridger's encyclopedic knowledge of the West. "With a buffalo skin and a piece of charcoal, he will map out any portion of this immense region, and delineate streams, mountains and circular valleys, called holes, with wonderful accuracy," stated an army captain. Hiring the old mountain man as chief guide and advisor would ensure that the grand hunt would be just that.

It was amazing that the two men got along. Bridger had no use for titles and did not distinguish between a nobleman and an Indian when it came to bestowing respect. He was illiterate and spoke with the distinctive twang of a mountain man. When Gore often quoted from Shakespeare after a leisurely dinner, Bridger complained that he "reckoned Shakespeare was a lettle too highfalutin for him." But Bridger liked the cultured and refined Sir St. George Gore. This friendly aristocrat had nothing to do in life other than to seek adventure and entertainment, spend money, and be pampered by an army of servants. Yet a friendship quickly developed, and the two men were almost constant companions for the next two years.

Shortly after their meeting in 1854, Gore and Bridger

decided to hunt the Colorado parks located south of Fort Laramie. The procession arrived in North Park sometime during the autumn. Details of the excursion are unknown, for Bridger could not write and Gore could not be bothered. Secondary records suggest that the hunting party set up a main camp in North Park and then traveled to Middle Park with fewer men and equipment than usual. Perhaps the bathtub and a few servants stayed behind in North Park, but it would be wrong to think that Gore did not live in luxury while in Middle Park.

The abundance of game in the Park at that time has been well documented, and presumably their hunting was successful. Indians were likewise abundant, so Bridger moved their camp to a new location every night in a successful effort to avoid them. Although Bridger was a skilled Indian negotiator and respected fighter if combat was the only way out, his usual policy when away from his fort was to avoid Indians altogether.

The hunters did not stay long in Middle Park, for it was late in the season and Bridger had a healthy respect for mountain winters. Yet the impact of the hunting party was sufficient to leave several named landmarks behind. Gore Pass, Gore Range, Gore Canyon, Gore Creek, and Gore Mountain carry the name of the eccentric playboy.

As they left Middle Park and a string of carcasses behind, Bridger was likely disturbed by the wanton slaughter of animals. The old scout probably agreed with the Indian philosophy of taking only what is needed and using all of what is taken. The Irish nimrod had a different point of view, and during his two-year hunt, thousands of buffalo and other big game species were slaughtered. According to one member of the hunting expedition, so many buffalo were killed that one Indian tribe "brought complaints of the needless and reckless destruction of these animals to their agents, and the government intervened." Bridger likely kept his opinion to himself, for the two men remained friends.

Bridger's next trip to Colorado was announced by the *Rocky Mountain News*. On May 8, 1861, the newspaper noted that

"James Bridger arrived here this morning by coach, and will proceed at once to lay out and locate a Government Road passing through Denver and on northwest through Bridger Pass toward the Pacific." Bridger had been hired by the Central Overland California to find a wagon road from Denver to Salt Lake City and beyond.

The citizens of Golden, who were actively seeking the title of territorial capital, were incensed that the proposed transcontinental route would miss their fine city. Besides, Edward Berthoud and other prominent men had reliable information that a breach in the mountain wall at the headwaters of Clear Creek provided an easy path to the west. Just a week prior to Bridger's arrival and the entry of the Central Overland California, the newspaper announced the formation of the "Middle Park Road" expedition. The Denver newspaper proclaimed that "the route is entirely practicable, and we look confidently forward to an early day when the main route of travel will be from this city directly westward . . . through the Middle Park, and so on westward to the Salt Lake Valley." The vigorous promotors of this route quickly convinced the directors of the Central Overland California to change their minds. Bridger's orders were modified and instead of heading north to Wyoming, he went west with Berthoud.

The expedition started on May 10, 1861. Berthoud, a highly respected and energetic surveyor, was in charge and represented the Golden interests while Bridger was guide and represented the interests of the Central Overland California. These interests coincided until the headwaters of Clear Creek were approached two days later. The Golden group insisted that the best route from that point was through Middle Park, while the Central Overland California group argued that a route through South Park held better prospects. Unable to come to an agreement, the group split. Bridger and three others headed for South Park and the mining camp of Tarryall. Berthoud stuck with the original plan and headed for Middle Park.

When the expedition returned to Golden two weeks later, Bridger had failed to find a suitable route. Berthoud, however, was exuberant, for he had discovered a pass. Unlike other Rocky Mountain passes, this one showed no signs of having been used before by Indians, buffalo, or any other creature walking on legs. Actually, Berthoud first described the pass as a "low spot on the range," and at an elevation of over 11,000 feet, that's about as far as it went. But if Golden was to be on the transcontinental route, this low spot represented the only way. Therefore, Berthoud Pass received much fanfare and the road idea flourished. The Central Overland California reluctantly decided to sponsor another, and more elaborate, expedition.

On July 6, an expedition that eventually consisted of seventeen men and thirty horses and mules left Denver and traveled to Middle Park via Berthoud Pass. As on the previous expedition, Berthoud was in charge and Bridger served as guide. Four days later they arrived at the summit of the pass and camped "in a most delicious meadow skirted by a beautiful forest of spruce trees." Their journey down the north side of the pass was "fatiguing" due to the dense timber and brush. Bridger guided them through Middle Park and westward via Gore Pass.

About a month later they arrived in Utah, having found a route from Denver to Salt Lake City that was almost two hundred miles shorter than the existing route through Wyoming. With Bridger in the lead, the trip was "eminently successful in every particular" and "we did not see an Indian, great or small, either going or coming, and we are very thankful that we did not."

One member of the expedition, C. M. Ferrel, wrote the following regarding Bridger:

> I cannot say too much of him; he is an old mountaineer in the broadest sense of the term, and convinced all of us that he had traveled this route before the majority of us were in existence. He is a kind, jovial old gentleman, and I trust that I utter the sentiments of the whole party when I say, that we all entertain the highest affection and regard for him.

Despite Bridger's skill as a guide and Berthoud's exuberant reports concerning the westward route through Middle Park, few paid much attention. The Civil War had broken out, and keeping the nation together took precedent over building a road through Colorado. Following the war, the idea of a transcontinental wagon road was replaced by a railroad to California. Once again Golden, now the territorial capital, campaigned to be on the route and Berthoud Pass was actively promoted as providing the best passage through the mountains. The Union Pacific Railroad expressed interest, and representatives arrived in Colorado in August 1866. The railroad officials quickly concluded that although the Colorado Rockies could be breached during the summer, there was little hope for keeping the route open during the winter. Berthoud Pass and Middle Park were forgotten as a transcontinental route.

Yet the publicity surrounding the early expeditions into Middle Park found a receptive audience. Ranchers, farmers, hunters, and even tourists soon headed for this grassland park surrounded by snow-capped mountains.

18
The Utes of Middle Park

About eighty lodges of Utes are camped here now, along the opposite bank of the river; their village presenting a novel and animated appearance. The number is daily increasing and it is said will reach three thousand persons by the middle of next week.

Rocky Mountain News, August 20, 1868

The Ute Indians loved Middle Park, for it was one of their favorite hunting grounds, and it contained sacred hot springs. Indians were not alone in their fondness of Middle Park. Although most of the Park lacked mineral resources, settlers and tourists found wealth in its rich grasslands, abundant game, and thermal waters. After Berthoud hacked a crude trail over a high pass that allowed access to Middle Park during the summer, the Utes found they had to share their sacred hunting ground and hot springs.

Early contact between the Middle Park Ute Indians and the whites was infrequent and usually peaceful; the Utes were not inclined toward hostilities and extended friendship toward the newcomers. Early writers described the Middle Park Ute Indians as friendly, affable, hospitable toward strangers, and good people who did not take themselves too seriously, except for their love of children, horses, and dogs. When conflict did arise, the Utes usually ordered the whites to leave within "two sleeps." On occasion, the Indians would emphasize their request with threatening gestures and by confiscating horses.

The relative peace in Middle Park was in sharp contrast to other parts of Colorado where Indians habitually attacked stagecoaches and raided farms, ranches, and outlying settlements. Realizing that peace might not last, in the summer of 1863 the government sent a delegation to Middle Park to negotiate a treaty with the Utes. These men set up camp at the hot springs – a favorite gathering place for the Ute – but they found no Indians.

Later that year, the government succeeded in contacting the Indians, and a formal treaty was negotiated with the Tabeguache Utes under which the Indians ceded a lavish extent of territory to the government. Although the treaty implied that Middle Park was no longer Indian territory, only one band of Utes having interest in the Park had been included in the treaty. The Indian problem in Middle Park had not been solved.

In 1866 another treaty was signed at the hot springs. For days the whites tried to induce another band of Utes to join their Tabeguache relatives on a reservation. Although the remaining Middle Park Utes had no desire for reservation life, the portion of the ten tons of gifts and a herd of cattle that had survived the rough trip over Rollins Pass bought partial accommodation. The gathered Utes ceded a right-of-way through the Park and promised not to molest any settlements that might be built along it. In turn they would be given livestock, blankets, and provisions. The treaty failed to pass the Senate, due in part to the opposition of some Colorado citizens who wanted the Utes confined to a remote reservation.

Although the agreement was not approved, western whites and Indians who cared little for political detail saw the Treaty of Middle Park as an informal agreement under which each party could use the Park according to its own inclinations. The lack of settlements, the scarcity of squatters, and the transient nature of the tourists and speculators did not unduly infringe on the Utes' traditional use of the area and helped implement this understanding. In addition, the good behavior on the part of the Indians may have been motivated, in part, by their anticipation of collecting the promised annuity under the rejected treaty.

Samuel Bowles, editor of the *Springfield Republican,* and his large traveling party entered the scene in the summer of 1868. As Bowles rode into Middle Park, he observed that "a hundred white tents, like dots in the distance, showed the encampment of six to eight hundred Ute Indians."

The whites set up camp in the vicinity of the hot springs, not far from the Indians. The Utes valued the hot springs for their sacred and medicinal attributes. Soaking in the springs was thought to cure a wide assortment of ills. Even sick or lame horses were partially immersed into the steaming water.

Bowles found the Ute Indians quite neighborly and later wrote:

> Curiosity, begging and good-fellowship were their only apparent motives; they did no mischief; they stole nothing, though food and clothing, pistols and knives, things they coveted and needed above all else, were loosely scattered about within reach; they only became a nuisance by being everlastingly in the way and spoiling the enjoyment of one's food by their wistful observations.

Bowles wrote that the Indians were rather short, under six feet, and of very comely appearance with fine hands, delicate feet, and shapely limbs. Most had bright complexions and clear, piercing eyes. Daubs of red and yellow paint decorated their cheeks and foreheads.

Clothing was an interesting mixture of cultures. A white man's cast-off hat, coat, or pantaloons combined with leggings and moccasins formed the basics for the men. When the weather was cool, a worn blanket or beaded buckskin jacket was added. Eagle feathers, brass ornaments, or tin trinkets hung from the head, ears, or down the back or chest. Bowles recorded that the combinations resulted in a disorderly and absurd appearance.

The women dressed much more plainly than the men. Some wore shabby calico dresses, long shirts of white cloth, or flour sacks (often bearing brand names such as "Hard to Beat") sewn into garments. Others wore traditional dress that consisted of two doeskins sewn together.

Bowles found no evidence of a desire for strong drink among members of this tribe. No one even asked for whiskey. But they did crave sugar and biscuits, and this weakness, plus their contact with whites, had disastrous effects, as observed by Bowles.

> Coughs are frequent, and dyspepsia; sickness and deaths are quite common among the children; and this incongruous mixture of white man's food and raiment and life with their own, which their contact with civilization has led them into, is sapping their vitality at its foundations. To make matters the worse, they have got hold of our quack medicines . . . with the vain hope of curing their maladies.

Other aspects of Ute culture were recorded by the Springfield editor. Horses constituted wealth, and the Middle Park tribe had several hundred horses that they either bred or stole from other tribes, especially the hated Arapahoes and Cheyennes. The Utes subsisted on wild game, nuts, berries, roots, and government handouts – a precarious living given disappearing game and undependable government agents. Politics also entered their lives. When Bowles arrived in Middle Park, an old chief had died, and the successor was being contested. He noted that the wrangling was not half so fierce as would arise over a contested election for mayor.

For the most part the Indian camp was quiet during the day. The men hunted, repaired weapons, sat around fires, or gambled. Horse racing was the preferred form of gambling, and an Indian with a fast horse might bet all that he owned, plus his wife, on the outcome of a single race. Women gathered wood and berries, tanned skins, wove coiled baskets, prepared meals, braided lariats, or made leather garments. The children helped their mothers, guarded horses, and played simple games. Grand pow-wows ruled the night. Music and loud shouting rolled into the Bowles's camp at a frightful volume, as if the Utes were getting ready to scalp someone. But it was innocent amusement.

Two years later, in 1870, the Utes were no longer amused. William Byers, editor of the *Rocky Mountain News*, had secured title to land surrounding the hot springs. There he constructed a log cabin, blacksmith shop, and an enclosure around the principal pool to keep the Indians and their horses out and the steam in. That summer the returning Utes looked with dismay at their desecrated hot springs. Later that year they burned the blacksmith shop and for the next several years the Utes made a habit of convincing whites, often at gunpoint, that leaving the Park would be good for their health. Yet settlers continued to trickle into Middle Park.

This encroachment into Middle Park was described in an 1875 article in the *Rocky Mountain News* stating that at Hot Sulphur Springs, "we find instead of the encampment of 400 Utes which were here four years ago, a flourishing village of 20 to 30 houses, two or three hotels, stores, post office, blacksmith shop, and livery stable." In addition, numerous ranches had sprouted up to feed Central City and other mining towns. The idea of a major road or railroad through the Park was vigorously supported.

Although the Utes were now aware that civilization had advanced far into Middle Park, they were unable to deal with the new situation and continued to treat the Park as their own. Thus, they cut fences that blocked their travel, burned fence posts for cooking fires, grazed their horses in the hay fields, coerced timid settlers into giving them food, and occasionally burned a building.

In 1878 a band of disgruntled and dismayed Utes, emboldened by liquor, entered the Park and set up camp at the Junction Ranch. They tore down fences, turned their horses loose in the hay fields, and set up a crude race track. A posse arrived at the encampment the next day, and during a scuffle one miscreant Ute, Tabernash, was killed. Later that summer some Indians retaliated by murdering a rancher. Panic spread among the Middle Park settlers, but peaceful Utes quickly arrived, and the matter was settled amicably.

The next year, 1879, the confused Utes relieved their frustrations with assaults upon the natural resources of Middle Park. Most of the antelope, nearly all of the mountain bison, and approximately half of the deer and elk were killed and left to rot. The Indians also set numerous fires in the forests surrounding Middle Park. R. D. Cox, who was working in the area, stated that he "constantly saw the smoke of fires. The atmosphere was blue with smoke, and on every hand we heard complaints of the fires started by the Utes."

George Grinnell passed through Middle Park in the summer of 1879. He viewed the destruction with dismay and reflected on the plight of the Indians:

> The Utes have always been friendly to the whites; and although occasionally wild spirits among them have robbed and murdered, these acts have been condemned by the tribe at large, and the perpetrators, when it was possible to capture them, have been punished. As to what inherent rights a few thousand Indians have to occupy as a hunting ground a section of country that would support ten times as many white men, I have nothing to say. This is a great question in ethics on which there are different opinions; but all will acknowledge that it is sad to see a nation of brave, fine people driven from their homes, as I fear the Utes must be soon.

Grinnell was right. Federal troops moved into Middle Park in the fall of 1879 and returned in the summers of 1880 and

1881. The troops encountered no Indians and instead spent their time racing horses and feasting on game and trout. The Utes had withdrawn from Middle Park, never to return.

19
Damn Bruin

When he recovered consciousness he found himself in a pool of clotted blood, but no bear in sight. His clothes were nearly all torn off, fifty wounds scarred his body from head to foot.

Rocky Mountain News, July 11, 1871

James Nugent, alias Rocky Mountain Jim, was described as a chivalrous gentleman, drunkard, poet, liar, mountain man, and ruffian. Arriving in the Rocky Mountains in 1854, this character roamed through the forests and plains, stopping only sporadically to work for the army as a guide, scout, or Indian spy when in need of cash. About 1870 he brought a small herd of cattle to Estes Park and tried to settle down as a rancher. Yet his desire to roam remained strong, and it was this desire that brought him to Middle Park.

On a bright Thursday morning in July 1871, Rocky Mountain Jim saddled his mule and left camp to visit a deer lick near Grand Lake. He left his rifle in camp, confident that his large-caliber revolver would do the job of bringing in venison for dinner.

Jim was in his early forties, thickset, about medium height, and with tawny hair that fell in uncared curls over his collar. Beneath his dark, bushy eyebrows resided a pair of large, deeply-set gray-blue eyes. His nose ended in a slight hook, similar to an eagle's beak. Jim's face was smooth shaven except for a dense, imperial moustache.

A traveler, Isabella L. Bird, once described Jim's remarkable walking wardrobe:

> an old cap on his head, and wearing a grey hunting suit much the worse for wear (almost falling to pieces, in fact), a digger's scarf knotted around his waist, a knife in his belt, and "a bosom friend," a revolver, sticking out of the breast-pocket of his coat; his feet, which were very small, were bare, except for some dilapidated moccasins made of horse hide. The marvel was how his clothes hung together, and on him. The scarf round his waist must have had something to do with it.

As Jim rode toward Grand Lake, his faithful dog, Ring, bounded ahead. He had the body and legs of a collie, both of which looked out of place with his head that may have been borrowed from a mastiff. It was this odd-looking dog that started all the trouble.

By mid-morning, Rocky Mountain Jim reached the vicinity of the deer lick. He tied his mule well away from the site and silently approached the opening. Ring stayed behind, as commanded, then disappeared into the brush. Several deer were at the lick, intent on the salt and unaware of Jim's presence. Suddenly the deer became tense and alert, and Jim turned to follow their stare and the noise coming from the brush.

A few seconds later Ring came running back, and for good reason. Right behind the dog was a huge cinnamon-colored bear and her two cubs. The bear instantly shifted her attention from the annoying dog to the man. Jim clearly knew what was about to happen and began firing his revolver. He lodged four bullets into the bear before she reached him. The *Rocky Mountain News* described what happened next:

> She seized him by the left arm at the elbow, biting it

> through and through and mangling it fearfully, hurled him to the ground and shook him as a dog would a rat. Jim still held on to his pistol, and placing the muzzle against her body fired the fifth shot. The sixth refused to go. She then let go of the arm and seized him by the head, ripping the scalp to the bone along the right side and across the forehead. Her weight settled down uponhis chest and he became insensible.

Rocky Mountain Jim was lying in a pool of clotted blood when he regained consciousness. The bear lay dead beside him. His clothes were in shreds, his left thumb bitten off, his right eye hidden by the torn scalp, and ragged, bloody wounds scarred his body from head to foot. Jim groped his way to his mule, dragged himself aboard, and headed for Grand Lake, about eight miles distant.

Rocky Mountain Jim later remembered hearing shouts and calls along the way. He feebly answered them, but no one came because the noise was the creation of his bewildered mind. He fainted often, and once found himself on the grass beside his faithful mule. Jim eventually reached the lake and holloed for help. Two men on the far shore heard the cry and rowed across the lake.

They bound his wounds and cared for him as best they could but realized it was a losing battle. One of the men headed out in the dim hope of finding a doctor. By the merest chance, Dr. Pollock was only fifteen miles away in a mining camp. He arrived in Grand Lake in the late evening and did what little he could to relieve Jim's suffering. The newspaper reported that the patient was no better the following morning:

> He was delirious, defying the Indians that he fancied surrounding him, calling them by name, and appealing to a comrade to bring his horse that he might go away, saying, "See, they have shot me through the head, and here, and here, but the balls are small and don't amount to much," and then he would bless the peace

> commissioners, in his way, and the white men who armed and fed the Indians at the Sand Creek camp and battle ground.

Almost a month after his fight with the bear, Rocky Mountain Jim walked into the newspaper office in Central City. He was covered with scars and oozing wounds. His right eye was bandaged, his face scarred, and his left arm hung limply in a sling. Jim's purpose in going to the newspaper office was to publicly thank all those who had assisted him since his misfortune with the bear. With a trembling voice and a moist eye, he especially thanked the doctor's wife, Mrs. Pollock, and others who had nursed him back to health.

As for bears, Rocky Mountain Jim promised to "make himself a terror to the whole bear family." He swore eternal enmity on the entire bear race and vowed to devote the remainder of his days exclusively to the business of eliminating bears.

He would have likely lived longer if he had stuck to his vow. Instead, he went back to his squatter's claim in Estes Park. He soon earned the reputation as someone to avoid, but that was difficult because his claim was located at the mouth of the only entrance to Estes Park. He took a dim view of tourists and settlers and was "dangerous with his pistols and it would be safer if he were not here," remarked a visitor.

In 1874 Rocky Mountain Jim found that people were far more dangerous than bears. While arguing with Griff Evans over a land claim, Rocky Mountain Jim drew his pistol. Evans was quicker, and the old mountain man was shot. He died a few months later.

Some wanted Evans charged with murder. However, the newspaper noted that Rocky Mountain Jim had been "going around the country" in good health. It attributed his death to "bad whisky and too much of it." As a final tribute to the old man, the paper went on to say that "some years ago he was terribly mutilated in a hand-to-paw encounter with a grizzly in Middle Park."

20
Maggie and Jimmy

In the spring freshness of a new day Maggie saw sagebrush and wild meadow land flecked with flowers; she saw bluffs and ledges and pine-covered hills far gentler than those of the great range behind. The wagons sloshed across willow-lined creeks, bank full with snow water.

Lulita Pritchett, on Maggie's
view of Middle Park, June 1874

The Crawford family – Maggie, Jimmy, and their three children – had arrived in Middle Park. The trip had been a long struggle that began the previous year when the family left Missouri. That year they traveled as far as Empire before winter closed the mountain roads. Temporarily deterred from pursuing his dream of raising cattle, Jimmy found work in Empire. "He leased a mine, worked hard all winter, and made nothing," remembered his granddaughter.

Early the next spring the family was anxious to be on its way, but the snowy trail up Berthoud Pass would not accommodate their wagon. Jimmy learned that John Rollins was building a road over Boulder Pass and into Middle Park. Impatient to start their Middle Park ranch, the Crawfords packed their wagons and headed for Boulder Pass. They arrived at the foot of the pass in early June, only to find that the road was still under construction and not passable.

Not the type to sit around, Jimmy joined the construction crew and for several days helped move boulders from the roadbed. Finally, on June 10, he decided to try the still unfinished road. He hitched up three mules and one horse to his wagon and started up the pass. The mules and horse played out after moving the wagon only a few feet. Undaunted, Jimmy borrowed two yoke of oxen, hitched them to the wagon with the horse and mules, and foot by foot, struggled to the top of the Continental Divide.

Maggie, with her infant son in her arms, and the two other children walked up the pass. "She was so busy picking her way that she paid little attention to the weather till a cannon clap of thunder jarred the granite, and a violent gust from the black overcast almost wrenched her sunbonnet from its strings," wrote Maggie's granddaughter. A howling blizzard of hailstones quickly followed the thunder. Fortunately, Maggie and her children found shelter under a saddle blanket lost by the road crew.

That night they camped just below timberline. Descending the west side of the pass the next morning was almost as difficult as climbing the east side, yet by evening they arrived in Middle Park. After two more days of travel, the Crawford family reached the hot springs.

There to meet them was William Byers, the energetic and sanguine owner of the Hot Sulphur Springs townsite. He had first visited the springs years earlier, probably in 1863. Both an ardent sportsman and entrepreneur, he promptly decided that he had to own the springs. A few years later he built a cabin near the site and, by dubious means, eventually became owner of the land surrounding the hot springs.

Byers had large-sized dreams for his town. Spas were in fashion, and Byers's watering hole offered "the most delicious bath in the world. The springs are what their name implies, 116 degree heat, and so strong of sulphur that the odor is borne on the breeze for a long distance." The waters cured a long list of socially acceptable ills, including "inflammatory rheumatism and kindred blood diseases." Just to make sure that people got the point, Byers advertised that "a choice lot will be donated to each person who will build thereon, this year, a neat and comfortable dwelling." The fact that Byers was owner and editor of the *Rocky Mountain News* ensured that his town would get all the free publicity it needed.

With these grandiose plans firmly in mind, Byers extended a warm welcome to the Crawfords and invited them to pick a lot. There were plenty of lots to choose from, for the "town" consisted of little more than Byers's partially finished cabin and the start of a log hotel. The Crawfords selected a lot well back from the river and near a spring supplying good drinking water.

Jimmy hauled logs to his lot and had started erecting walls when an unwelcome neighbor, a Ute chief named Colorow, suddenly appeared. Colorow was not happy with what he saw. He was about sixty years old, perhaps five and a half feet tall, and weighed well over two hundred pounds. This "unlovely specimen" made a habit of threatening settlers intruding on Indian land. He was first classified by the *Rocky Mountain News* as a "Ute nuisance" and later as a "devil incarnate by nature."

As this nuisance devil sat on his pony and watched Jimmy haul logs, he complained about too many houses and too many settlers. He ordered the Crawfords to leave within "two sleeps." Jimmy and Maggie ignored him, and the infamous Ute chief rode off. The time allotted to the Crawfords passed without consequence. Other Indians arrived who were friendly and hungry. Maggie baked batch after batch of biscuits for them. Later, the Indian women came to Maggie's cabin to trade their buckskins for calico.

Work on the Crawford house continued and soon Jimmy was nailing on the roof. It consisted of spruce bark covered with dirt. This arrangement worked well in dry weather but leaked whenever it rained. Maggie did not complain, for at last she had a house. She covered the dirt floor with elk skins and hung a wagon sheet down the middle to curtain off bedrooms. Jimmy nailed a split-pole table to one wall. Crudely made beds and chairs completed the furnishings.

The log cabin finished, Jimmy went off in search of both cattle and grazing lands. Maggie set out to turn her cabin into a home. Cleanliness came first, so the elk skin rug received a daily sweeping. Baking was a close second, and Maggie baked almost every day. On one particular day she had just punched down her bread dough and placed it on the table to rise when trouble arrived. She glanced out the window to see seven-year-old Lulie and five-year-old Logan playing near the woodpile. John, just over one year old, was taking a nap. She sensed someone in the cabin with her and whirled around to see Colorow standing at her shoulder.

The old Indian had not come to order Maggie away from the springs, but to trade. He first proposed selling his old pony to Maggie, but she claimed poverty. Undaunted, Colorow looked around for something else. His sharp eyes fastened on John and his red hair. He proposed to swap his pony for John. Aghast, Maggie hid her fear, viciously jabbed at the dough, and refused to trade. Meanwhile, her two children ran for help. Help soon arrived, and Colorow left with a grunt.

As a neighbor, Colorow was not working out. However, he was not as bad as some of the "tourists" who had begun coming to Hot Sulphur Springs, thanks to the completed road and Byers's advertising. During the summer of 1874 a tent saloon opened, and business immediately boomed. After a few slugs of red-eye, the rowdies enjoyed shooting up the town. There wasn't much of a town to shoot up, but that didn't stop the imbibers. Maggie feared the loose bullets more than she feared Colorow.

Her bad luck with neighbors changed when the Gansons – William, Sarah, and two children – moved into town. They promptly completed the two-story log hotel started by Byers and soon had a thriving business. For those who wanted to soak in the "magnificent bath tub," William hauled them across the river on a wagon. But that arrangement worked only when the river was low, so he built a narrow, swinging footbridge.

With the neighbor problem solved, Maggie's attention

focused on the roof. It was now mid-summer and afternoon showers had started in earnest. When the dirt on the roof became rain-soaked, water ran between the spruce bark shingles and dripped mud all over her house. Now that Jimmy was back, it was time to fix the roof. He took the wagon to the Cozens Ranch where a blacksmith made him a froe. Jimmy then found suitable timber, cut it into boards, and shaved the boards into shingles. When he arrived back in Hot Sulphur Springs, he brought a load of shingles and, just as important, a cookstove for Maggie. She soon put the stove to use, but the shingles had to wait. Scarlet fever had struck.

Logan was the first to come down with a red rash and fever. Lulie and John soon caught the disease. Replacing the roof was out of the question with three desperately sick children. So Jimmy rigged up a wagon sheet, tent fashion, over the children to keep them dry, and Maggie caught the other drips in pots and pans. Long, anxious days and nights followed before the children recovered, and at last Jimmy was able to roof their cabin before it snowed.

The promise of snow and closed passes meant one last trip to the outside for provisions. Jimmy and a friend loaded the two wagons with elk meat to trade for supplies and headed for the outside world. When they returned, the men brought over a ton of flour, cornmeal, dried beans, sugar, molasses, dried fruit, and salt.

With winter in the air, all the tourists and even some of the townsfolk left. When the proprietor of the saloon, Mr. Moss, headed for the outside, Jimmy agreed to keep his brandy for the winter. Maggie was furious. The last things she wanted in her house were barrels of peach and apple brandy. But Mr. Moss explained that Jimmy and Maggie were the only people he could trust because they never patronized his saloon. So the brandy stayed. Several times during the winter, men tried to talk Maggie out of some brandy, but she would not dispense one drop. She would not run a saloon, regardless of how much money the men offered for just one drink.

As the winter days became shorter, the children reminded

their mother that Christmas was not far off. Although Maggie explained that Santa Claus could never find Middle Park, they insisted on hanging their much-darned stockings at the foot of their beds. After the children fell asleep on Christmas Eve, Maggie stirred the fire and started to make some candy. It would not be much of a Christmas, but at least her children would have something in the morning. Just as she began to make the candy, she heard a knock. When she opened the door, there stood Charlie Royer, bundled against the bitter cold. Her granddaughter recorded what happened next.

> "Howdy, ma'am." The man's chapped face cracked into a grin. He held out a gunny sack. "Here's some oranges. Hope they're not froze. And some candy and nuts and a few trinkets for the young ones. And I picked up a little mail for you." Maggie stood there like a ninny, grasping the sack, unable to speak. Through blurring eyes she watched Charlie stump away on wooden feet. He had left the gaiety of the mining camps and ridden sixty miles across a lonesome winter wilderness just so a handful of children at Hot Sulphur Springs could have a Christmas treat.

21
The Great Fishing Caper

Those who are fond of good trout fishing should start at once for Grand Lake. The fishing here is superior to that of any other section of Colorado. John Mitchell is pulling the trout out of the lake at the rate of from fifteen to twenty-five pounds a day. For these he receives thirty-seven cents a pound here.

Grand Lake Prospector, July 12, 1883

Irving Hale and his friend Frank Dimock knew all about the good fishing in Grand Lake five years before the *Prospector* proclaimed the news. These two teenagers were among the first who attempted to profit from the teeming fish in the lake.

The boys, age sixteen, left Denver on July 2, 1878, and headed for Middle Park. Their first night away from home was spent at a railroad camp near Floyd Hill. Hale's diary stated that they "passed the night in close communion with nature," manifest in the form of bedbugs that lived in the old quilt the railroad men had furnished.

On July 4, the two tired boys were in Georgetown where they decided that help was needed. So they rented a mule with no name and headed for Berthoud Pass. The steep, boggy road that snaked up the pass did nothing to enliven their spirits. To make matters worse, it started to rain. That night, Hale spent several hours trying to start a fire from soaked wood while mosquitoes feasted. He finally made a roaring inferno that kept the mosquitoes several feet away. Unfortunately, the bugs could stand the heat better than the boys, so the mosquitoes still had the upper hand. Supper consisted of cornmeal mush with lumps of uncooked meal and mosquitoes.

The cornmeal wasn't the only thing that had lumps. When Hale woke up the next morning, he had a "bad sore throat with big lumps in it." He had the mumps, and it was painful to choke down their breakfast of dry bread and crackers. Later that day the travelers arrived at Cozens Ranch, which occupied the southern edge of the level, treeless plain that formed Middle Park. They continued and crossed four streams within five minutes. Both had their boots filled with water more than once. Dimock decided to dry out his feet, so he flopped down on the ground and stuck one leg in the air for Hale to pull off his boot. "His pants are in his boots and the water starts on a tour of inspection down his leg," recorded Hale. "Results can be imagined."

Having exhausted their culinary skills the previous day, the boys ate bread and milk for supper. They burned off their excess energy by playing a game of ball before going to bed.

The next morning the mule with no name was gone, and Hale feared that it might have headed back to Georgetown. However, after a thorough search, they found the critter in a distant pasture where the grass was greener. That day they tried to cross the Fraser River, but after several dunkings, Hale concluded that the water was too deep. Fortunately, George Proctor came along about then. He was returning to his cabin on Grand Lake from his Sunday ride to Hot Sulphur Springs. He told the boys of a blind trail to the lake that avoided the worst parts of both the Fraser and Grand Rivers.

With Proctor in the lead, they started along the back trail. The rough trail went up and down hills, over labyrinths of fallen timber, and along steep hillsides. They eventually crossed the

Grand River and arrived at Grand Lake. "After cutting fishing poles, looking around the lake a little, and playing cards, we went to bed," wrote Hale.

Tired of living in the open, the boys scouted the lake for better quarters and found an old cabin once occupied by Dick Anderson. A day's work made the structure livable. An old scow came with the cabin, and after applying a few rounds of caulking, they launched the row boat. Next came the live box that resembled a large crate with slats for sides. It was towed behind the scow and allowed the caught fish to swim around and eat before the boys ate them. After digging grubs and catching grasshoppers, Hale and Dimock cast off and started fishing.

Unfortunately, it was late afternoon and a storm was brewing. After they had caught four trout, the storm hit. With Hale at the oars, they headed for shore. "The old scow, retarded by the live box behind it, pulled like an ironclad," wrote Hale, "and the thunder and lightning and rain, wind and rising waves, made me feel a little skittish." They could not find the cabin in the darkness, so they beached the boat and walked home. During the night, the boat came loose and drifted out into the lake, and the live box broke.

Their fishing expedition had not begun on a very good note. Undaunted, the boys returned to the lake the next day, retrieved the boat, fixed the live box, and set the pace for the following two weeks. Fishing started in the early afternoon. After a few hours, a storm usually chased them off the lake. Most of the time they ended up on the opposite side of the lake from their cabin. So they found the remains of another cabin that offered some shelter and waited for the storm to move on. Often they built a fire for warmth and took naps while marking time. Once the lake was calm again, they fished well into the night. Finally, they rowed back to the cabin and slept most of the morning.

Although this schedule guaranteed that they got chased around by storms, they managed to catch an impressive number of fish. Their biggest problem was maintaining a supply of fish hooks. When they snagged a large fish, the ensuing battle often ended in a snapped line. The fish was gone, and so was the precious hook. Another problem arose from napping near a fire while waiting for the storms to subside. During one such nap in mid-July, Hale awoke to find his boot on fire. A few days later Dimock was asleep by the fire when he and Hale woke to the smell of burning rubber. Dimock's coat was burning this time.

By now Hale had recovered from the mumps, but other ailments had appeared in the form of injured hands. Both hands sported rows of raw blisters from pulling on the oars. In addition, scabs occupied a significant portion of the three fingers farthest from the thumb on his left hand. The forefinger supported a large blister donated by a frying pan, and he had smashed his thumb with an axe while he pounded nails. "So much for the left hand," complained Hale. "The right hand cannot make as extensive an exhibition, but what it lacks in numbers it makes up in quality, its only blemish being a felon of the genuine stock." The felon was the size of a large bean and was deeply infected. The pain was equal to that of all the other injuries.

Yet the fishing continued to be good, and by July 22 the boys decided they had enough fish to sell in Central City. They cleaned the fish that night and, after searching long and hard for the mule with no name, left the next morning. The mule was not in a traveling mood and refused to cross the river. Although they "belabored" him with clubs and rained "blessings" on his head, the mule with no name refused to move. Finally, Hale stripped and, with the halter rope in his hand, pulled the critter across the river. The mule thoroughly enjoyed this arrangement and crossed without any problem.

After a cold, rainy night, the boys arrived in Central City. Although they survived the trip in good shape, the fish did not. After two days on the trail, the fish smelled just like dead fish. Unwilling to give the fish a decent burial, Hale went to the butcher shop and bought twenty pounds of ice. A few hours on the ice cut the smell considerably, and the boys sold most of their fish, getting thirty-five cents a pound. In all, they made a disappointing $18.65. They left town the next day, perhaps in response to numerous complaints about two boys selling rotten fish. They walked to Georgetown where they gladly returned the mule with no name. However, despite their efforts to beat down the rental price, the mule cost them $16.50.

Ignoring their financial disaster, Hall and Dimock returned to Grand Lake. They fished both the lake and nearby streams. The fishing was now necessary, for the boys needed something to eat and they had to pay off their Grand Lake debts. Now that August had arrived, it started raining in earnest. The old cabin could not handle the daily deluges, and soon there was almost as much water inside the cabin as in the lake.

The storms complicated fishing. For example, on Tuesday, August 13, Hale rowed out to a good fishing spot. Just as he settled in, the wind picked up and the waves drove him to shore. No sooner was he on shore than the lake became quiet, so he returned to fishing, only to be driven to shore once again. After repeating this sequence several times, Hale became "thoroughly disgusted with the eccentricities of the fickle lake" and quit fishing for the day.

The fish were also not cooperative. When they did bite, the fish often broke the line or sometimes took the pole. On one occasion, Dimock frantically rowed after a fishing pole snatched by a fish. The fish would dive, taking the pole with it, only to surface a minute later. Dimock eventually caught the pole and the thieving fish.

Social life was virtually nonexistent that summer, with one exception. One Saturday afternoon, as Hale was chasing grasshoppers for bait, the pretty Miss Bartlett of Denver arrived with a message for him. "I was dressed in a shirt, buckskin pants (fearfully ripped) and moccasins, also an apology for a hat. I blurted out something and ignominiously fled." So much for social affairs.

By the end of August the boys were tired of eating fish and tired of the rain. So they packed up their few belongings and returned to Denver. Two years later the *Rocky Mountain News* noted that "Master Hale was the valedictorian of the first class that graduated from the Denver High School, and his standing as a student and position as a young gentleman is well known in Denver, and it is needless to say that he will be a credit to Colorado as a cadet at West Point." Yet throughout his distinguished career in the military and as a civilian, Hale never forgot the vivid memory of his "five hundred miles of tramping from place to place" in Middle Park during the summer of 1878.

22
The Buffalo Soldier

I arrived at the crossing of Grand River, near the mouth of Troublesome Creek, in the Park, August 17, and there established a supply camp. My orders required me to prevent any collision between the Indians and settlers in that region.
Captain Francis Dodge, October 27, 1879

Company D (Ninth Cavalry) under Captain Francis Dodge had arrived in Middle Park. Orders directed the captain to sort out settlers' complaints against the Ute Indians and to prevent any further "collisions." This strategy also placed Company D within two hundred miles of the White River Agency where Nathan Meeker was having a difficult time converting Indians to dirt farmers. If trouble started, Dodge and his black troopers would be near at hand. But trouble was not expected, and at least some of the men enjoyed the peace of late summer and the change of scenery during their first, and only, service in the northern Colorado mountains.

For twelve years, Captain Dodge and his soldiers had served along the Mexican border. There they had fought Indians who had no use for reservation life, tracked down bandits and revolutionaries who raided and murdered with impunity, escorted stages, and protected wagon trains. The troopers had built military posts, strung telegraph wire, and helped restore civil authority when greedy cattle barons, dishonest Indian agents, scheming politicians, and other scum threatened to take over towns and counties. Food had been poor for the Ninth, horses and equipment were substandard, violent death patiently waited for the unwise or unlucky, and prejudice often robbed them of well-deserved recognition. Yet morale had remained high in the Ninth Cavalry, the desertion rate the lowest of any unit on the frontier, and the troopers among the bravest and best fighters in the army.

Indians had quickly recognized the fighting ability of the black men on horseback and dubbed them "Buffalo Soldiers." The name appeared to originate from the similarity between the hair of the black soldier and that of the buffalo. Because the Indians regarded the buffalo as sacred, the name implied respect. The troopers readily accepted the title, and some units even featured a buffalo as part of their regimental crest.

Now the Buffalo Soldiers resided in Middle Park, trying to keep peace between the settlers and Indians. As they scouted throughout the Park, Dodge made careful notes about the settlers' complaints. At the scattered settlements and isolated ranches, the people complained that the Utes had "fired the timber," slaughtered game out of season, burned grass, hay, and buildings, and threatened settlers. Dodge concluded that these complaints "were so positive and uncontradictory that I am obliged to believe in their accuracy," with exception of the forest fires.

Although the Utes were undoubtedly responsible for many of the fires, Dodge felt that it was unfair to blame all the fires on the frustrated Indians. The captain noted that the summer had been unusually dry, and lightning may have started some fires. He also found that "great numbers of hunting parties frequent these parks during the summer and fall months, and doubtless many of these fires are due to their carelessness."

During the scouting activities in Middle Park, it appears that only two Indians were found. Returning from a visit with

Governor Pitkin, these Indians professed friendship with the settlers. When asked about the fires, they replied that a few bad Indians might be responsible but "that the greater part of the tribe was entirely innocent of such practices. However, a few days after their visit, a fire broke out on the Gore Range, which was said to be the work of these same chiefs."

After Captain Dodge and his Buffalo Soldiers concluded that Indians were not threatening Middle Park, they scouted farther west and in the vicinity of Steamboat Springs and the Bear River. They made no contact with the Indians. When the troops moved to within forty miles of the White River Agency, they "heard that Agent Meeker had been roughly handled by an Indian named Johnson." However, the accounts of the problem were "so contradictory that I was inclined to give them little credence," later reported Dodge. The captain concluded that troops were not "necessary to protect life and property" at the Agency, so the Buffalo Soldiers returned to Middle Park.

When Company D arrived at their supply camp, a telegram ordered the troops back to the White River Agency. After they had moved to within about ninety miles of the Agency, one of the men found a piece of paper attached to the sagebrush by the trail. The paper contained a terse message: "Hurry up, the troops have been defeated at the agency." They pushed on as fast as possible and eventually found a civilian named John Gordon who knew the situation.

Several days earlier, claimed Gordon, Major Thornburgh from Fort Steele in Wyoming had entered the White River reservation with about one hundred sixty men. As they rode through a narrow canyon along the Milk River, a large force of Indians hidden in the surrounding bluffs ambushed the soldiers. The deadly Indian crossfire immediately killed twelve men, including Thornburgh, wounded fifty, and killed about two hundred mules and horses. The troops, now led by Captain Payne, were surrounded and outnumbered, and it would be just a matter of time before all of them were killed, concluded Gordon.

Although it appeared unlikely that the small force of Buffalo Soldiers could free the surrounded men, they had to try.

Company D moved out and headed for the Agency as fast as possible. Late in the afternoon they made camp as a ruse to fool any spying Indians. At sunset, Dodge ordered the wagons repacked and, with a guard of eight men, sent them north and out of immediate danger. To the rest of the command, now numbering only two officers and thirty-five soldiers, Dodge issued each man one hundred rounds of ammunition and three days' rations. That night Company D rode seventy miles and arrived at Milk Creek about an hour before sunrise.

A soldier under Captain Payne described the arrival of the Buffalo Soldiers:

> We were getting pretty d---d tired about that time. It was the third morning after we were corralled, and of course we didn't know whether any of our messengers sent out from camp had struck help or not. Suddenly that morning in the dusk we heard a noise. Even by that time some of us had begun to fear that the Indians would charge us, as we all then supposed it might be Indians. If it hadn't been for the voice of John Gordon, the scout, who was riding in the advance, we might have poured in a volley at them, but you bet your life there wasn't no volley except cheers when Captain Dodge came up at a canter, leading the rest of his men. We didn't take much account, except of wonder a little at the color of their faces. We forgot all about the danger of exposing ourselves, and leaped up out of the pits to shake hands all around.

However, the celebration was short lived, for the Indians began pouring down a deadly fire that kept up for the next three days. Although providing moral support, the Buffalo Soldiers could not break the siege and were pinned down in shallow pits fortified with dead horses and mules that rotted in the hot October sun. Food was in short supply, and water could be obtained only by crawling to the river under the cover of darkness and hoping the Indians would not spot them. Finally, on the morning of October 5, reinforcement arrived and the Indians quickly melted into the mountains. Although no one in Company D had been killed and just one man wounded, only four of their horses survived the Indian crossfire.

A few days later Company D escorted the remnant of Captain Payne's command back to Rawlins. The Buffalo Soldiers then boarded a train for New Mexico. On their trip south, they passed through Denver where Governor Pitkin had arranged a celebration. When the "celebrated company of brave volunteers who went to the rescue of Captain Payne's command in the trenches of Milk River" arrived at the train station, the "air was rent with cheers, and everything assumed the aspect of a grand jollification," reported the *Rocky Mountain News*. The troopers marched up Sixteenth Street to Lawrence, and then to the hall of the Young Men's Christian Association where a large crowd had gathered. After the speeches finally ended, the soldiers moved "to another portion of the hall where an elegant repast was in waiting for them." The next morning they left for Fort Union, New Mexico, "to be ready to move against the Indians in that section should it become necessary."

The short sojourn of the cavalry in Middle Park left a permanent impression on at least one member of Company D. James Milton claimed to be a Company D Buffalo Soldier, and following his discharge from the Army, he returned to Middle Park. Milton took a job at the Pharo Ranch and quickly proved his worth as a cowboy. He apparently spent most of his time breaking horses, yet he worked with cattle enough to become known and respected as the best roper and rider in Middle Park.

While working on the Pharo Ranch, Milton met Julie Bullette who was employed there as a maid. Julie was an attractive, buxom lady with a round face and friendly eyes. Jim and Julie were married at the Pharo Ranch. As they prepared for a Wyoming honeymoon, cowboy pranksters struck. They switched the wheels on Milton's buggy, placing the large wheels in front and the small ones in back. But that trick in no way hindered the honeymoon.

After his marriage, Jim bought breeding stock and started his own cattle herd. He wintered them along Reeder Creek, not far from the old cavalry bivouac area along Troublesome Creek. In 1898 Jim registered his own brand, B-J, perhaps reflecting the first letter in his wife's maiden name and his first name. Later he filed on a one-hundred-sixty-acre parcel of government land along Reeder Creek and became a small homesteader like many others in Middle Park. The couple built a one-story log house, about twenty feet square, that faced south. Corrals and perhaps a chicken coop completed the improvements. The Miltons used a flat meadow adjacent to the creek as a hay field. The native grass was harvested in the late summer and used as feed during the long winters.

While homesteading, Jim continued to break horses for area ranchers, and Julie served as a midwife. She likely followed the typical midwife role of that time, using home remedies, lots of hot water, and unlimited kindness to assist mothers during childbirth. After spending several weeks with the mother, she probably received payment in the form of meat, a weaner calf, a load of hay, or perhaps a sack of flour.

The childless couple was well-liked and respected throughout Middle Park. As they advanced in age, they decided to move back to Texas where apparently both had been born. The Miltons sold their homestead to a neighbor, Mrs. Oaks, around 1915 and moved to Texas. This decision may have been unwise, for within a year Julie wrote to friends in Middle Park saying how much she missed the mountains and friendly people. Yet they never returned to the Colorado mountains.

23
Waldron Walks

The invitations for the New Year's ball at the Grand Lake House have been issued. A large attendance is looked for, and an enjoyable time anticipated.

Grand Lake Prospector, December 23, 1882

Most residents of Grand Lake attended the ball, and most had an enjoyable time. After all, New Year's Eve was a time to celebrate, and the revelers who came to the Grand Lake House from all directions had celebrating in mind. Dancing and drinking formed the menu of the night. It was unfortunate that Mr. Waldron spoiled the affair.

The Grand Lake House was an obvious place to hold this important event. It was one of the first and, for many years, the largest building in town. The dining room alone could seat seventy-five. Wilson Waldron, who built the hotel in 1878, furnished it with all the modern amenities, including "bedsteads, spring mattresses, chairs, wash stands, marble topped bureaus, toilet stands, and looking glasses." The two-story frame structure was erected before the town was surveyed, and when the streets eventually came into existence, the Grand Lake House stood at an odd angle and was distinctly out of line with the orderly arrangement of buildings that the surveyor obviously had in mind.

Waldron was a young, ambitious man from Canada with a cluster of children and an English wife named Eleanor. His financial interests extended beyond the hotel, for he was a principal figure in at least one mining company. Both friendly and politically inclined, Waldron was elected county commissioner. He used this office to vigorously promote Middle Park in general and Grand Lake and his hotel in particular. On at least one occasion his promotional efforts got out of hand.

Shortly after he built the hotel, a debate started as to which side of the lake should be promoted as the town of Grand Lake. Homes and cabins were scattered around the lake, and although the consensus seemed to be that the north side of the lake should be the town site, not everyone agreed. Waldron forced the issue by staking out a road that diverted traffic from the south side of the lake to the north side where his hotel stood. He then put up a sign stating, "This is the road to Grand Lake." That was too much for Billy Murphy, apparently a south side resident. He tore the sign down, pulled out the stakes, and blocked the road with logs and rocks. Waldron came unglued. Following a battle of words, Waldron used his fists on Murphy. "After some rough pounding, Billy promised to replace the sign and stakes and quiet was restored," reported a witness.

It wasn't until New Year's Eve of 1882 that Waldron lost his temper again and spoiled the celebration. The celebration began with no sign of foreboding. As with most social events, this one probably began in a subdued fashion while the children were still awake. Once the young ones were settled down in the many upstairs rooms of the house, their parents wasted no time winding up for a festive night.

Waldron joined the revelers and was soon drinking heavily. His behavior degraded from excusable to unacceptable, especially toward his wife and infant child. Eleanor was sitting in a rocking chair nursing her child when her husband approached. As Andy Eairheart remembered the incident, "Waldron began fooling with the baby, drunkenly teasing it and annoying its mother." Noting the condition of her husband, Eleanor became concerned for the safety of her child. When Waldron turned away for a moment, Eleanor asked her friend, a miner by the name of Bob Plummer, to quietly get Waldron away from her and the baby.

"Bob tried to persuade him to go out of the room, and when he wouldn't do so Bob got a little rough and tried to force him to leave," recalled Eairheart. Being forced out of his own home infuriated Waldron, and he went for a rifle hanging on the wall. Plummer realized the situation could get out of hand, so he abruptly left the house. Waldron watched as Plummer quickly walked across the street to a small log building. "Just as he entered the building, Waldron shot him dead," testified a witness.

Waldron was promptly arrested and locked in the newly built jail – a frame building with walls made of two by sixes placed flat and spiked together for strength. The strength of the walls didn't bother Waldron, for he "had the utmost freedom; people would go in and out of the jail at will, and if the prisoner decided to take a walk around town, there seemed to be no hindrance," according to the Teller newspaper. For appearance sake, the jailer sometimes lurked in the neighborhood during Waldron's walks around town, but often the jailer was busy and just let his prisoner go by himself.

Waldron's trial, originally set for August, was postponed because of county turmoil. Yet Waldron appeared content with his casual incarceration and was confident that his political connections as a former county commissioner would serve him well during his trial. However, as the October trial date approached, Waldron had second thoughts. On one of his walks around town he picked up a "big Navy revolver." During the evening of September 14, 1883, when the sheriff was conveniently out of town, Waldron used the revolver to knock the jailer insensible. The prisoner then walked out of jail. "The only astonishing thing about the story," complained the *North Park Miner*, "is the barbarity displayed by the said Waldron against the jailer, a harmless fellow, who had treated Waldron like a prince, and allowed him to go just about where he wanted to."

Sheriff Burton made a feeble effort to capture Waldron, but his heart was not in the chase. He was preoccupied with finding delegates to support his candidacy for sheriff. Although scattered reports surfaced regarding Waldron, no definitive leads developed. He had simply walked out of jail and disappeared.

The newspaper concluded that it would be useless to blame the jailer for the escape, "for from what we saw of him we should judge that if the prisoners told him they would not leave, he would take it for granted that they would stay." The newspaper praised the jailer's faith in human nature, "but when it comes to prisoners indicted for murder, we would rather see the jailer have faith in good iron and a strong cell."

Eleanor Waldron apparently had little faith that she would see her husband again, so she and her children left Grand Lake for Golden in October. A year later she sold the furnishings of the Grand Lake House. Most of the furniture was bought by Walker McQueary and used in a hotel in Hot Sulphur Springs.

The untimely death of a helpful miner known as Robert Plummer had closed the Grand Lake House as a hotel. Although occupied to some extent, the former hotel was considered haunted. "The house is full of ghosts, they say," begins a poem about the hotel. Few people had any interest in living with ghosts, and the once grand hotel was eventually torn down.

24
County Cauldron

The long impending storm in Grand County has descended. While the nation throughout its length and breadth rejoiced on its 107th anniversary of independence, county officials at Grand Lake were shooting each other.

Colorado Miner, July 7, 1883

The cauldron was simply a political mess that boiled out of control. Middle Park, which dominates Grand County, was a tranquil political backwater until a mining boom started in the late 1870s. The influx of miners and the services they required quadrupled the population within a few years.

Other areas of Colorado had experienced booms without political turmoil, but this was not to be the case in Middle Park. Miners flocked to the mineral-rich eastern portion of the county around Grand Lake, well away from the county seat in Hot Sulphur Springs. Worse, most newcomers claimed to be Republicans. The smooth running Democratic political machine centered in Hot Sulphur Springs suddenly developed mechanical problems.

In the fall of 1880 a petition was sent to the county commissioners requesting a special election to decide the permanent location of the county seat. The petition was signed by a large number of voters, presumably Republican, from Grand Lake. This action hit a raw nerve among the Democrats who wanted the county seat to remain in Hot Sulphur Springs. After numerous delays, a referendum was held, and Grand Lake received the majority of votes. Those from Hot Sulphur Springs immediately challenged the results; a protracted court battle ensued. Two years later the District Court finally ruled that Grand Lake had been legally chosen as the county seat.

Not everyone accepted the court ruling. "Some of the people – or rather politicians of small bore at Hot Sulphur Springs – think the county seat ought still be at the Springs, notwithstanding the fact that a majority of the voters cast their ballots for Grand Lake," grumbled the *Colorado Miner* in 1883. To make matters worse, the county cauldron churned with other issues. Poor roads, high taxes, extravagance on the part of the commissioners, deficit spending, territorial disputes with adjacent counties, poor county services, and general financial uncertainty boiled in the county pot. The county was thoroughly "stirred from center to circumference," claimed a newspaper.

Worse, the dispute no longer ran along political lines where there existed at least some acceptable procedures to sort out problems. The conflict left the political arena and centered on the ambitious personalities of Edward Weber and John Mills. Weber was an attorney and mine superintendent who had business dealings in Grand Lake but defended the interests of Hot Sulphur Springs. Mills was a self-proclaimed attorney who was involved in mining; he served as a county commissioner and had substantial control over Grand Lake politics. Both Weber and Mills claimed the same political affiliation.

The battle intensified when Weber was appointed as a county commissioner to replace a commissioner-elect who suddenly decided he was ineligible to hold office. Weber and Mills immediately started hurling verbal mud at each other; phrases such as small brain, perjurer, miserable sneak, cowardly tool and thief, and an assortment of other incendiary accusations punctuated editorials and flavored conversations. Libel suits followed.

Verbal mud changed to physical threats early in 1883 when Weber seized the political advantage by winning the support of Commissioner Barney Day. With only three county commissioners, Mills was the odd man out. Weber was able to replace the county attorney with an individual supporting his politics; then he presented a number of political reforms and drafted an ordinance that would return the county seat to Hot Sulphur Springs. Mills countered with threats of violence. Weber and Day took the threats seriously and boycotted the commissioners' meeting, leaving Mills sitting alone and unable to transact any business.

Important individuals lined up behind the combatants. Thomas "Cap" Dean, acting county clerk, joined Day in supporting Weber. Mills recruited Charles Royer, sheriff of Grand County, Undersheriff William Redman, and his deadbeat brother, Mann. Others took sides until the political cauldron was about to boil over.

Several episodes stirred the pot in the late winter and spring of 1883. Weber had the county treasurer and others arrested for trying to collect supposedly illegal taxes from Day and Dean. Then Weber and Day jointly urged Middle Park residents not to pay taxes. Mills quickly made matters worse by suggesting that a "committee" would soon clean up the county. Undersheriff Redman had a "series of bitter quarrels with both Dean and Weber" over mining and ranching properties. More arrest warrants were issued by Weber, including one for Undersheriff Redman. Mob violence against Weber and Day was threatened, and "Grand Lakers took steps to prevent a threatened unlawful seizure of the county records by Hot Springs parties." County business was at a standstill during the spring of 1883 as the cauldron boiled over.

The law required a commissioners' meeting on July 2, so the fractious men met at the courthouse at Grand Lake. There is no record of what happened at that meeting, but both factions emerged in good humor. Peace seemed possible, but that was only an illusion.

Mills was unable to attend the commissioners' meeting scheduled for the next day, but Weber and Day had assured him that "only routine business" would be transacted. Once behind closed doors, Weber and Day got down to business that was anything but routine. They promptly drew up eight summons that would crush Mills's patronage structure. Mills heard about the ploy, but there "was not the faintest sign of trouble." He merely asked what time the commissioners' meeting would be held the next day, July 4.

During the morning of July 4, no one noticed that a small group of men strapped on revolvers, donned rough masks made of sacking, and disappeared behind a pile of boulders near the shore of Grand Lake, not far from an abandoned cabin used as an ice house. There they waited.

Meanwhile, Weber, Dean, and Day enjoyed a leisurely breakfast at Mrs. Young's Fairview House. What happened when they left to attend the commissioners' meeting at the courthouse has never been fully sorted out. Dean, the only surviving witness, made the following statement:

> Between half-past 8 and 9 o'clock E. P. Weber, Barney Day and myself were walking along side by side, near the old Anderson cabin. I heard the report of a pistol or rifle; couldn't say which. Mr. Weber said, "Oh! I am shot." Mr. Barney Day and myself caught hold of Mr. Weber to ease him to the ground and see where he was shot. About that time I heard a report; then I looked up. I saw three masked persons within a few feet of me. Apparently two revolvers were pointed directly at me. I jumped. At the same time I drew my revolver. I was shot in the face near the eye, which partially blinded me. I found I had lost control of myself. I turned to see if I could get behind something for protection, and at that time I received a bullet in the right hip that felled me to the ground. At that time one of the ruffians

> jumped me and gave me a severe beating with some heavy revolver, then turning left me lying on the ground.

While the bushwackers' attention was focused on Dean, Day pulled his gun and started firing. His first shot sent one man pitching onto his face, and another shot hit a second man. Yet Day was not ignored by the assailants, for a bullet soon tore into him. Shot through the heart, he dropped his pistol and toppled headlong into the shallows of Grand Lake. The surviving attackers ran for their horses and disappeared.

As gun smoke drifted over the lake, Weber, shot through the lungs, staggered to his feet and tried to stumble back to the Fairview House. He didn't make it. Dean also made it to his feet and started walking. By that time a few Grand Lakers realized that something was amiss and came running. Several assisted Dean and Weber while Deputy Sheriff Max James went over to the prone man and tore off the mask. It was Mills.

A call went out for Sheriff Royer and Undersheriff Redman. Neither one could be found, so Deputy Sheriff James took charge. Day was fished out of the lake and placed next to Mills. Deputy James examined the guns and found that Dean's revolver had not been fired. Then he followed a trail of blood leading away from the crime scene. It ended where horses had been tied about one-quarter of a mile from the ambush.

The men carried Weber and Dean to the Fairview House where Weber soon died. However, Dean was fully alert and provided details about the attack. The physician from Teller arrived and examined his injuries. He concluded that operating would be fruitless and that infection was almost certain. Although Dean was determined to live long enough to bring his assailants to justice, he failed and died of his wounds.

The missing Sheriff Royer abruptly appeared in Hot Sulphur Springs during the afternoon of July 4. Riding a lathered horse that was almost dead, he assured everyone that things were normal in Grand Lake and that the commissioners were meeting as planned. When a frantic rider arrived with news of the shoot-out, Royer first expressed disbelief, then fell into a depression. He later left for Grand Lake.

The immediate response to the Grand Lake tragedy was an influx of Denver reporters to cover the "most sensational thing that has ever occurred within the borders of Colorado," according to the *Rocky Mountain News*. These reporters arrived with "couriers, private telegraph lines, and other wondrous appliances." But according to the local newspapers, they failed to get the facts. The "tenderfoot pencil-shovers swallowed" even the wildest rumors and subsequently printed "extravagant and unreliable reports" about a "reign of terror" in Middle Park.

Like the Denver reporters, Sheriff Royer couldn't find any reliable information when he finally arrived on the scene. He conducted a cursory investigation and found no clues and no suspects. He bristled at criticism voiced against him and insisted that he "was doing all he could to catch the murderers." That investigation abruptly ended in Georgetown on July 16 when the "best man of all blew his brains out."

Sheriff Royer was found dead in his hotel room with a bullet through his head. The revolver found at his feet pointed to suicide. His involvement in the ambush was uncertain. One person claimed that at the time of the ambush he saw Royer on the road to Hot Sulphur Springs. Yet several years later a transcript surfaced containing the alleged confession of Sheriff Royer just before his suicide. The confession stated that on July 4, Royer was invited to "see a little fun" and "give Weber a little scare." Royer accepted and in the melee that followed, he shot Barney Day. "Ever since," claimed the confession, "old Barney has been looking me in the eye, and I can't stand it any longer."

Little doubt lingered that Undersheriff William Redman and his brother were involved in the ambush. Some thought they saw the form of William stumbling from the scene, wounded in the ambush. Other stories followed, claiming that the undersheriff was murdered, died of his wounds, committed suicide, and was living in Arizona, New Mexico, and Wyoming. Documentation is limited to the fact that he left a wife in

Middle Park and was never seen again. His brother left nothing behind and likewise disappeared for good.

Although the investigation continued, nothing definite was established. Two men from the Mills faction were arrested for murder but later acquitted. No other arrests were made, for all of the known participants were buried. If any conspirators remained above ground, they kept quiet.

Middle Park was also quiet. "Allow the dead to rest in peace," urged the *Grand Lake Prospector*. Middle Park wisely took that advice and buried the issues along with the commissioners. Four months after the bloody affair, a Denver newspaper stated that "the people of Grand County are disposed to dwell together in peace and harmony and the spirit of sectionalism which was shown with so much bitterness when the tragedy was enacted is fast disappearing."

Five years later, when the mining boom died, the county seat was moved back to Hot Sulphur Springs. This time no one objected.

25
Texas Charlie

If not the very hardest, certainly one of the worst characters that ever entered Middle Park, bit the dust at Hot Sulphur Springs last Tuesday. He died with his boots on.

Rocky Mountain News, December 14, 1884

Charles W. Wilson, alias Texas Charlie, swaggered into Hot Sulphur Springs sometime in 1883. He was a young man of about twenty who had spent at least part of his life in New Mexico and Texas. Although idle much of the time, he did take occasional jobs at area ranches where he was regarded as a conscientious worker and helpful when in the mood. But Texas Charles was rarely in the mood, and his long and frequent periods of idleness proved to be his undoing.

When idle, Texas Charlie often rode into Hot Sulphur Springs. He was a fancy and particular dresser when in town. His getup included a large sombrero that looked out of place in Middle Park. One, and sometimes two, .45-caliber revolvers hung from his hips. Just in case the pistols failed to get the job done, he could use the large bowie knife that was jammed in his belt. Fancy boots completed the outfit. He looked as if he had just stepped out of a romantic western novel. People may have been inclined to laugh at him but thought better of it. Texas Charlie wanted a reputation and he didn't care how he got it. He was deadly serious about his dress and a crack shot with his pistols. So no one laughed. All kept their distance and hoped the nuisance would go away.

But this wannabe bad man had no intentions of going away. Texas Charlie craved action, yet in the sleepy town of Hot Sulphur Springs, there was no action to be had. He corrected this deficiency by creating his own excitement.

One of his favorite forms of amusement at Hot Sulphur Springs and elsewhere was to shoot between men's legs and at their toes. The *Georgetown Courier* reported that Texas Charlie "entered a saloon, and drawing his revolvers, compelled a man to go through the evolutions of a dance." Such antics went unappreciated in Hot Sulphur Springs; verbal rebukes followed, and he was pointedly asked to leave town on a number of occasions.

Charlie's answer to those who failed to recognize his bravado was to classify them as "sons of bitches." He was in town less than two years and had most of the prominent citizens of Hot Sulphur Springs – Frank Byers, E. Marker, Calvin Kinney, Walker McQueary, George Lee, W. L. Pattison, David Gardner, and W. L. Veatch – so classified. Texas Charlie even wrote some of the names down in a pocket notebook that he carried. "He never hesitated to threaten the life of any man who incurred his displeasure, and as he was an expert shot, and was always armed to the teeth, no one cared to take their chances with him," warned the *Rocky Mountain News.* Texas Charlie had changed from a nuisance to a serious threat.

He was also a threat in New Mexico where he supposedly killed a man. While riding the stage to Hot Sulphur Springs in November 1884, he confided to a passenger that he was wanted for murder in New Mexico, and that wanted posters would probably show up any day. Documents carried by Texas Charlie showed that he had been in Springer, New Mexico, earlier that fall. It is doubtful that he was in trouble there, for he renewed his subscription to the local newspaper, the *Colfax Stockman*, left them his forwarding address in Hot Sulphur Springs, and wrote a travel itinerary that suggested a leisurely departure. The story was probably no more than an empty brag intended to increase his growing notoriety.

Charlie arrived in town for one of his frequent visits during the evening of Friday, December 5. With him were two drifters of dubious character, J. V. Thompson and J. H. Colthrap. Charlie and his cronies walked into the Byers & Briggs general store that also served as the town's post office and social center. Texas Charlie spoke pleasantly to those around, then started up the stairs for the second level. Colthrap began a conversation, or an argument, with Veatch. Veatch was a mild-mannered man who, together with his brother, owned a mine and commercial property in Hot Sulphur Springs.

Perhaps it was something that Veatch said to Colthrap or some previous petty grievance against Veatch that set Texas off. Whatever the cause, Charlie abruptly changed directions, pulled his pistol, and jumped down the stairs. Without saying a word he clobbered Veatch with his pistol. Unarmed and taken by surprise, Veatch offered no resistance.

Pattison, the town constable, ran over to separate the two men. Before he got very far, the drifter Thompson pulled his revolver and made it clear that no one would interfere. Texas gave Veatch another vicious whack with his gun, this time tearing his scalp open. He then cocked his pistol, pointed it at the head of Veatch, and threatened to kill him.

Pleased with himself, Texas Charlie released Veatch. The confused victim quickly headed for safer ground at the Kinney House where Calvin Kinney, justice of the peace, was in his office. His face covered with blood, Veatch burst into the office and demanded a gun. Kinney wisely declined. Calming down a bit, Veatch then told of the attack. His story was verified by several men who had followed Veatch out of the general store. Acting on Kinney's advice, Veatch swore out an affidavit.

As Kinney was writing out the arrest warrant, Texas Charlie barged into the office, leaving his friends Thompson and Colthrap guarding the door. The bully said he was willing to give himself up and pay the fine then and there. Kinney told him that he would deal with any fine after Texas was safely behind bars. The town plague pulled his gun and, waving it in the air, threatened to kill everyone in the room if there was any attempt to arrest him. He demanded that the warrant be torn up, but Kinney held his ground and Charlie left.

The warrant was soon completed and handed to Constable Pattison for delivery. “He said he would be back in a few minutes to get it,” later testified Kinney. Pattison did not return for the warrant, perhaps remembering that Texas Charlie threatened to kill anyone who tried to arrest him.

Kinney then asked another man in the room to deliver it, but he also declined. Finally, George Lee agreed to deliver it to Constable Pattison. As Lee was looking for Pattison, Texas Charlie found him first and demanded the warrant. Lee handed it over, and Texas tore it up. Then the town terror left.

Four days later, December 9, he was back. Texas Charlie and the two drifters arrived in town on the buckboard that carried the mail. As they rode through town, Texas spotted John Gardner, age fifteen, on his way to school. Gardner later testified that Texas asked him if “they were going to pull him when he reached town,” and “if the papers were made out.” Gardner didn't know. Unknown to the teenager, a warrant had been prepared, but no one had plans to arrest Texas Charlie.

The buckboard stopped at the Byers & Briggs store and everyone climbed down. Perhaps in a magnanimous mood, Texas Charlie carried the mail sack into the post office. The town menace and his cronies then headed for the Kinney House, presumably to discuss the outstanding warrant with the justice of the peace and to make appropriate threats. He passed David Gardner on the way. Calling Gardner over, Texas “said he supposed there was a warrant in Pattison's hands for him and to tell Pattison to not try to arrest him.” He added a warning for Veatch, directing Gardner to “tell Veatch to not come into court and if Veatch did come in, to keep out of range as he should kill Veatch on sight.” Texas Charlie then continued on his way.

Down the street from the Kinney House stood the Hook Building, a vacant store with a few missing windows. Just as

Texas Charlie and his cronies passed this landmark, two warning shots rang out from the building.

"Seems to be getting pretty warm around here," said Texas Charlie, according to the newspaper. Apparently pleased with the situation, he drew his pistol and searched for the assailants. Unwilling to share his lust for violence, Colthrap and Thompson immediately backed away.

A volley of shots rang out from fifteen men and as many guns hidden in the shadowy recesses of the Hook Building. One bullet tore into Charlie's right hand. Texas Charlie changed the pistol to his left hand and coolly faced the bushwhackers. The next fusillade of lead was the last. Bullets and buckshot riddled Texas Charlie.

The noise brought out everyone in Hot Sulphur Springs. Some carried guns, and all stopped to looked at the young man who once terrorized their town. Coroner Bock took possession of the body and hauled it into the nearby carpenter's shop. Within a few hours a coroner's jury was impanelled and a dozen men summoned to appear.

Without exception, all those summoned to testify knew Texas Charlie and his bad character. All of the men heard the shots, none had any idea who did the shooting, and all claimed to be "busy" at the time of the shooting. Byers was at his stable when the shots were fired, Marker was in the Kinney House, Kinney was in his office, McQueary was at home, and Veatch was down the street. Constable Pattison, George Lee, and David Gardner didn't explain where they were at the time of the shooting, but all three indicated that they were quite busy. The jury concluded that "C. W. Wilson came to his death by gunshot wounds at the hands of some person or persons to us unknown."

The *Rocky Mountain News* summed up the incident by stating that this "beastly enemy to man" was "shot down by fifteen of his fellow citizens." Texas Charlie was the "victim of this vengeance of the people." Yet Texas Charlie could be considered the winner that day in Hot Sulphur Springs. He finally achieved the reputation that he craved, and in the only way he knew how.

26
A Year with Mary

Sometimes, especially when a member of the family is away and the skies are cloudy, it seems inexpressibly lonely and desolate here to me.
Mary E. Cozens, Thanksgiving Day 1887

Although Mary Elizabeth Cozens, age twenty-two, lamented her loneliness in her diary, she also expressed her appreciation to "Divine Goodness" on that Thanksgiving Day. Mary's family – her mother, Mary, father, William, younger sister, Sarah, and older brother, Will – gathered around the large dinner table for their Thanksgiving meal. Hunting was poor in Middle Park that fall, so they ate roast beef rather than the traditional turkey.

A month earlier, when her mother, escorted by Will, went to Denver to have her teeth pulled, Mary remarked that "it is lonely, of course, without the dear ones. It would be horrible to live here alone now." Although Mary never lived in Middle Park alone, few opportunities for social contact existed. During the year that she kept a detailed diary, Mary mentioned only one social event. The family attended a dinner party given by Mrs. Hammonds in Fraser, a town of about twenty people located just one mile north of the Cozens Ranch.

Even the holidays brought little contact with friends and neighbors. Christmas and Easter passed without mention of social activities, and the only notation about the Fourth of July was that someone in the family made ice cream. With exception of occasional walks, sled rides, and other brief excursions, usually on Sunday, Middle Park offered Mary few opportunities for fun. Mary's lonely plight was no secret, for her diary stated that "relatives have taken us to their hearts, pitying our lonely condition here." Some thought marriage might relieve the loneliness, but Mary did not think so. After hearing complaints from an unhappy wife, Mary concluded that "married life in the Park is anything but fascinating so far as I can see."

To ease her loneliness and isolation, Mary Elizabeth Cozens kept her diary, which "makes time fly faster." She was a prolific letter writer as well and kept in contact with the outside world by sometimes writing four letters a day and receiving as many.

Mail was important to Mary, and not just for the letters she sent and received. The Cozens Ranch served as a post office for almost thirty years. William Cozens was appointed postmaster in 1876, yet Mary seemed to be the one who actually ran things. The mail arrived on Monday, Wednesday, and Friday; time of arrival was rarely as scheduled and ranged from sunrise to well after midnight. The erratic arrival of the mail did not agree with Mary's sense of punctuality. On April 18, she was particularly annoyed because Curley Lewis, one of the mail carriers, did not arrive until 2 a.m. "Seems to me we were awake half the night," she griped. Fixing a meal for the carrier was part of the contract, but Mary thought that "if the mail carrier didn't make better time, I think he ought not to be fed here."

Late arrival of the mail was a particular problem in the spring. The snow was soft during the day, so the carrier waited until it crusted over at night before attempting to cross the pass. Crossing Berthoud Pass at any time of the year was difficult, but the journey during the snowy spring was particularly taxing. After one such run from Cozens to Georgetown, Curley

Lewis dropped dead of heart failure after arriving in Georgetown with the mail.

Although letters dominated the mail, anything that could fit in the large leather bags came along. Horse medicine, shoes, hams, hair curlers, rosebushes, and steel traps often arrived with the letters. Newspapers dominated the mail during the early part of the week. Mary had little use for these, perhaps because politics often dominated the news.

Her attitude toward politicians was summed up shortly before the November election when she wrote, "I wonder where they keep their self-respect, these office seekers, running about with whiskey and tobacco, begging votes." The day after the election her opinion didn't change. Her brother, Will, won the office of justice of the peace, "and they put Papa on the Democratic ticket against him. How cute! Lord grant their nonsense makes no trouble for us."

Although there were no repercussions from her father's election loss, the politics of organized labor provided lively debate. During breakfast on a January morning, Mary wrote that the family discussed "labor and monopoly questions to the point of an angry outbreak; fortunately, we stopped on the extreme edge." With exception of her father, the family was prolabor. A few days later, the debate continued and the family had another "warm time at breakfast over the labor subject. Papa sees no right in strikes; we, the rest, do."

Others came to the Cozens' house to discuss politics, particularly Mr. Sprunk, who consistently arrived with "disagreeable ideas that he ventilates here whenever he comes." Mary's diary entry for June 7, tartly noted that Sprunk "makes Will and Papa angry; evening ends in brimstone."

Mary saved most of her brimstone for relatives who persistently asked for money "as if we were made of it and when they are advised to get it for themselves by honest, hard labor as we do." Mary was right on the hard labor part. In addition to running the post office, the Cozens managed a well-known way station for the stage coach.

The ranch was a stop on the run from Georgetown to various points in Middle Park. Except during the winter when few people traveled very far, four to six travelers often spent the night at the Cozens' house. This number was just about right, for the upstairs of the house was remodeled in the late 1870s and contained five small rooms that the travelers used.

The almost constant stream of people kept Mary and the entire family busy. To help ease the load, a cook and chore boy were hired during the summer. Mary helped with everything but the cooking. She served meals to the guests and washed the dishes. The demands of travelers for meals at all hours of the day and night made Mary's job even harder. After helping with a 10 p.m. supper, Mary complained that "if I had my way, there wouldn't be meals at all hours here." Perhaps someone listened, for a few days later a traveler wanted supper at 10 p.m. and breakfast at 4 a.m.; he got neither.

Mary did not cook – and for good reason. One fall day she tried to make biscuits without soda; it was a "dreadful mess." The cook, Mary Rohracher, was mad, probably because she took meticulous care of the kitchen and Mary had created turmoil. Six months later Mary tried to cook some beans and created another "fine mess." Reflecting on the disaster, Mary concluded, "I never was cut out for a cook anyhow."

Other chores added to the hard work that was part of Mary's life. Monday was wash day, and presumably Mary's mother and sister helped with this chore. If the weather was good and the wash dried, they ironed on Monday. Otherwise, Tuesday was reserved for ironing. Cleaning took place on other days. Mary mentioned scrubbing the kitchen, office, and bedrooms, and sweeping the kitchen ceiling.

Finally, Mary was the family seamstress. She always had at least one sewing project, such as a shirt for her father or a dress for her mother. Other projects included aprons, sun bonnets, sheets, rag rugs, jackets, and apparently all the family clothing. Dresses appeared to be the most challenging, for Mary remarked that her "dress making means almost endless sewing, ripping, and sewing over again." Mary insisted on getting things right, and this included spiritual as well as secular matters.

The Cozens were devout Catholics, with the exception of Mary's father. He professed no religion, and despite prayers for his conversion, he never joined the Catholic Church. Yet he converted the second story of a water tower (it might have been an ice house) to a family chapel. Mary took immaculate care of the chapel and likely went there daily for prayers. She observed the Catholic holidays and asked forgiveness for even a minor transgression, such as forgetting to fast. Her diary was punctuated with quotes from the Bible, words of wisdom, and praise for the Catholic Church. Jesuit priests rarely came to Middle Park, but when they arrived it was an important event for Mary. She wrote about one such visit and expressed her disappointment that the priest had to leave before he could hear confession. Mary regularly corresponded with church officials, and their letters to her apparently provided holy sustenance in a lonely land void of religious nourishment.

Presumably some of Mary's prayers received answers, for she had a beautiful garden. A successful garden in Middle Park usually requires divine intervention. When she started her diary in the fall, she sadly chronicled the passing of each flower. Carnations and morning glories departed early while the pansies, poppies, and daises lasted until mid-October. With the flowers gone for the season, Mary put manure around some of the plants and spaded the fertilizer into other parts of her garden. Some plants were dug up and put in kegs for the winter; others received a layer of mulch for protection. Her garden was winterized by early November, but Mary still worried that it might not survive.

The seed catalog arrived in January, and late in the month she optimistically planted nine beech nuts under a window board. In February she ordered seeds, including caraway, tomato, pansy, morning glory, phlox, and dandelion. Anxiously watching her garden for signs of life, Mary happily wrote that poppies and dandelions emerged on April 2; carnations and daises soon followed. Then she watched the mail for her seeds and was disappointed when they did not come in April. Finally, the seeds arrived in early May and were soon in the ground.

Then the typical mountain gardener laments started. Mary wrote that the "seeds came up indifferently," and in late May the "heavy frosts and sudden warm spells, storms, etc. seem to check the growth of everything." On June 22 "all my tomatoes but one froze" and the lone survivor froze two days later. Next came the bugs, and Mary wrote that the "garden is again the prey of the aphids." Lack of rain, too much rain, hail, wind, and hungry animals made gardening a challenge for Mary. She wrote about her discouragement, yet she kept on and produced one of the finest gardens in the Park.

Thus, a year passed in the life of Mary Elizabeth Cozens as recorded in her diary during 1887 and 1888. It is unlikely that her life was much different before and after her diary, for change came slowly to Middle Park. During the lonely year of the diary, Mary made no mention of suitors. Although she was a beautiful woman with fine features, she did not marry. And with the exception of her early childhood in Central City and a year at boarding school in Kansas, she never left the Cozens Ranch.

When Mary became seriously ill in December 1928, medical and spiritual assistance was summoned. Both a physician and Father Ryan made a difficult winter trip from Denver to Middle Park. Despite medical help and prayers, Mary Elizabeth Cozens died on December 7 at the age of sixty-four. "A large concourse of friends gathered to pay their last tribute of respect to her," printed the *Middle Park Times*. She willed the ranch to the Jesuits of Sacred Heart College (now Regis). Mary joined the rest of her family in a small cemetery on their ranch, not far from where a Catholic Church was built years later.

27
Chew Pie, the Avenger

In the winter . . . there occurred but little to enliven the monotony of existence for those who, from necessity or choice, resided in the camp [Grand Lake] year round.

Charence Lower, on winters
in Grand Lake, 1892

The monotony of existence could be enlivened by going to Hank Brown's general store. Seasoned orators surrounded the pot-bellied stove; each sought to outdo the other. By early December, the competition invariably centered around two contestants, Old Man McGee and Don Slocum.

McGee recounted the events of one stormy night when he and a partner hunted for something or other. Slocum countered McGee's fascinating tale with his own story of how he tried to kill his worthless dog. Years earlier when dog fighting was popular, Slocum had placed a fifty-dollar bet that his dog could whip an unknown bulldog pup. When it came time to fight, Slocum's dog took one look at his opponent and headed for safer ground. In a fit of anger, Slocum tried to kill his cowardly canine with a blast of dynamite but only succeeded in almost killing himself. These two tales were told over and over, the details never varying, as winter slowly passed. It was small wonder that when someone mentioned a play, only McGee and Slocum grumbled. Any change would be an improvement.

Theatricals were a tradition in Grand Lake. During better times in the early 1880s, the Grand Lake Dramatic Society regularly performed for the captive winter population in this corner of Middle Park. Plays such as *No Thoroughfare*, *Our Boys*, *Engaged*, *A Cup of Tea*, and *Lunatic* were performed for an appreciative audience. A decade later there was no doubt that a play would again add sparkle to a dull landscape.

Edward Smith, who claimed to possess limited literary talent, volunteered to write a play. In short order he cranked out a melodrama entitled *Chew Pie, the Avenger*. It contained all that a good melodrama should – love, betrayal, abduction, and murder. The plot was as follows:

> Inezilla de la Fuenta, a Spanish beauty, flings her lover away in favor of a wealthy suitor. As the fickle fair goes off to her wedding, the broken and bitter lover, known as Captain Midnight, renounces his allegiance to civilization and heads for the hills. Here the Captain collects a rowdy bunch of villains and takes to robbing the overland stage and terrorizing travelers.
>
> With this background, the curtain opens on act one. The overland stage is due to pass through Dead Man's Gulch at midnight. When the stage arrives, Captain Midnight and his villains are waiting with drawn guns. The stage is stopped and the strong boxes containing gold thrown down to the road agents. Unsatisfied, the villains decide to rob the passengers, so they force the three travelers out of the stage. Down steps the Señora Inezilla, her six-year-old daughter, and their valet, the faithful Chew Pie, a young Ute Indian.
>
> Upon seeing his former mistress, the evil heart of Captain Midnight grows even darker. In a fit of rage, he condemns her to death and carries her off. As the

Señora exits the stage, she shouts, "Remember, if you kill me, I shall die!" She is right on both accounts, for the evil Captain Midnight kills her in cold blood. The remaining villains stalk off stage, their bent bodies taking long and careful strides.

During the melee, Chew Pie is knocked over the head and left for dead, the stage driver runs off, and the daughter overlooked. The Indian regains consciousness and vows to avenge the murder of the Señora. He then takes the daughter to a Ute village where she is adopted into the tribe and given the name of Beautiful Snow. As she grows into womanhood, Chew Pie instills the sentiments of revenge toward the slayer of her mother. Thus ends act one.

Act two takes place ten years later in the barroom of a mining camp saloon. Captain Midnight enters and immediately sees a hauntingly beautiful girl of sixteen dancing on the stage. Among the crowd is a Ute Indian collecting money in an old hat. Beautiful Snow immediately recognizes Captain Midnight, and bestows upon him a look so full of hatred that the villain is seized with a nervous chill and runs from the saloon. With the patience of a skilled hunter who has waited long for his prey, Chew Pie follows Captain Midnight.

The evil Captain runs to his lonely cabin in Dead Man's Gulch and there proceeds to fill up with tanglefoot to drown out past memories. As the villain is seated on a stool, bottle in hand, the voice of the murdered Señora informs Captain Midnight of his approaching dissolution. The eery voice of the Señora floats across the stage saying, "Base villain, tremble! for your doom draws nigh! Prepare to see your victim's ghost and die!"

Wrapped in a shroud, the Señora appears and points an outstretched arm at the villain. Captain Midnight springs up from his stool in dismay. At that moment the faithful Chew Pie sends a bullet crashing

> through the window and into the evil heart of the Captain.
>
> Beautiful Snow and Chew Pie are later married and live near the Indian agency where he becomes superintendent of the Sunday School. Both live happily ever after.

With the play written and the props under construction, casting became the central issue. Two members of the Dramatic Society, Andrew A. Eairheart and Jack N. Pettingell, contended for the lead role.

Eairheart, former foreman of the Hidden Treasure Mine, prospector, boat builder, and machinist, was considered to be competent in nearly every capacity. He was the "useful sort who commonly acquires more respect than worldly goods." Eairheart also played a bull fiddle that took up as much room as a person.

Pettingell had a variety of occupations including postmaster, insurance agent, attorney, justice of the peace, and county clerk. Judge Pettingell had impressive credentials in the theater. He was stage manager when the Grand Lake Dramatic Society was first organized, and in 1882 the *Grand Lake Prospector* stated, "Jack Pettingell as the admiral in *Pinafore* is a gigantic success." He played important roles in most of the Grand Lake plays.

Pettingell got the lead role as Captain Midnight, and Eairheart was sore. He may have considered joining the orchestra, but his bull fiddle was more often tuneless than tuneful. So Eairheart took the job of stage manager and started looking for a chance to get even. Chew Pie was not the only one seeking revenge.

As stage manager, Eairheart arranged and rearranged the props during every practice, so no one paid any attention when he drilled a hole in the seat of the stool. He was likewise ignored when he carefully arranged a bodkin (still sharp from poking holes in leather), a cork, a few small pieces of wood, and a long piece of string. He then placed the stool in precisely the right place, tried his contraption a few times to make sure it worked properly, and waited for the right moment.

After several weeks of daily practices, the melodrama was ready for opening night. Most of the town crowded into a hall behind a saloon. The hall was fitted with a stage, drop curtain, homemade scenery, benches, and other amenities that made it a respectable theater for homegrown plays. The audience anxiously waited for the curtain to rise on the first play of the winter season.

Captain Midnight and the beautiful Inezilla appeared on the stage, and the melodrama was off. The audience immediately fell into the play, enthusiastically cheering and booing in all the right places. Stage manager Eairheart directed the offstage maneuvers with professional competence. The play proceeded without a hitch until the final scene in which Captain Midnight sat on the stool and the ghost of SeZora Inezilla appeared.

Just as the ghost appeared, Eairheart gave the string on his contraption a vicious jerk. The bodkin shot up through the hole in the stool and impaled itself into the captain's rump. The captain departed from the stool as if belched from a cannon. Without missing a beat, he completed his lines and died in good form when the shot from Chew Pie rang out. The curtain descended amidst wild applause from the audience.

The applause continued, with calls for Pettingell. So the curtain was hauled up and Captain Midnight stepped forward for a bow. Working the ropes on the curtain, Eairheart saw another chance to strike a blow at his rival. As Pettingell bent at the waist to acknowledge the audience, Eairheart released the curtain. The pole attached to the bottom of the curtain walloped Pettingell on his already injured rump and propelled him headfirst into the orchestra pit. There he tangled with at least one fiddle and several surprised musicians. The audience howled with laughter as Pettingell and the orchestra members picked themselves up. Eairheart quietly left the theater by a back door.

Pettingell swore he would get even with the perpetrator of

the joke. He conducted a methodical investigation, as only an attorney would do, to positively identify the culprit. By the time he identified Eairheart as the responsible party, his rump felt a lot better. The whole matter was quietly settled with a chuckle and most likely a few beers. After all, Eairheart and Pettingell were fast friends.

28
The Old Sheriff

As the Old Sheriff, seated contentedly on the porch floor, was enjoying the outlook down the Fraser Valley where it opened so prettily into Middle Park, I said to him that it seemed to suggest a peaceful and contented neighborhood. His reply was, "Not so peaceable as you think."

L. Hanchett, about 1900

The Old Sheriff, William (Billy) Cozens, had given up law enforcement years earlier when he moved from Central City to Middle Park. Although his sharp, piercing black eyes still spoke of courage and unquenchable determination, the thinning white hair and neatly trimmed Vandyke beard mellowed his once threatening appearance. So now the Old Sheriff liked nothing better than to reminisce about the old days in Middle Park and Central City when "angry disputes were arbitrated on the instant. A flash, an explosion, a dead man, a funeral. The proceedings were brief, explicit, final," claimed a Denver newspaper.

Life was not like that in northern New York where Billy spent most of his childhood. As a young man, he learned the carpenter trade and specialized in building barns. Anxious to see more than New York, Billy left home when he was about twenty-five and worked his way west. While in St. Louis he heard about the Pike's Peak gold rush and in the spring of 1859 he arrived at Gregory Diggings with a horde of other gold seekers. Out of money and realizing that there was more gold in the miners' pockets than in the ground, Billy went to work for Jack Keeler as a bartender and grocery clerk. A year later Keeler was elected county sheriff, and he appointed Billy as deputy.

During his first year in Gregory Diggings, the young deputy met Mary York. Orphaned at age twelve and without relatives, this Irish girl was forced to make a living on her own. Mary went to work as a servant and eventually found employment with the McGees, a Boston family. When they decided to move to California in 1859, Mary went with them. Her hopes for a new life disappeared when she learned that Mr. McGee had plans to use her as a prostitute. Mary's choices were few: commit suicide or run away. Her strict adherence to Catholicism put the damper on the suicide option, so at the appropriate time, she quietly walked away from the wagon train and hid in the willows along the Platte River. That evening a man came to the river for water. Mary crawled out of her hiding place and asked for help. The man, John Gregory, was returning to his gold claim near what would soon become Central City. He agreed to provide Mary with safe passage, and she arrived at Gregory Diggings about the same time as Billy.

Once settled in the mining camp, Mary earned her keep by washing clothes and cooking meals for the miners. She was one of the few women in camp and by far the best catch. How Billy caught her is unknown, but his tall stature, friendly nature, and good looks certainly helped. The couple was married in 1860 by Father Machebeuf, a missionary priest.

Billy soon became county sheriff. "I had a lot to do in getting started off right," remembered the Old Sheriff, "and precious little to do with – just a couple of Colt revolvers, a Sharp rifle, and some handcuffs and leg irons. We had no jail, so when we arrested someone we had to see to it that he got a pretty speedy trial."

But a speedy trial was not always possible, much to the dismay of Mary. One night Billy captured two husky horse rustlers, but the court was closed until morning. So he brought them home. Mary was not happy about sheltering thieves and "she wasn't mealy-mouthed about what she had to say to me, either. I told her I was in a hell of a fix, that I had to keep those men in our home because I had no other place to put 'em." Billy handcuffed the rustlers to their bed and told them that if he heard even a cough he would start shooting. The men kept quiet all night, but in the morning, Mary made it clear that the bedroom would not be used again as a jail. So in 1862 Billy built a jail of "hewed logs, weathered-boarded on the outside." It was a two-story affair, with wooden cells on the first floor and a courtroom on the second. This edifice became known as the Hotel-de-Cozens, and Billy collected a sizable annual rent of twenty-five hundred dollars.

With or without a jail, nothing stopped Billy from tracking down a criminal. One spring he trailed a mule thief to Denver and nabbed the purloiner while he was "leisurely occupying a first class seat at the Denver theatre." On another occasion a man named Kelsey took several head of stolen cattle to Central City and sold them. When officers tried to arrest him, he managed to hide in one of the drifts in the Gregory Extension Lode. "But Billy Cozens was after him, and he finally had to cave," stated the newspaper. Disguised as a miner, Billy descended the shaft in a bucket. Searching the mine, he caught sight of a man in a dark corner. The sheriff opened a conversation and the man turned out to be Kelsey. It took another half-hour to convince the cattle crook that jail was safer and a lot more comfortable than a mine.

Yet the case that sealed Billy's reputation didn't involve capturing a criminal but simply holding on to one already in custody. During his first term as sheriff, a man named Van Horn arrived in Central City and set up a saloon and hotel. His Kansas housekeeper was a "large, but comely women with a tendency to drink and fast ways." Joe Coleman, a hotel clerk, became acquainted with the flirtatious housekeeper. One

Saturday night, as Coleman and the housekeeper quietly strolled along the main street of Central City, three shots rang out and Coleman lay dead.

Sheriff Cozens took to the trail and in a few hours captured Van Horn. A preliminary examination was held the next day in a large theater that accommodated only a small portion of the gathered crowd. The victim was a popular man, and Billy quickly recognized the ugly mood of the miners.

As soon as the hearing ended, he "rushed his prisoner out the back way, which had been left unguarded and unwatched by the mob." He hustled Van Horn down the street toward the jail. The mob quickly realized what had happened and pursued the two men. Billy and Van Horn arrived at the jail first. The sheriff "opened the door and literally threw Van Horn to the inner stairway, reckless of how or where he landed." Then he whirled around and pointed his revolver at the mob. "I'll kill the man who attempts to take him," shouted the sheriff.

The mob fell back along the narrow street and stood there, angry and threatening. Cozens then went "deliberately down among them and called for a posse to aid him in guarding the jail, but no one came." Realizing he was alone, he drew a line in the dust with the toe of his boot and stepped back. "I'll kill the man who crosses that," the redoubtable sheriff shouted as he pointed to the line. A few of the more rowdy miners looked as if they might try but thought better of it. The mob slowly dispersed, most of them heading for their favorite saloon.

Billy guarded the line throughout the day and well into the night. Before daylight the next morning, Van Horn was spirited away to Denver. He was tried, convicted, and sentenced to hang. Sheriff Cozens carried out the sentence in January 1864; it was the first legal execution in Colorado Territory.

Billy enforced the law in Central City and was well liked for his fearless efforts. "He has the reputation of being the best sheriff Colorado has ever had," printed the Central City newspaper. But his wife was not happy with his occupation. Now that they had three children, Mary did not think Central City was a safe place to raise a family. The local newspaper disagreed, pointing out that the police court "has not exhibited enough business activity upon the dockets for the past three months to warrant a respectable newspaper item. Whether the fault is with the people – who seem to be ill-disposed for any excitement – or with the marshal or police, is a matter for investigation." Mary ignored the newspaper and insisted that they move, so Billy gave up law enforcement and became one of the first Middle Park ranchers.

The Cozens moved to the Fraser Valley in 1874, and it wasn't long before Billy had more than ranching on his mind. He soon won a coveted appointment as postmaster and added a room onto his house to serve as a post office. With the mail came passengers, so he enlarged his house to provide overnight accommodations and built a huge kitchen to serve the guests. Later a small store and blacksmith shop were added, then another barn to stable the stage horses. Mining interests in the western portion of the Park and a term as county commissioner provided more diversions. With all these distractions, Billy had little time for ranching, so he hired out most of the work.

Billy was still a sheriff at heart and at times acted like one. When a band of about forty disgruntled Utes tried to eject him from his ranch, Billy calmly walked out to them, rifle in hand, and ordered them off his land. Once the Indians realized who they were dealing with, they left. That was the end of his Indian problems, although these Utes created problems for other Middle Park ranchers.

Then the railroad surveyors showed up. They started placing stakes for the right of way through the middle of Billy's best pasture. He suggested that they move their stakes out of his pasture and to the western edge of his land. They unwisely ignored the suggestion. So Billy took down his rifle and found a comfortable place on his porch. Taking careful aim, he shot the stakes off at ground level. At first the crew ignored him, but it soon became apparent that Billy could shoot the stakes off faster than they could put them in. The surveyors relocated the right of way as suggested by Billy.

During his thirty years in Middle Park, Billy had to deal

with only one horse thief. A horse was stolen from a neighbor's barn, and Billy's son tracked the rustler all over the range without success. Then the old sheriff took to the trail and within a few days a horse thief named Lomax was in jail.

Disagreements over livestock were common in Middle Park. For example, Frank Vulgamott and Richard McQuary had an argument over the branding of range cattle, and Vulgamott filed charges against McQuary. On the date of the trial, both men and their friends arrived early. Having nothing to do, they started milling around and arguing; harsh words followed. Vulgamott and McQuary traded a few preliminary blows and the fight was on. McQuary's father took charge of the event and was having a great time, for his son had the upper hand. When Billy and his son, Will, appeared, McQuary's father told them to get back in the house and "let these men settle things their own way." The Cozens did just that, and the fight went on with McQuary on top and Vulgamott taking a beating. Then the unexpected happened: Vulgamott was on top and "mussing up the McQuary face quite a considerable lot." His father ran to Billy, shouting that the law couldn't just stand by and let a terrible thing like this happen. The fight was broken up and the trial moved to Hot Sulphur Springs. Vulgamott showed up, but McQuary did not. The judge wanted to continue the trial to another date. Vulgamott refused and allowed his charges against McQuary to be dropped. When the judge proposed to charge McQuary for court costs, Vulgamott, in another moment of compassion, paid the costs.

Dropping charges and volunteering to pay court costs wouldn't have happened in the old days. Just ask Billy Cozens, the Old Sheriff. He'll tell you all about the old neighborhood that once was not peaceful and contented.

29
Doc Susie

My first patient? He was a horse, but I'm afraid I never got his name. He'd cut himself on a wire fence and I stitched him up. Those stitches never lasted – the critter tore them out with his teeth. But I pulled him through.

Susan Anderson, 1908

Susan Anderson did not move to Middle Park to treat horses. She was a physician, not a veterinarian. But the horse needed help, so Doc Susie's first patient in Fraser had four legs and a bad attitude.

In reality, Doc Susie came to Fraser to die. After graduating from medical school in 1897, she set up practice in Cripple Creek where her father lived. The rough and rowdy miners in that boomtown accepted her without protest, although "some were a little bashful about having their barroom wounds sewed up by a lady – but they learned to accept it." Her father, however, was not comfortable with his daughter's role of keeping miners in one piece. He insisted that Cripple Creek was no place for a lady, and after three years of nagging, he finally convinced her to leave.

Susan Anderson visited Steamboat Springs but saw little

opportunity because there was no railroad. Doc Susie tried Denver and quickly concluded that she "didn't like it." Greeley was the next stop and there she found plenty of work, for a diphtheria epidemic was in full swing.

She accepted a position in the Greeley hospital as a nurse and soon found herself responsible for the care of twenty-six diphtheria patients, mostly children. The toilsome job often required her to work twenty-two hours at a stretch. She served as a hospital nurse for six years, but her health slowly failed under the strain of overwork. Then she started to cough – a deep, hacking cough that sometimes brought up blood. Doc Susie suspected tuberculosis and moved to Fraser because "I thought I was going to die, and I didn't want to bother anyone."

So on a cold winter morning in December 1907, Dr. Susan Anderson, now thirty-seven years old, arrived in Fraser via the Moffat Road on steam locomotive Number One. With Doc Susie was a small, white spitz dog. She and her feisty dog found lodging with Cora and Charlie Warner who owned and lived in a store on the west side of the tracks.

Before long, her first patient arrived, and Doc Susie started her Middle Park practice sewing up a horse. A steady stream of human patients quickly replaced the horse, and robust health replaced her tuberculosis. The "tiny, wispy, soft, and pretty" Susan Anderson, with a "sharp mind, sympathetic manner, quick wit, and burning ambition" to be a good physician, settled down to a busy and rewarding life in Fraser.

She soon moved out of her rented quarters and into a place of her own. But it wasn't much of a place, only a "box-car like cabin" adjacent to the railroad tracks. The structure offered shelter and little else. Her cabin was hardly fit for treating patients and left much to be desired as a home.

Although Doc Susie was not one to dwell on creature comforts and had little use for material goods not related to treating patients, she did long for better accommodations. An opportunity came one day when a rancher offered her a log barn about four miles away, provided that she moved the barn into town. Doc Susie soon had the move organized and was delighted when most of Fraser showed up to assist her. Before the workers tore down the barn, Doc Susie "took a hammer and drove an eight-penny nail in the first log, leaving only the head showing, two nails in the second log, three nails in the third log, and so on." The barn was quickly disassembled and moved to Fraser; by using the nails as a guide, the workers were able to reassemble the logs in the right order.

Windows, a stone fireplace, interior walls, and an upstairs floor eventually turned the barn into a real home. Doc Susie didn't consider a foundation necessary, so the house had none. Cardboard from old boxes was nailed to the log walls to serve as insulation against the cold winters.

The house soon had the clutter of a packrat's nest, for it was filled with everything imaginable, just in case someone might need something. On the main floor Doc Susie had her desk and a white metal examination table with adjustable back and leg rests. Both surfaces were piled with bottles of medicines, medical books, and bandages. One patient claimed that if he were seriously ill, he would be dead by the time she found and cleared her examining table. An ancient combination bookcase and writing desk occupied a corner. The desk was perpetually open, revealing letters, a worn Bible, and general disorder. Other furniture consisted of three classroom chairs with arms for writing, a table, and an old oak chair with a back that could be lowered for comfort. Oil lamps provided light. Pictures of roses cut from calendars and seed catalogs adorned the walls. The upstairs was used as a bedroom during the summer. The one and only notable piece of furniture in the house was her bed. It was made of cherry wood with a carved head six feet high.

In a typical day, Doc Susie might attend to a logging accident, a horse with a bellyache, and a maternity case. "I've delivered babies in kitchens without any assistance and I've performed major surgery under similar circumstances. But it only sounds dramatic when you discuss it. Actually, I had no choice in those matters."

Her usual charge for a visit was twenty-five cents or some firewood. Often, her patients were too poor to pay and that didn't bother the doctor in the least. "They need me," she often said, and "I got my pay by seeing my patients get better."

Doc Susie was a familiar and welcome sight in the small towns of Fraser and Tabernash, and at the lumber camps and isolated ranches in the southern portion of Middle Park. She quickly discarded feminine frills for heavy wool clothing and felt boots. "I wear the long boots and the long-handle underwear – just like everybody else up here," she once told a reporter. "Course I don't wear them when I go to Denver – they'd probably throw me in jail if I dressed the same down there as I do up here."

The country doctor walked whenever possible, but if the distance to a patient was great, she used whatever conveyance was available. She often rode a horse or took a wagon. For a ride in a locomotive cab, Doc Susie only needed to stand near the track and wave down the first train. "Any train would grind to a stop on Doc Susie's signal," noted the *Rocky Mountain News*. "Engineers and firemen were proud to take her aboard on her missions of mercy."

In the winter she traveled to her patients by sled, snowshoe, or skis. "Never was much of a skier," she admitted, and the doctor often wound up in a ditch. "And I lost my way now and then in a blizzard, but nothing to get worried about. Once all the townspeople thought I was lost and had searching parties out for me – but it was silly, I wasn't lost." But the citizens of Fraser worried about their beloved physician, for she went out on calls regardless of the weather. She was out treating patients even when it was fifty degrees below zero and in a blizzard where "I couldn't see the horses in front of the sleigh for the snow."

But she did draw the line on some means of travel. Late in her life when airplanes came on the scene, she would have nothing to do with them. She claimed that an airplane was just like poison – "one drop and it'll kill you."

One foggy night another type of drop almost killed her. It started when a sick engineer arrived in her office. The man was in anguish from stomach pains and his heart was "acting up." As soon as Doc Susie relieved his pain, the engineer insisted that he return to his locomotive. He had to meet the schedule and arrive in Tabernash on time, and it was getting late. The sick man was helped back to the locomotive, hauled up the ladder and placed on the fireman's seat in the cab. Doc Susie held him upright as the fireman ran the engine. Just as the locomotive got underway, Doc Susie yelled that the train must stop. When she hastily left home, she forgot about her dog that was now running after the engine. The train ground to a halt and Doc Susie climbed down the iron ladder, picked up her dog, and handed it to the fireman. With the throttle wide open, the train thundered down the tracks for Tabernash and arrived on time.

Immediately after arrival, the fireman called for help. Doc Susie had given detailed instructions on how to make a stretcher and move the sick man. The engineer was gently taken from the cab and placed in a hotel room where the Doc could give him proper care.

After the engineer was comfortable, Doc Susie remembered her dog. He was still in the locomotive, and the small creature would probably use his sharp teeth on anyone trying to get him out. She threw on a coat and headed for the train station, forgetting to grab a lantern on the way out. It was a black, foggy night and the only light came from the busy roundhouse near the station. She ran down the tracks toward the light. Seconds later she plunged into the engine pit sunk between the rails. Her cries for help went unheard, for the hiss of steam and confusion in the busy roundhouse muffled the sound. Besides, with several broken ribs, Doc Susie had no lung power to yell.

Worse yet, no one had seen her arrive because they were preoccupied. A small creature had jumped from a locomotive cab and landed in another portion of the engine pit. The men stood around, watching in amazement as a small dog clawed its way out of the pit. The next thing to appear out of the gloom and ashes was Doc Susie. One of the men later told her, "I will never be more scared when I see the dead come out of the grave than when I saw you come out of that pit." Undaunted by the fall, Doc Susie borrowed a corset and laced it tightly around her broken ribs. After checking on the sick engineer, she tucked the troublesome dog under her arm and caught the train for Fraser.

Although treating the sick was her life, Doc Susie had a social side. The newspaper commonly reported in the local news section that "Dr. Anderson of Fraser was visiting several days last week at the home of" a local resident. Gregarious and friendly, she rarely missed a dance or social event, loved to recite poetry, and often broke into song for no apparent reason other than she was happy.

Doc Susie was also quite happy with an axe, both for splitting wood and carving up stills. After witnessing the often devastating effects of excessive alcohol on the lives of her patients, she became a staunch prohibitionist. The doctor was even deputized in 1924 to assist with raids on moonshiners in the Fraser Valley. Presumably, she took her favorite axe with her on raids and put it to good use.

Dr. Susan Anderson came to Fraser to die and instead put her life to good use by providing gracious and loving service to the sick for almost fifty years. The talented country doctor dedicated her life to her patients. When she died at age ninety, all of Fraser mourned.

30
Pipe Dreams

The pipe line still continues to be frozen in the upper part of town and remains a matter of considerable inconvenience to a number of water users.

Middle Park Times, May 23, 1913

Leon Almirall may have chuckled over the lament of the frozen water pipe in Hot Sulphur Springs, for he knew all about pipes that refused to work. His pipe problems started in 1912 when he bought a three-hundred-twenty-acre ranch along the Williams Fork River.

Although Almirall was still new in the West when he arrived in Middle Park during the summer of 1912, he had shed most of his resemblance to a pilgrim and tenderfoot. Escaping New York City for both his health and his dislike of city life, Almirall worked as a ranch hand in Colorado and New Mexico for three years. He carefully saved his money and by combining it with a sizeable inheritance from his parents, he was able to buy a rundown ranch.

The new ranch owner, a bachelor, wasted no time getting to work. His first priority was the house; cattle and fences could wait a bit. So he bought a wagonload of lumber, shingles, nails, and wallpaper and started to make the old house not only livable but attractive and comfortable. Almirall also hired Adolph Brown, a blue-eyed, towheaded youth with a winning smile.

As the two of them worked on the house one day, Almirall faced the fact that his new home was not equipped with indoor plumbing. Few ranch houses had plumbing at the time, but Almirall's proper Eastern upbringing told him that a house was not a home without running water.

Before purchasing the ranch, he had located a bubbling spring in a draw above the house. So Adolph and Almirall hiked to the spring and started clearing out the tightly woven thicket of willows and followed the water into the meadow. Then they staked out the location of a pipeline from the spring to the house and barn. The distance was seventeen hundred feet!

Undaunted, Almirall plunged ahead and hired a surveyor to locate the final grade for the pipe. With all the work that a pipeline would take, he didn't want to make any mistakes. Almirall also sought advice from two cowboys looking for stray cattle. Attracted by the hammering, sawing, and flapping wallpaper at what had once been an abandoned house, the cowboys rode in to see what was going on. When Almirall mentioned his intentions of piping water to the house for a bathroom, the cowboys "gave a kind of suppressed start, but they made no remarks." Almirall wanted to know how deep to bury the pipeline so that it would not freeze in the winter. Both men thought about it for a minute or two before speaking. "Kind of depends on the winter," replied one of the cow punchers. "If we catch a usual one, with plenty of snow, I'd say three feet down oughter be deep enough." His companion agreed, perhaps with an inward smile.

That settled, Almirall ordered the pipe and hired more men. For the next two weeks, five men grubbed out willows and dug their way through the rocky soil. The day they finished digging, the pipe arrived from Denver. The task of laying and connecting the pipe was hard work but nothing compared to digging the trench.

Finally, the pipe was in the trench and the last hookup at

the spring completed. The men then ran back into the house and watched the kitchen faucet. At first there was just a drip, then it steadily grew as the punchers, turned plumbers, congratulated themselves. The Almirall Pipeline worked and was duly registered at the state engineer's office.

But the work was not done, for seventeen hundred feet of open trench had to be filled in. A week later the project was officially completed and, with exception of Adolph, the crew went home.

The indoor bathroom was the subject of much comment in the ranching community. It was called the "wonder room" and Almirall wondered how he could live without it. He soon found out.

On one particularly cold winter morning, Almirall entered the wonder room, turned the faucet, and waited. Nothing happened. He ran to the kitchen and then to the barn. There was no water. The rancher correctly concluded that he had a seventeen-hundred-foot icicle!

Adolph and Almirall tried to thaw the pipe, but the only thing they accomplished was to burn up most of their winter wood. Almirall wasn't about to wait for summer to have running water, so he contacted plumbers in Denver. Several days later a crew of three plumbers arrived and quickly concluded that thawing the pipe wasn't going to be easy. They decided to set fires at three spots along the pipeline, thaw the soil, dig down to the pipe, and use gasoline torches to melt the icicle.

Although it sounded simple, digging the three pits was a tough, backbreaking proposition that took three days. Then the torches were lit and aimed at the pipe. Everyone waited expectantly, convinced that the pipe would quickly thaw. Two hours later the boss plumber growled, "Hell! It ain't gonna work. We gotta dig up the whole damn trench."

And they did just that. Almirall failed to mention how long it took to thaw the ground and dig a trench seventeen hundred feet long, but it must have taken at least several weeks. Finally the digging was done and the torches soon thawed the pipe.

Backfilling the trench was just as much work as the first

time, but Almirall was convinced that this would be the end of his problems. The wonder room worked again. Yet as a precaution, he left the water running day and night in the house and in the barn.

The next time the wonder room went dry was in the summer. "It isn't frozen," griped Almirall, "but it might as well be if we have to yank the ditch apart and take the pipe up again." The Denver plumbers returned and quickly concluded that they had no option but to dig up the damn pipe a second time.

So all seventeen hundred feet of pipe was exposed and most of it disconnected. This time the problem was a small stone that had worked its way into the pipe and eventually had become stuck. Now that the trench was open they decided to bury the line six feet deep. This was the end of the wonder room problems, and Almirall's pipe dream finally became a reality.

But another pipe dream took its place. By this time Almirall had acquired some stock, including two horses that looked as if they could run. He needed a diversion from the pipeline, so he decided to enter his two runners in the Kremmling rodeo. Then Bill Duncan showed up and put a new wrinkle in the rodeo plans.

Duncan drifted in one day riding a rangy roan and leading a white mule. He had dark hair and eyes, a straight nose, and high cheekbones. About medium height, Duncan supported a frame that resembled a well rope. He looked as if he could handle horses.

The drifter was looking for a job. Almirall had no need for an extra hand at that time, but he convinced the drifter to stay long enough to represent the ranch at the Kremmling rodeo. Duncan agreed and within a few days he, Almirall, and Adolph arrived in town for the rodeo.

Kremmling was a "raucous, ribald cow town" jammed with cowboys, most of whom were either bellied up to a bar or gambling at one of the tables. "Good and bad women rubbed elbows with men of the same caliber," remembered Almirall. The three men ate dinner, then roamed the town. Duncan found an old friend and drifted off. Almirall and Adolph continued roaming until Adolph found a saloon to his liking. They entered, and soon Adolph was at the roulette table, hit hard by the gambling fever. Almirall turned away, for he didn't want to see the ranch hand who was still a boy lose all his money. Adolph gambled for hours, then found Almirall. "Broke up the game and the feller who ran it ruled me out," reported Adolph. Both of his pockets were stuffed with money.

At the horse race the next day, there was a short squabble when Almirall's horse, Streak, came to the starting line. "She ain't no cow horse," objected a cowboy. "Look at her. She's a runnin' horse." Streak was a cow horse all right, but her long legs and sleek body gave another impression. It looked like a sure win for Streak, judging from the competition. Most of the other contestants were coarse, wringy-looking broomtails owned by Indians. The quarter-mile race was on and Streak was quickly left in the dust of the Indian ponies. Adolph grumbled something about a new variety of Indian broomtail as he paid his bet. Their horse-racing pipe dream was just that.

Their only hope for winning now rested with Duncan. He drew a large, mean-looking buckskin with wicked eyes that rolled and showed the whites. The horse was pulled into the arena and blindfolded with a sack. Two men held the bronc, and one gave the horse's ear a vicious twist when the critter started to act up. The saddle was cinched in place and Duncan climbed aboard. He took the hackamore rope in his left hand and his hat in his right, then yelled to let the horse loose. Almirall recorded what happened next:

> Into the air went the eleven-hundred pounds of animated, four-footed dynamite, and it came down with a nerve-jarring jolt. But Duncan was still there, raking the outlaw from stem to stern, and slapping him along the neck with his hat.

The bucker went up again with a twisting, rolling motion, and when the buckskin came down it swapped ends and reared on its hind legs as he did a "cloud hunt." A rapid series of high, rocking, crooked jumps followed as the cayuse tried every trick he knew; but Duncan stayed on his back. He won first money.

As with most pipe dreams, this one came to fruition in an unexpected way. Almirall lost the horse race that he expected to win, but his ranch hands won at the roulette table and in the arena. Pipelines were not the only things that had unexpected twists.

South Park

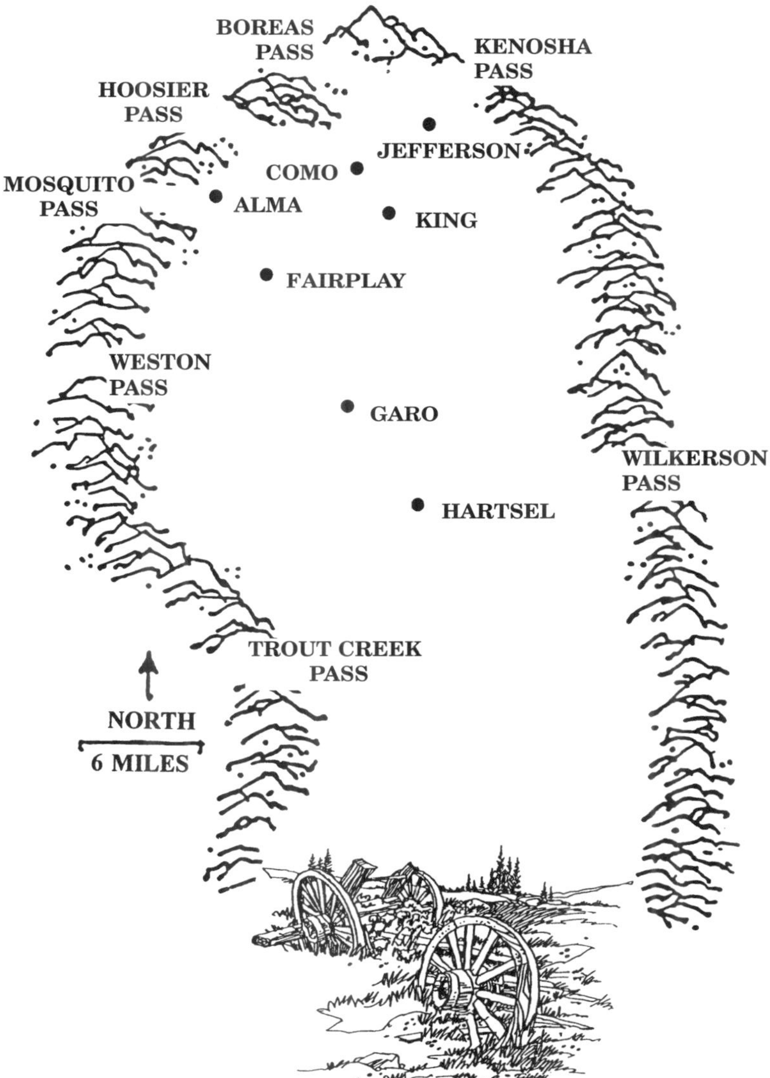
BOREAS PASS
KENOSHA PASS
HOOSIER PASS
JEFFERSON
COMO
MOSQUITO PASS
ALMA
KING
FAIRPLAY
WESTON PASS
GARO
WILKERSON PASS
HARTSEL
TROUT CREEK PASS
NORTH
6 MILES

31
Trappers' Reunion

I rigged up a party of eighteen men to go trapping, I taking charge of them. We went to the Balla Salado [South Park].

Kit Carson, on his trapping expedition, 1852

The idea of a trappers' reunion in South Park was presumably born during the idleness of one winter when Carson was living on a ranch along Rayado Creek near Taos, New Mexico. He decided to gather some of his old trapping friends and have one last fling at a happy way of life that had all but disappeared.

The trapping bonanza had ended in the early 1840s, primarily due to depleted beaver populations and different hat styles that demanded silk rather than fur. A decade later the style had not reverted to fur, and the price for a prime beaver skin was only about one dollar a pound. But the beaver had made an amazing comeback from near extinction, and former trapping grounds now had respectable beaver populations.

So in the spring of 1852, Kit Carson, forty-two years old, led a group of eighteen men north out of New Mexico and into their former trapping grounds in South Park and the vicinity. This was the first, and last, trapping expedition that Carson led. He was never a leader among trappers, apparently preferring to let others take on this worrisome responsibility. Why he chose to lead this last expedition is unknown.

Perhaps his physical appearance had something to do with his avoidance of leadership among trappers; Carson did not strike a commanding profile. In 1851 a newspaper correspondent wrote that he was "disappointed at first sight of the man." Carson was not wearing the outlandish clothing of a mountain man but "genteel American costume." He was short with stooped shoulders and long, curly, auburn hair that fell back from a face that was "not handsome." His eyes "almost monopolize your attention," wrote the correspondent. They were "gray, searching, piercing, as if with every glance he would reach the well-spring of thought and read your very silent imaginings." Carson's voice was soft and gentle, and his manner unobtrusive and polite. Although the old trapper was unable to read and could write no more than his name, he provided an excellent example that literacy is not a measure of intelligence.

The route from Taos to South Park most likely took the men along the east flank of the Rocky Mountains to the Arkansas River and then up the Arkansas to the vicinity of what is now Buena Vista. From this point it was only a few miles across Trout Creek Pass and into the southern portion of South Park.

Unfortunately, Carson did not elaborate on this trappers' reunion other than to state the bare facts of where they went. It is safe to assume that reminiscences around the evening campfire formed an important part of their social life during the trappers' wake. Such men were known for their enthusiastic embellishment of former experiences. Carson was different. Simplicity and modesty were two of his outstanding traits, and he was a slow and reluctant talker until certain that his lack of education would not matter to his audience. Yet he was considered good company and was highly respected among mountain men.

Campfire talk undoubtedly involved Carson, for he had much to tell about the old trapping days in Colorado. As a young man Carson was reckless and daring, especially when it came to

Indians who resented the presence of the trappers and coveted their horses. Although he never started a fight with Indians, he never failed to take up a fight they had started. This was especially true during 1833 when Carson was trapping in Colorado. That winter, Crow Indians ran off nine horses when Carson and a party of trappers wintered in the vicinity of what is now Pueblo. Twelve of the trappers, including Carson, took the trail of the thieves. They recovered their horses without firing a shot, then went back for an unnecessary battle with the fortified Indians. Carson remembered that the trappers "opened a deadly fire, each ball taking its victim. We killed nearly every Indian in the fort." The trappers returned to their camp and had no further trouble with Indians that winter.

That spring the trappers headed for Laramie on another trapping expedition under command of John Gantt. However, when they arrived at the South Fork of the South Platte River, two men deserted and took three of the best horses with them. Carson and another man followed the deserters back to the Arkansas River, only to discover that the thieves had exchanged the horses for a canoe and the trappers' beaver cache. Unable to continue their pursuit, Carson and his companion remained on the Arkansas until Jefferson Blackwell, partner of Gantt, found them. Blackwell informed the two trappers that Gantt's trapping expedition was now in South Park.

Four days later Carson joined up with the Gantt party in the Park. The next morning, as the trappers ate their breakfast, and the horses – some hobbled and some loose – peacefully grazed nearby, Indian troubles began anew. One of the men spotted Indians, probably Arapahoe or Cheyenne, among the horses. The trappers grabbed their rifles and ran for the herd. Only a few shots were fired, perhaps because they feared hitting the horses. Carson summed up the encounter: "One Indian was killed. They only stole from us one horse, one of the Indians having been lucky enough to have mounted one of the loose horses and made his escape."

That was not the last Indian encounter for the trip. Some of the trappers left South Park that day and thought they had lost the Indians. As a precaution, that night the men staked their best horses and placed a dog with them. Soon the dog started barking, and the trappers suspected Indians. After guarding the horses all night and not seeing any Indians, the men concluded that the dumb dog was barking at the moon. So Carson and three others left the camp to examine a nearby stream for signs of beaver. The Indians may have been waiting for this division of force, for soon after the trappers departed they charged the camp and ran off all the loose animals. Four men immediately mounted the staked horses and once again pursued the thieves. The trappers quickly overtook the Indians and recaptured all the horses. During the fray, one Indian was killed and one of the trappers wounded.

The trappers then crossed a rough mountain pass and journeyed into a valley but found no beaver. On their return to South Park they took a different route, presumably to avoid the Indians. As the trappers approached their former trail, Carson spotted four Indians along a distant ridge. He proposed to charge them, perhaps in retaliation for their previous troubles. All the trappers expressed willingness, and the charge was on. They were almost upon the Indians when the men realized it was a trap. Hidden from view were upward of sixty Indians, looking for blood because of their two unsuccessful attempts to steal the trappers' horses.

Quickly surrounded on three sides by the enemy, the trappers reversed course and made a hasty retreat. As the Indians opened fire from all directions, Carson remembered that they "ran the gauntlet for about two hundred yards, the Indians were often as near as twenty yards from us." None of the trappers fired their rifles. Carson explained their fear by saying: "We durst not fire, not knowing what moment our horses might be shot from under us and the idea of being left afoot, your gun unloaded, was enough to make any man retain the shot which his gun contained." All of the trappers escaped, although one man was wounded. He quickly recovered, and four days later the trappers, worse for the wear and carrying few pelts, rode into Gantt's camp.

These are among the experiences that Carson had when trapping the parks and mountains of Colorado. Such stories may have been told and retold around the campfires during the trappers' reunion. The expedition left South Park and, according to Carson's memoirs, traveled

> down the South Fork [of the North Platte], through the Plains of Laramie to the New Park [North Park], trapped it to the Old Park [Middle Park], then again to the Balla Salado [South Park], then on the Arkansas where it goes out of the mountains, then followed on under the mountain, thence home to the Rayado, through to the Raton Mountains, having made a very good hunt.

This beaver-trapping expedition into the Parks of Colorado was apparently the last one for the disappearing mountain men.

32
A Lesson in Claim Jumping

On the 13th day of July, 1859, good pay was struck, and the company made preparations to tarry-all. The different branches of the stream were prospected, with varying success, and Tarryall soon began to make a noise in the world.

Miner's Record, July 27, 1861

This noise carried all the way back in Sidney, Iowa, where William Hawkins Hedges heard it. The short, wiry, red-headed civil engineer promptly arranged for the care of his wife and newborn son, and together with two partners named Charlie and Blinn, headed for the Colorado goldfields and the "acquisition of wealth." After a "reasonably uneventful trip," they arrived in South Park during June 1860.

Gold "in scales nearly as large as watermelon seeds" had been found in Tarryall Gulch a year earlier. By the time Hedges and his partners arrived, two rival towns, Tarryall and Hamilton, had been established in the area now called Tarryall Diggings. Visitors described Hamilton as a "long, narrow town with one principal street" lined with tents and dirt-roofed log cabins. Constant traffic made the road through town a dust bowl in dry weather and a mud hole in wet weather. Large numbers of gold seekers arrived every day and, at the same time, many disappointed ones left for other mining camps.

Tarryall Diggings suffered from a poor image almost from the start. When gold was first discovered in Tarryall Gulch, the prospectors immediately claimed the most promising ground and set to work. Soon a horde of other miners showed up, so the first miners took measures to protect their discoveries. The size and shape of their claims did not fit the accepted practice in other mining areas of Colorado. To make matters worse, the upstream miners diverted most of the water into their claims, leaving little for those working the lower claims. The diggings were soon dubbed "Grab-all."

Although greed was the founding principle of Tarryall Diggings, some generosity could be found. The local newspaper reported that "a pit in the richest part of the gulch, on a claim the owner of which had gone east, was the bank of deposit, from which the hard-up drew their means of subsistence." Subsistence in a mining town meant whiskey, so the miners dubbed the bank "Whiskey Hole." It was the salvation of many unlucky miners who could quickly pan out the price of a drink and drown their disappointment.

Hedges, a religious man, didn't need the Whiskey Hole. He needed a claim, but all the ground was occupied by eager men and their sluice boxes. After a careful search, Hedges and his two partners found a promising claim about half way down the gulch. It had no sluice box and only one man leisurely working the ground. Talking with this man, the partners realized he suffered from a serious case of homesickness.

"Just got a letter from home last night," said he. "I must start for home at once, and will sell my claim for one half the lowest valuation any one in the Gulch will put on it. Won't you buy it? Big chance for you."

Hedges and his partners wanted to buy the claim, but they didn't have three thousand dollars – the going price for a piece – or anything close to half that amount. "We carefully considered the matter," remembered Hedges, "and decided to make him an offer of everything we could rake and scrape together for his claim." That consisted of their mules, covered wagon, tent, watches, almost five months' provisions, and two hundred dollars in cash. Much to their surprise, the lonely miner reluctantly accepted their offer. The necessary papers were filed, and the three men from Iowa found themselves the owners of a mine in the middle of Tarryall Diggings.

They could not, however, work their claim without sluice boxes. To make the boxes, they needed lumber, and the nearest sawmill was more than sixty miles away. The only way to get lumber at Tarryall Diggings was to cut down a tree and saw it into planks. So Hedges and his two partners found a tree about the right size on the mountainside, cut it down, and then rolled it onto a platform. The platform was "so arranged that one man could stand on top of the log and another on the ground underneath it, and between them work a big long saw up and down" and slowly cut the needed boards. Hedges grumbled that "of all my personal experiences in the labor world, this making a sawmill of myself was certainly the most trying." They hauled the boards to their claim and built the sluice boxes.

Irving Howbert was in Tarryall Diggings at the same time as the Iowa partners. He described how to build and work sluice boxes.

> These sluice boxes usually were from twelve to fifteen feet in length and from fourteen to eighteen inches wide, with sides six to eight inches high. In some of these boxes strips were nailed fairly close together across the bottom, making the riffles necessary to catch the gold. Six to eight lengths of these sluice boxes were then joined [and] . . . placed at a pitch sufficient to cause the water to flow through it rapidly. The next work was to dig up and throw into the sluice boxes the gravel on either side, which was supposed to contain gold. The rapid flow of water would carry off the gravel and small stones, leaving the gold, which was heavier, to settle on the bottom and be caught by the riffles.

Now the only problem facing the partners was to get enough water to run their sluice box. Although it appeared that the Iowa men might get sufficient water, they joined with the miners below them and demanded that the upper miners make certain changes that would allow more water to flow into the downstream claims. The upper miners finally agreed. Better yet for the partners, this affair endeared them to their neighboring miners, particularly a "grizzled old gold miner" from North Carolina who worked an adjacent claim.

So with "high hopes and expectations," the partners started digging and washing gravel. A few days later, three men suddenly appeared on their claim. One of the men, with much indignation and profanity, demanded to know what the hell they were doing on his property. Hedges calmly explained that he and his partners had bought the claim and showed the purchase papers as proof. "Well," he said, "that was my hired man that I left to take care of the claim while I was away."

So Hedges and the rest of the men, including the North Carolina neighbor, marched off to the recorder's office to examine the records. Sure enough, the belligerent man was the legitimate owner. The "lonely" miner that sold the claim never owned it in the first place.

The nasty owner pressed his advantage. He demanded that they stay off his claim and tapping the butt of his revolver, threatened that it would be bad for their health if they tried to work his ground. Without making a reply, the shocked partners left for their tent.

As they discussed the dismal situation, they were certain something could be done, but they didn't know what. Then the North Carolina neighbor came in. He was suspicious when the partners had been able to buy the claim so cheaply, and now he knew why. It was an old mining trick, he patiently explained. The original owner of the claim hires a man to work the ground and then leaves. If anyone shows an interest in the claim, the hired man sells it and disappears. Then the original owner returns, throws the new owner off, and splits the purchase money with his hired hand.

The scam usually worked, explained the old miner. But the unwritten mining law stated that if the owner left his claim for more than two weeks, anyone could jump the claim. Hedges and his partners had been on the claim for three weeks, so it was theirs if they could hold it.

The partners decided to do just that. Before they turned in that night, Hedges recorded that "our revolvers were carefully cleaned, oiled and reloaded and our belt knives made as keen as razors." They got up at the first streak of day, quickly ate, buckled on their "belt-rigs," and took possession of the disputed ground before sunrise. Much to their surprise, the miners on the claims below them were also out early, and each had a gun.

The partners waited for the owner to show, but he apparently thought he had scared the Iowa men away. So they started working, with Charlie and Hedges "down in the pit throwing dirt up into the sluice and Blinn tending the sluice boxes." About mid-morning the owner and two other men came running down the gulch. Charlie and Hedges stopped shoveling and, "leaning on our long handled shovels, hitched our revolvers and knives around handy and loosened them in their sheaths."

The three men came to the edge of the pit and the owner, roaring forth with a venomous ten-jointed oath, demanded to know what they were doing on his claim when the purchase papers were no good. Hedges told him that he didn't care about any papers because mining law held that his absence allowed the claim to be jumped. He and his partners had jumped, and they intended to stay.

As soon as Hedges said that, the owner's hand dropped to the butt of his big revolver. But before anyone could draw a gun, Hedges heard a cool, challenging kind of voice saying, "No shootin' in the hole." About thirty feet away their North Carolina friend was leaning carelessly on his sluice box, his left hand on the box and his right hand holding a cocked revolver. "With a slight shake of his head," wrote Hedges, their friend repeated, "No shootin' in the hole."

Hedges expected that the owner and his two cronies would demand that they climb out of the hole and fight on level ground. "We were keyed up for quick action and if he had spoken the words, we should have been on a level with him and firing inside a half a minute," remembered Hedges. Instead the owner exhausted his large vocabulary of profanity. Hedges politely listened, then calmly told him that "wind was cheap and he could amuse himself in that way as long or as much as he wished."

The owner and his men stalked off and were soon talking to a small knot of upstream miners. From the excited gestures, it was obvious that the owner was trying to entice a crowd to come down and deal with the claim jumpers. Once again, the North Carolina friend assisted. He gave some kind of signal and thirty to forty armed miners quickly gathered around the claim, ready to help the men from Iowa. The upper group didn't like the odds and melted away, and soon everyone was back at work and the argument forgotten.

Hedges and his partners peacefully worked their claim until late in the mining season. But the "acquisition of wealth" eluded them. The largest return for a day's work was sixteen dollars while the claims above them yielded two hundred dollars a day. The discouraged miners decided to return to Iowa. They sold their claim and sluice boxes that "cost so much labor" for fifty dollars and headed for home. Their only solace was knowing that they were in the majority, for "nine out of every ten who dared the trail came back far poorer than they went."

33
Reign of Terror

Never before in the history of the United States has a community the size of that of Colorado been the theatre of so many murderous outrages in the same length of time as we have been called upon to record in the month or six weeks just past.
Rocky Mountain News, May 7, 1863

The newspaper account went on to say that "one cold-blooded murder follows another in such quick succession that they cease to strike with surprise." Dead men were piling up in South Park at an alarming rate, and no one knew who was responsible.

Mr. Addleman was the first victim; then two men camped near Kenosha Pass were found murdered. Next, between Fairplay and Alma, Mr. Carter was killed. "Just after they had rifled his pockets and taken his pistol and most of his clothes, Mr. Metcalf came along with a wagon and oxen," recalled Father Dyer, a Methodist preacher. Lead started flying at Metcalf and one bullet slammed into his chest. Fortunately, the ball hit a thick pamphlet in his pocket and did little harm. The startled teamster yelled to his oxen and, in a rare burst of energy, they actually ran. A house was not far off, so he got away. "One of them had a broad-rimmed white hat" and was dark complected, claimed Metcalf. That was all anyone knew about the assassins that had killed four South Park men. But the reign of terror had not ended.

The unknown killers soon struck again, this time on Red Hill. "There they waited until two men, Lehman and Sigg (or Sayga), came along on their way from Denver to California Gulch. They shot one dead, and it was supposed wounded the other in the arm. He retreated down the hill . . . where they caught him and knocked a hole in his skull," wrote Father Dyer. Those in South Park armed themselves to the teeth against the unknown villains with unknown motives. Some even carried a wad of documents in their breast pockets as a Metcalf "improved patent life preserver."

Robbery may have been the motive, surmised the *Rocky Mountain News*. Each victim was robbed of money and, in some instances, of horses; personal effects were also taken. But in many cases the amount of money or valuables was "so trifling that it seems incredible that it should excite the cupidity of the most black-hearted murderer to commit so terrible a crime." So the newspaper concluded that revenge might be the motive and that "these acts will probably go on until the people take the matter in hand and make a terrible example of some of the suspected."

Unfortunately, some South Park men did just that. Heavily armed volunteers were sent out to bury Lehman and Sigg. Just as they arrived at one body, they saw a man coming along the road. The traveler, John Foster, also saw the armed men, and having "heard of the numerous murders on the road, he thought they would surely kill him." So he dropped his coat and ran. The burial party thought Foster was the killer, so they ran after him. "By remarkable speed and endurance he escaped after a six hours' run over the mountains and through the woods," reported the *Rocky Mountain News*.

He finally arrived in Fairplay without his shoes, coat, and hat. Those in town quickly concluded that the ragged-looking man was the murderer; they immediately prepared for a short trial and a prompt hanging. Luckily, Father Dyer recognized Foster, for he was a good Methodist from California Gulch. Dyer placed himself between Foster and the gathering mob, for good Methodists were in short supply in the mountains and he wasn't about to lose one. Father Dyer took Foster into a house "and it was some time before he could relate his feat, as he was very short of breath and badly scared." The burial party finally arrived in Fairplay, even more winded than Foster. Although annoyed at being outrun, the men accepted Foster's story and the hanging mob put their rope away – but not for long.

As the people of South Park buried the five murdered men, they wondered who would be next. "A vague, undefined sensation of dread and fear restrains the free actions of persons who . . . have been accustomed to traverse the Park and the mountains without a shadow of doubt as to their safety," printed a newspaper.

Several posses roamed the Park, hunting for the culprits. One group, looking for a suspicious character named Baxter, stopped by the Snyder Ranch below Kenosha Pass to get warm. When they knocked on the door, Mrs. Snyder answered that she was alone and could not let them in. The men assured her that they only wanted to warm themselves and would soon be on their way. She still refused. "But the quick ear of the outsiders had detected a sound inside like the shuffle of heavy booted heels." More questions were asked and the answer came in the form of bullets. One shot killed a mule and another plowed into a pack saddle.

"The party now withdrew a short distance from the house, and not knowing how many might be concealed within, it was decided to scatter around the house at a safe distance." A call went out for more help, and soon the posse grew to a formidable force. The men renewed negotiations, and finally Mr. Snyder agreed to come out. He "sallied forth, pushing his wife in front of him as a sort of living shield against a fire which he believed might be opened upon him." Snyder insisted that no one else was in the house, but one of the posse, standing near a window, heard the distinctive sound of a rifle being cocked. He shouted for Baxter to come out, threatening to burn the house down if he didn't.

Baxter finally surrendered and both he and Mr. Snyder were hauled to Fairplay for questioning. "Nothing, however, was elicited" except that Baxter confessed to having escaped from the Park County sheriff several months earlier. The only charge against Snyder was his reputation as a bad character, so he was given twenty-four hours to leave the country. Baxter was not as lucky. An informal Fairplay jury concluded that Baxter was a "notorious cattle thief" and probably responsible for the recent killings. He was taken to the vicinity of the Red Hill murder scene and hung.

Yet the mystery had not been solved. Shortly after the hanging, word got around that two brothers, Vivian and Filepe Espinosa, were wanted for a series of murders along the Arkansas River. For unknown reasons, the Espinosa brothers had started a private war against all Anglo men. Authorities suspected that the two men had fled to the South Park area. Those in Fairplay suddenly remembered Metcalf's description of the man that tried to kill him; the gunman was dark-complected and wore a broad-rimmed hat. That description didn't fit Baxter but would apply to someone with the name of Espinosa. They had hung the wrong man!

Now they were determined to hang the right men. Armed with names and descriptions, the citizens intensified the hunt for the "Mexican guerrillas." One posse of sixteen men followed the tracks leading away from the murder scene on Red Hill. The trail led east and out of South Park. They kept on the trail and eventually found fresh signs in the vicinity of what later became Cripple Creek. The fresh trail turned hot when a smoldering campfire and remains of dinner were found. The posse split; one group followed the trail and the other detoured around the killers to block their escape.

Those following the trail soon spotted smoke and then a small opening in the brush where three horses stood hobbled. Only a few moments elapsed before a burly man who was later identified as Vivian Espinosa appeared in the opening and stooped to fix a hobble. One of the posse members cut loose with a full charge of buckshot. "He fell," later reported the *Denver Republican*, "but partly raising himself, commenced emptying his revolver at the crowd and cursing them in Spanish." His shots went wild. One posse member then took careful aim and sent a bullet squarely into Vivian's forehead.

Just then another man appeared wearing an English hunting suit. Bullets were about to fly when one of the posse yelled, "For God's sake, don't shoot, that's Billy Young." The posse held its fire and the man whirled and looked at them. The face was not Young's but that of Filepe Espinosa. With a bound, Filepe disappeared into the brush.

Fortunately, Mr. Young was alive and well, but another man, previously dressed in an English hunting suit, lay dead and stripped of his clothing. The posse decided not to go after the other Espinosa brother. They were tired of the chase, and tracking a man through thick timber and brush would not be easy. Vivian was left unburied, for the posse did not think that a murderer of his caliber deserved burial. The posse went home.

Yet a desperado thought to be responsible for at least thirty (some claim more than fifty) murders in Colorado was at large. Territorial Governor Evans offered a one-thousand-dollar reward for the capture, dead or alive, of Filepe Espinosa. That was enough cash to interest Thomas Tobin, a former mountain man who "could track a grasshopper across the Rocky Mountains." He was also known as a "splendid shot and an all-round fighter."

Tobin followed the trail from where the posse lost interest and eventually tracked Filepe to Fort Garland. The Espinosa clan lived in that area, so Tobin asked a few questions and patiently waited. Suspicion settled on Filepe's nephew. The young man took frequent trips into the mountains, and on each trip he carried more provisions than one person needed. One day Tobin and a contingent of soldiers from Fort Garland followed the young man. The trail ended at a "cleft in the rocks near which a smoldering camp fire sent up a thin wreath of smoke." Directing all but two of the soldiers to stay behind,

Tobin and the two men "stealthily advanced" until they spotted Filepe, sitting by the fire roasting meat. Tobin took careful aim and killed the second Espinosa brother.

Now Tobin faced a problem. To collect the reward, he needed proof that Espinosa was dead. But the man was too big to haul all the way back to Denver. So he dug out his knife and "deftly severed Filepe's head from his shoulders." He placed the head in a sack and later preserved it in whiskey. It was not difficult for Tobin to track down Governor Evans, but getting the reward proved to be a different matter. The territorial legislature had not approved the reward, and it took Tobin over thirty years to collect.

Meanwhile, other issues came to a head. The pickled head of Filepe Espinosa disappeared, and many Colorado visitors wanted to see the remains of the notorious outlaw. "Curator Ferril of the State Historical Society would like to have someone inform him as the disposition of the head of Espinosa," announced the *Denver Times*. Ferril wanted to display the gory relic, but it proved to be more elusive than the reward. Perhaps the head was given a decent burial.

34
Sojourners

Ah Yot, an ancient Chinaman, who has been long known in Fairplay as the water carrier, was crossing Front Street last Friday, just as Wall & Whitter's coach was swinging around.

Fairplay Flume, April 10, 1879

Thomas Wood sat in the driver's seat of the coach as it turned on Front Street. He saw Ah Yot crossing the street and whipped the horses into a gallop, "probably with the intention of scaring the Chinaman." No longer fast on his feet, Ah Yot scrambled to get out of the way. He wasn't quick enough and the wheels of the heavy Concord coach loaded with passengers ran over him.

Bystanders rushed to Ah Yot's aid. "Upon picking him up it was feared that he had received fatal injuries," the *Fairplay Flume* reporter wrote. Ah Yot would be missed, for at age fifty-three he was a hard-working water carrier. Six days after the accident, the newspaper reported that Ah Yot was "much better and in no danger of dying." Wood had agreed to pay the doctor's bill and other necessary expenses. Yet the citizens of Fairplay remained annoyed at the cruel joke.

Although the Chinese living in South Park were victimized

on occasion, most people respected the industrious, hard-working Asians. They first arrived in South Park during the early 1870s. Once the placer claims in Tarryall and Fairplay became too poor to work as small claims, companies bought up the ground and hauled in machinery that used water jets to wash gravel from the banks into long flumes where the gold was recovered.

This often-dangerous process required cheap labor, and the Chinese had no equals when it came to hard labor for low wages. In 1875 Edward Thayer arrived in South Park with two hundred Chinese to work the Fairplay placer claims. Thayer had many years of experience in contracting Chinese labor and was well respected by the Chinese as a generous friend and compassionate employer. Although Thayer quit mining and left when a cloudburst destroyed his placer improvements, most of the Chinese stayed.

The industrious Chinese men filled all vacuums in the labor market. They soon found that South Park was short of laundry facilities, so some of the unemployed Chinese started washing clothes. By 1880, nine Chinese "washees" competed for business in Fairplay. The *Fairplay Flume* was amazed when one ambitious washee, Sing Kee, "gave notice to his patrons that he reduced prices to fifty cents a dozen for washing, starching and ironing" shirts.

The willingness of the Chinese to work for low wages was incredible only to the Americans. A majority of the Chinese came from Canton where devastating wars and natural disasters forced most of the people into poverty and reduced their income to less than sixty dollars a year. Their best hope for a better future rested in venturing to America where the average salary was more than thirty dollars a month. With just a few years of work in this country and frugal living, they could return home with enough money to last a lifetime. So the men left their families and sailed to a strange land for the sole purpose of making a quick fortune and then returning to China. Many of them succeeded.

Because most Chinese planned to stay only a few years, the

"sojourners from the Celestial Empire" kept themselves culturally isolated from the rest of society. Their dress consisted of baggy black cotton pantaloons that barely reached the ankle and a shapeless blouse of the same material and color. The blouse was fitted around the neck and hung loosely down to the knees. The material overlapped down the front and was fastened with buttons or loops. Most wore a wide umbrella-shaped hat made of bamboo or grass. Although this dress was distinctive, the shaven head and long braided queue that trailed down the back and often ended at the knees was even more foreign than the clothes.

The South Park Chinese lived in camps separated from the adjacent community; in Fairplay their camp of small frame houses was located across the river and immediately south of town. Here they re-created a portion of China where they could practice their ancient customs without interference. Rice, fish, and tea imported from China dominated their diet. More than food was sent to America; almost every article of clothing and furniture was imported from their homeland.

The Chinese even had their own judicial system that worked well with exclusively Chinese problems. When Ah Oun, a placer miner in Fairplay, lost heavily during a social game of draw poker and found himself unable to pay, threatening words followed. Ah Oun "broke away and ran across the gulch barefooted, and hid in Jacob Radcliff's house, to the great consternation of his family." A few days later Ping Kee of Denver arrived and held a "judicial inquiry that has made all things right," according to Chinese custom.

Another placer miner, Ah Yot, found himself in trouble trying to catch the person who habitually cleaned the gold from his sluice boxes. When the thief cleaned up to the tune of almost two hundred dollars on a single night, Ah Yot decided to follow the footprints. They led to Ah Quong, a "young dandy that made his living off of his fellows." Ah Yot questioned the dandy, and the answer came in the form of a bullet that almost removed his ear. "This abrupt way of answering a civil question irritated Ah

Yot," and he went hunting for a gun. Although he found one, Chinese law prevailed and the matter was settled peacefully.

Chinese law extended only so far and it had no jurisdiction over the important issue of land ownership. Only American citizens could own land, and few Chinese were citizens. So those involved in mining had no choice but to lease the land. By 1882 the placer claims in the Fairplay area were leased and worked by a growing Chinese population. Those in Fairplay welcomed the newcomers, and the local newspaper stated that it was "glad to see this boom in the Chinese camp as adding its might to the prosperity of the town." The Chinese held the lease for many years and through their hard work recovered substantial amounts of gold.

As long as jobs remained plentiful, no one in South Park complained about the cheap Chinese labor used to work the unproductive placer claims. Yet some tried to take advantage of the second-class status of the Chinese. If a Chinese-leased placer showed more color than expected, some excuse was found to cancel the lease. So the Chinese became defensive when white miners showed interest in their placer deposits.

One such incident became deadly. A group of about twenty Chinese had leased a rich placer bed west of Fairplay. When a group of armed whites approached them in September 1881, the Chinese immediately became excited, threw down their shovels, and ran for their cabins. As the confused whites came closer, the Chinese reappeared, armed with pistols, rifles, and shotguns. Fearing attack, the whites sent a volley of lead at the Chinese. One was hit in the stomach as the rest headed for cover. A truce was called and it was only then that the Chinese realized that the whites were just hunting and intended no harm. Because one man was wounded, word was sent to Fairplay for a doctor. The miner died a few hours after the doctor's arrival. "There had been a mistake," concluded the *Rocky Mountain Sun*, "and the Chinamen had been the sufferers."

Mistakes occurred in other portions of South Park. Edward Thayer, friend and contractor for the Chinese, had returned to Fairplay and was again working the placer claims with Chinese labor. Continually looking for opportunities, he accepted a contract from the South Park Coal Company to supply Chinese laborers for the mines near Como. In doing so he started the "Como War."

Eight Chinese soon arrived and started digging coal. The other miners, predominantly Italian, feared they would lose their jobs to the lower paid newcomers. They held a meeting and decided that the "Chinamen must go." Then "they marched in a body, about thirty in number, to the Chinese camp, and by the aid of an interpreter, demanded of them to leave the place, never to return, under the penalty of being scalped, or something to that effect." The Chinese promised to leave the next day but instead returned to the mines. Their patience gone, the Italians armed themselves and began hunting for an explanation. They found Thayer and presented their demands.

Thayer calmly listened, then refused to remove the Chinese. Threatening words followed. Outnumbered and outgunned, Thayer made the mistake of drawing his revolver. The Italians surrounded him and demanded that the gun be dropped. Thayer obeyed. "The mob then threw him down, stamped on him with their feet and pounded him with the butts of their rifles." One of the mob shot at Thayer and fortunately missed. The specter of murder unnerved the miners and they quickly left.

The Chinese also left and returned to Fairplay. Although they lost the first battle of the Como War, they had no intentions of losing again. The *Fairplay Flume* noted that the Chinese had taken up pistol shooting, and the crack of guns could be heard every day. The newspaper concluded that the Chinese were "becoming pugnacious and intend to resist when tackled again by Italians."

It was the mine superintendent, not the Chinese, who tackled the Italians. He tried to negotiate a compromise with the Italians, but they insisted that no Chinese be allowed to work in the mines. Coal production came to a halt and soon two hundred cars from Leadville crowded the rails because no coal was available for the locomotives.

Prompt action followed. The striking miners were fired and Chinese miners hired. Governor Evans stated that "these people [Chinese] have been peaceable and industriously at work in various parts of the state and in large numbers in Park County for years. They certainly had acquired the right to live and work in that part of the state as well as other foreigners."

Soon almost two hundred Chinese dominated the workforce at the coal mines near Como. But their victory was hollow. Many of the Chinese apparently did not like underground mining and returned to the placer deposits. An explosion in 1885 that was rumored to have killed over thirty Chinese may have further dampened their interest in coal mining. Italians and other Europeans slowly returned to the mines and the Como War was soon ended.

Labor squabbles became part of the Chinese life in South Park. Yet the Chinese continued to prosper and to share a portion of their wealth with others. Their generosity was particularly obvious during the Chinese New Year celebrated in February. Fireworks that put the Fourth of July to shame punctuated this important holiday. The Chinese opened their homes to visitors and many non-Chinese paid social calls to their foreign neighbors. The tradition of gift-giving formed part of the celebration, and the local newspaper commented that if the New Year came more frequently, the Chinese would likely spend "all their profits buying silk handkerchiefs, fans, and other seasonable gifts for their patrons."

Most of the Chinese left South Park when the mining industry collapsed in the 1890s. With them went a colorful and important segment of South Park history.

35
Horrible Hoover

He was of a violent and irascible temperament, and when under the influence of stimulants, as was frequently the case, he was subject to no control. It has been held by his friends that he was insane, and this is the most charitable view that we can take of the matter.

Fairplay Flume, April 29, 1880

John J. Hoover came to Colorado during the gold rush in 1860 and started mining in California Gulch. A year later he moved over the mountain to Buckskin Joe, and for the next ten years he worked mining claims on both sides of the Continental Divide. Hoover eventually became "one of the owners of the celebrated Five-Twenty lode in California Gulch." When silver discoveries replaced the played-out gold mines in the early 1870s, it appears that Hoover lost interest in mining. But he did decide to mine the miners' pockets, so he opened the Cabinet Billiard Parlor in Fairplay. Actually, his establishment was a saloon with a billiard table.

The biggest threat to Hoover's saloon was a nearby irrigation ditch on the property of the Fairplay House. This ditch habitually overflowed, probably because it was half full of rocks and other debris. Whenever it flooded, the water came into Hoover's establishment; this damp event did not enhance business. So he complained about the ditch and probably made a few threats. The proprietor of the Fairplay House, J. H. McLain, finally got the message and hired Thomas Bennett to clean out the troublesome ditch. Bennett was an Iowa man and known to be a "very peaceable, quiet young fellow" who had lived in Fairplay for about a year. He worked as a stage driver for Wall & Witter but for some reason quit.

On Monday, April 7, 1879, Bennett started working on the ditch. The next day "Bennett found it necessary to dam a portion of the ditch to clear out the rocks and brush from the bottom. This caused a portion of the water to flow over the ground belonging to Hoover."

When Hoover saw the water at his front door, he quietly went behind his bar, gulped a big slug of whiskey, dug out a pistol, and headed for the Fairplay House. He stormed into the hotel office and there found Bennett leaning on the counter.

"I own that house and lot, and I'm not going to have my family imposed upon," shouted Hoover as he pointed the revolver at Bennett's face.

Bennett drew himself up and said: "Hold on, I don't want any trouble." He then politely told Hoover that he had not intended to cause any problems.

Without another word, Hoover shot him in the chest; the bullet passed entirely through Bennett's body and landed on the floor behind him. Bennett slumped forward onto the counter as Hoover covered him and cocked his pistol for another shot. At that moment one of the boarders stepped forward and knocked his arm, shouting: "For God's sake, don't shoot him again!"

Unable to stand, Bennett fell to the floor. Hoover stood over him yelling, "Get up there, God d--n you."

Bennett didn't get up, so the irate saloon owner quickly left. Runners immediately left the hotel to find the sheriff and the physician. Sheriff Ifinger was at home eating dinner when the clerk of the Fairplay House arrived with the news. Ifinger went to the Cabinet Billiard Parlor and found Hoover with his wife.

When the sheriff entered the saloon, Hoover simply said, "You can consider me your prisoner." He handed the sheriff a .38-caliber Colt revolver and a knife.

Although Hoover was easy to find, locating a physician proved to be difficult. While they waited for medical help, Bennett was questioned by the sheriff. When asked if he knew of any reason for the shooting, Bennett weakly replied, "No, No, No. Oh my God, he did it in cold blood." Dr. Ramey finally arrived later that evening, but there was nothing he could do. Bennett died the next day.

The *Fairplay Flume* noted that Hoover, who had "kept a stiff upper lip until the death of Bennett, appears now to be much depressed and to fully realize his fearful position." Yet Hoover was not without a friend. "His wife, a most estimable woman, is with him a good deal of the time."

During his preliminary examination, Hoover was charged with "deliberate murder" and was ordered held without bail. Sensing the ugly mood in Fairplay, Sheriff Ifinger took Hoover, accompanied by his wife, to Denver for safe keeping.

Legal maneuvering delayed the trial for a year, but on Monday, April 26, 1880, Hoover was back in Fairplay standing trial for murder. The upstairs courtroom was packed, for the people of Fairplay had not forgotten the brutal murder. J. Q. Charles, one of the two attorneys hired by Hoover, requested a continuance, "which disclosed the fact that a plea of insanity would be set up for the defense." District Attorney Burris didn't like that idea because two continuances had already been granted and the trial had been delayed for a year. So the prosecuting and defense attorneys huddled together and agreed to settle matters by changing Hoover's plea of "not guilty of murder" to that of "guilty of manslaughter." On Tuesday Hoover did as instructed and Judge Bowen accepted the changed plea.

The judge then said, "Let the prisoner stand up." Hoover rose and listened attentively as Judge Bowen summarized both sides of the case. He then stated that the maximum extent of punishment for manslaughter was ten years' imprisonment. Judge Bowen was amenable to consider the year that Hoover had already spent in prison and the plea for leniency, so he pronounced a sentence of "eight years' service in the penitentiary at Canon City."

"A smile of satisfaction irradiated the countenance of the condemned man," reported the *Fairplay Flume*. As he walked from the courtroom, he nodded to his friends and smiled, knowing that he was a lucky man. He apparently did not hear the whispers of dissatisfaction among the courtroom crowd and the muffled cry of "Bring a rope!"

Little was accomplished in Fairplay that afternoon, for everyone was debating the trial. The "hot-headed part of the population made many rash and imprudent assertions," but it was just talk. Sheriff Ifinger listened to the mutterings and decided to place two guards, James Beach and Walter Taylor, in the jail. The combination sheriff's office and jail was located in the basement of the court house. The sheriff stayed with the guards until half-past two o'clock Wednesday morning. By that time the town was dark and quiet, so he considered Hoover safe.

The sheriff went home and had no more than dozed off when a knock on the door woke him. He asked who was there and a voice replied that the sheriff was wanted. Ifinger asked what they wanted, but the voice only repeated that the sheriff was needed. Ifinger then raised a corner of the window curtain and "discovered that a mob of between twenty and twenty-five disguised men was waiting impatiently about the door." When the mob hammered on the door and threatened to knock it down, Mrs. Ifinger opened the door. The mob swarmed in. Pointing a gun at the sheriff, the men demanded the jail keys, but Ifinger refused. Then they demanded that the sheriff go with them to the jail. "He consented, wishing to get them out of the house as his family was frightened and his wife half sick."

Once the mob was away from his home, Ifinger's cooperation abruptly ended and he refused to go any farther. The sheriff scorned yet another demand for the jail keys. Tired of this stubborn man, the vigilantes left a guard over Ifinger and went to the jail without him and the keys. There the "midnight avengers" pounded on the door and demanded entrance to the sheriff's office.

When the guards opened the door, the mob poured in and quickly disarmed both men. They demanded the jail keys, but the guards didn't have them. Forgetting about the damn keys, the avengers hammered down the outside jail door.

Hoover knew what was coming and tried to raise an alarm. He smashed the small cell window, using first his shoe and then a tin can. Through the broken glass he "raised a shrill cry which aroused many, but was not understood nor heeded." When the mob reached his cell door, Hoover turned and cried, "Must I die like a dog!" One of the vigilantes snarled, "Bennett died like a dog."

Hoover begged them to add ten years to his sentence, but the vigilantes didn't have jail in mind. Then he begged them for time to see his friends and to pray. The mob was not listening. "They wrestled the cell door from its fastenings, gagged him, bound him, and hustled him to the front steps of the court-house." A rope was thrown out of the second story window and "in a minute more Hoover's lifeless remains were suspended in mid air."

When Sheriff Ifinger finally got away from his guards, there was nothing to do but cut down the body. At the coroner's inquest held later that day, the jury concluded the obvious – Hoover "came to his death by hanging at the hands of parties unknown."

Both Judge Bowen and District Attorney Burris took the untimely demise of Hoover as a personal threat against them-selves. "They lacked nerve," concluded the *Fairplay Flume*. "They became frightened unnecessarily and no doubt they imagined themselves in actual danger, but had they been nervy they would have stood at their post of duty." Instead, the two men "ingloriously" skipped town, and they didn't bother to tell anyone except the district clerk. Bowen and Burris left behind an unfinished docket and a court that was never officially adjourned.

Although both the judge and district attorney bolted from

town, some concerned citizens wanted to identify the midnight avengers. "A tendency in this direction was promptly checked by the posting of a warning from the vigilantes, which was found tacked up on the corner at the post office building," said the *Fairplay Flume*. The notice was written in a "very good imitation of blood" and stated, in part:

Citizens
We have organized to make this
a county of safety!
105 men, true and brave, in this county alone
have sworn to enforce the laws and punish
MURDERERS
If one single member of our organization
is arrested or tampered with for the hanging of
Hoover, the MURDERER,
those suspected parties will share Hoover's
fate without a moment's delay!
Awake! Arise!
Or be forever fallen!
Strike the death blow to all murderers now
that the work has begun.
Beware of the Vengeance of the Vigilantes!

None of the vigilantes were identified, so perhaps the concerned citizens followed the proclamation's strong advice. More importantly, only a few wanted to "make a bad matter worse by seeking to know who were the parties interested in the lynching." The midnight avengers of South Park melted away and never struck again.

36
The American Game

On the afternoon of the 5th the Alma base ball nine is to meet the Sacramento nine on the diamond field near Fairplay and a good and closely contested game is anticipated.

Fairplay Flume, July 1, 1880

The newspaper called it the "first very considerable game of base ball" in South Park, and this sporting event was played on July 5, 1880. July 4 would have been a better choice, but playing baseball on Sunday was frowned upon, even in remote mining towns. So at half past two on Monday, the game was started by umpire W. H. Price. The diamond was just across the South Platte River from Fairplay. Several hundred fans lined the field that day to watch this first "considerable" game.

Although baseball was new to South Park, by 1880 it was over thirty years old and had evolved from bumbling competition rife with acrimony and hostility into a struggling, albeit respectable, national sport. Betting was still common, and in the West the firing of a six-shooter just as a fielder was about to snag a fly ball was practiced on occasion. Fans heckled umpires, razzed players, and rioted when the game took an unexpected turn. Yet everyone loved a game of baseball, especially in a town such as Fairplay where the usual entertainment consisted of booze and brawls.

On this warm Monday afternoon, the Alma nine won the toss and took the field, with team captain George Snell in the lead. The local newspaper failed to describe what the men wore. The *Official Baseball Guide of 1878* required professional players to wear white knickerbocker pants, white shirts, and socks and hats of appropriate color. Additionally, most pros wore leather shoes that laced at the ankle. It is safe to assume that the Alma and Sacramento teams wore none of this garb for their game. Floppy hats, baggy wool pants and shirts, and heavy shoes were probably the dress of the day for men who were miners first and baseball players a distant second.

Yet on that Monday afternoon mining was forgotten as the Alma nine took to the field and the Sacramento team prepared to bat. What they used for a bat remains a mystery. Bats of the 1880 vintage were made from any piece of seasoned hardwood. Fence posts, wagon tongues, cart shafts, and even jailhouse scaffolding were often handy and, therefore, served as raw material. Specifications concerning length, style (round or squarish), and weight did not exist. For the South Park game, the bat was probably made from aspen or pine, both decidedly inferior wood for swatting a ball. But that did not bother the Sacramento team. Captain John Lacey and his teammates hit the ball far enough for eight runs during their first inning at bat.

High-scoring innings were not unusual for early baseball. Batters quickly learned not to hit high fly balls that could be easily caught by fielders not wearing mitts. Line drives were the ticket for running up the score. Protective equipment for players was almost nonexistent at this time. Albert Spalding, a baseball player, started making thin, lightly padded baseball gloves in 1876. Yet fans and players alike considered those who wore gloves as sissies; taunts and jeers greeted a player foolish enough to use one. Baseball was a rough-and-tumble sport for the manly type such as South Park miners, so protective garb was not needed. The catcher was often an exception. The "bird cage" catcher's mask was commercially produced in 1877. But it cost three dollars, so it was unlikely that anyone in South Park would spend that much money just to protect a few teeth.

At the bottom of the first inning Alma was at bat, but they made no progress against the Sacramento pitcher named Pike. "It looked blue for the Alma boys," stated the *Fairplay Flume,* "but by making a change in pitchers they managed to hold the thing level until the sixth inning." The new pitcher was McKenzie, and he pitched for the remainder of the game.

It was during the sixth inning that Alma finally got into the contest. They did some "splendid batting and ran up a score of nine," wrote the reporter. From this inning to the end of the game, the baseball saw plenty of action. The Fairplay newspaper did not mention any problems with the baseball, so it must be assumed that it held together. Perhaps the ball was made by Albert Spalding, for he had exclusive rights to produce National League baseballs. Because there were no regulations and no quality control, each baseball had a personality of its own. Teams with good fielders preferred the softer balls while teams with good hitters wanted the harder balls. Judging from the final score of the South Park game, the ball was probably of the hard and lively type.

From the seventh to the ninth innings, the game was "hotly contested and the slightest advantage on either side was cheered" by a crowd now thoroughly into the game. The newspaper coverage continued: "At the end of the first half of the ninth inning the Sacramento nine stood one ahead, when their opponents went to the bat and made three runs, thus winning the game" with a score of twenty-two for Alma and twenty for Sacramento.

Although forty-two runs were not unusual for early baseball games, the newspaper attributed the high score to "the fact that each nine became rattled in one inning, as is liable to be the case where men are not used to play together and practice daily." But there was no time for daily practices, and no one objected to rattled players and high scores.

So the first baseball game in South Park was a success. The spectators wanted more of the sport, and the newspaper noted on July 8, 1880, that "another game of baseball is talked of and after the good start of last Monday it would seem a pity not to carry the game on at times during the season." The miners intended to do just that, and a week later the newspaper reported that the "Alma base ball boys say that if the Sacramento nine will meet them on their own grounds near Alma, they will raise a purse to play for and get up a ball for the evening."

Unfortunately, baseball was quickly forgotten in South Park. The public hanging of Cicero C. Simms, the first legal hanging in South Park, furnished far more entertainment than baseball. The newspaper remarked that "it is a sad commentary on human nature, no doubt, but it is a fact that in the west a hanging out draws a circus" and a baseball game.

37
The Lost Head

Quite a buzz of excitement occurred a few days since by the digging up of a human skull which had been enveloped in an old blanket . . . It was buried minus any other portion of the human anatomy, and speculation was rife as to who lost it.

Fairplay Flume, February 16, 1882

The old timers knew who had lost the head, and no sympathy was expressed for its owner. The loss occurred in 1864 when Jim Reynolds and a band of about ten men entered South Park to plunder the gold and silver from its mines. Some contended that the men were Confederate soldiers sent on a desperate mission to extort money for the Southern cause; others argued that they were simply criminals taking advantage of the war to collect loot for their own use.

Whatever the motive, their leader was quite familiar with South Park. Reynolds, a Texan, was thought to be among the early waves of gold miners in the area. When these men arrived at Tarryall, they found that the first miners had used unethical means to grab all the valuable ground. So Reynolds and other disgruntled miners pushed farther south and eventually found gold deposits along the Middle Fork of the South Platte River. Once a mining camp was established, Reynolds and others insisted that it be governed by rules of fair play. Soon thereafter, the camp was named Fairplay.

With the start of the war, Reynolds disappeared and then returned to Colorado a few years later with a gang of thieves that had no interest in fair play. Although the details have been clouded by time, the Reynolds Gang was credited with the capture of two wagon trains in New Mexico. What they did with the wagons, stock, and loot remains unknown, but the property they stole en route to Colorado was often given to the next person along the road. "They played some curious freaks in taking and disposing of property," concluded the *Rocky Mountain News.*

Their South Park crime spree started with the capture of Major DeMary and James McLaughlin near Trout Creek. The major was relieved of his money while McLaughlin was apparently lucky enough not to have anything of value. The jayhawkers took their prisoners to a stage stop at McLaughlin's ranch and waited.

When the Buckskin Joe coach arrived, only William McClellan, owner of the stage line, and Abner Williamson, the driver, were aboard. That made no difference to the Reynolds Gang as they surrounded the stage and ordered the men down. They robbed McClellan of "about four hundred dollars in currency, a very fine gold watch, and a revolver." The express box was thrown down and chopped to pieces with an axe; it contained about three thousand dollars in gold dust. They rifled the mail sack looking for currency and other valuables. Meanwhile, some of the gang disabled the coach by chopping the spokes from the wheels. Finally, they apparently liked the looks of McClellan's horses, so they took the team. As was their curious habit, they later turned the horses loose.

The Reynolds Gang left South Park via Kenosha Pass, followed the North Fork of the South Platte River, and waylaid travelers headed for the Park, robbing them of valuables. Two victims, Charles Hall and William Berry, reported that the robbers "seemed very jovial, talked freely, and said that they didn't mean to hurt anyone, but that they came to this country for money and they were bound to have it." The rebs freely stated their plans to move on to Denver. Berry passed off the city as "devilish dull" and not worth the trouble. Disappointed, the freebooters appeared undecided and in no hurry as they talked to the two men. They even showed Berry and Hall some of the loot, including a bundle of mail. "Berry asked if they had any letters for him, which they seemed to take as a very good joke." The robbers decided to let the two men go and even allowed them to keep their horses.

Berry and Hall continued up the road to South Park, but as soon as they were out of sight, they doubled back and headed for Denver. Along the way they warned the settlers of the robbers and advised them to drive their stock away from the road. When interviewed by the *Rocky Mountain News*, Berry concluded that the Confederates appeared new to the criminal business and "acted in a very unsophisticated manner."

Colorado was not in the mood to entertain Confederates in any form, and several posses took to the trail of the thieves. Smarting from the indignity of being robbed, "Major DeMary promptly organized a company of thirty-one men from Summit and Park Counties, and started in pursuit." At the same time Captain Maynard and a contingent of soldiers left Denver and joined in the chase. But the Reynolds Gang was not as "unsophisticated" as they appeared. They melted into the mountains adjacent to the Platte River where they watched "everybody that passed and all that was going on." After about a week of searching, both DeMary and Maynard gave up.

Not everyone was ready to forget the "guerrillas." Jack Sparks rounded up a dozen men from the vicinity of Breckenridge and rode into South Park via Hoosier Pass. More men joined the posse at Montgomery; the most notable new member was a physician.

They rode through South Park and started down Hall's Valley just below Kenosha Pass. By pure luck, someone in the posse spotted the light of a campfire in the rugged mountains along the South Platte. Tying their horses in the dense trees, the men crept within seventy-five yards of the bandits. "A number of men were collected about the fire, but our boys were in doubt whether they were friends or foes," reported the newspaper. While they debated the question, the rebels overheard them and went for their guns. The posse fired a volley as the bandits scattered into the forest.

It was growing dark and "prudence dictated a retreat from a locality of which nothing was known." The posse returned the next morning and found the camp strewn with saddles, guns, and plunder; even the gang's horses were left behind. More important, one of the bandits, later identified as Owen Singleterry, was found dead. The posse collected everything of value, but this did not include Owen. However, the Montgomery physician, a generous man of jovial and bibulous temperament named Doc Bailey, considered the rebel a prize worth keeping. Bailey decided that he only wanted part of Owen, so after downing a healthy slug of whiskey, the physician cut off the head, reverently wrapped it in canvas, and tied the trophy on the back of his saddle.

It was a common practice at that time for physicians and other men of science to keep the skulls of violent criminals, perhaps with the idea of discovering the cause of their unacceptable behavior. However, the *Fairplay Flume* thought that the doc was just a bone kleptomaniac who wanted to study the human noggin at leisure. Doc Bailey returned to Montgomery and put Owen's head in a jar of alcohol. He placed the pickled cranium in a prominent spot from which Owen's benign stare filled the room with an eerie aura.

In the meantime, most of the Reynolds Gang was captured and taken to Denver. The stockade at Denver was not considered strong enough for the criminals, so they were transferred to Fort Lyon. During the trip they became "impudent and insulting to the soldiers." As they halted for water, the "prisoners made a concerted attempt to escape, when they were fired upon by the guard and all instantly killed." In reality, the military was tired of the Reynolds Gang and this was the easiest way to solve the problem.

Owen Singleterry presented no problem to Doc Bailey. When Montgomery declined in the late 1860s, most of the residents left, including Owen. The bandit did not go far, only down the valley to Alma where the doc set up office. The *Fairplay Flume* picked up the story:

> Time passed, and after a while the comrades of the jovial Doctor used to shun the side of the cabin where the "pickle" was stored, and during the Doctor's absence in Denver, they passed resolutions condemning the same and wrapping it in a faded coat of blue, they threw it into a shallow prospect hole.

The above is not the only version of how Owen's head disappeared. Some miners claimed that an "inebriate," most likely Doc Bailey, was consumed with a thirst for alcohol but had no money. So he took the jar to an abandoned mine shaft, tossed Owen in, and drank the alcohol.

Regardless of the story, Owen ended up in a mining shaft. Almost twenty years later, as an old mining shaft was being dug out for renewed exploration, Owen's head was uncovered. Doc Bailey was long gone, so Owen found a new home, which was described in the *Fairplay Flume*:

> Lovers of the beautiful in nature and in art are invited to step into the Flume office and admire the piece of choice bric-a-brac, mentioned last week at some length. Some unknown friend has sent us in a box the skull . . . and its open countenance smiles benignantly down upon us as we write, flanked on either side by the paste pot and *Webster's Unabridged*, from which it is expected to draw mental and physical nourishment.

38
Old Mose

Mr. Radcliff had only time to draw up his gun and fire at random. The brute caught his ankle with its paw.

Fairplay Flume, November 29, 1883

Jacob Radcliff and his two companions, Henry Seymour and a man known only as Cory, were in no hurry to start the day's hunt. They left their camp around noon, with each hunter going in a different direction. Radcliff preferred it that way, for this seasoned hunter was a dead shot and required no assistance to bring game home. Yet on that Thursday, November 22, 1883, he would find himself in desperate need of help.

Radcliff headed north from camp and soon discovered fresh bear tracks in a snow-covered meadow. He was hunting deer and had no intention of following tracks that could lead to trouble. But trouble came on its own accord when a huge bear bolted from the underbrush and headed for Radcliff. The hunter had barely enough time to fire one unaimed shot. The sting of the bullet just infuriated the beast, and now Radcliff's only defense was an empty rifle. He used it to push the bear away, but that only deflected the first charge. The brute came again and this time caught Radcliff by the ankle. As the bones broke beneath its teeth, the bear tossed the hunter into the air.

As reported by the *Fairplay Flume*, the situation changed from bad to worse for poor Radcliff:

> As he fell to the ground the brute pounced on him, crushing the bones of his legs, tearing his cheek and clawing his body frightfully. Mr. Radcliff was perfectly conscious. He knew of his danger, uttered repeated cries and endeavored to raise and escape, but the infuriated brute again tossed him in the air, and as he fell bit him nearly from ear to ear and tore off his scalp.

Radcliff finally lost consciousness; the bear lost interest and left. Cory had heard the screams and soon arrived. Seymour was close behind and together they hastily made a litter of poles and carried the mangled remains of Radcliff to the Mulock Ranch along Badger Creek. Mulock took one look at the hunter and summoned two of his best cowboys. Catching their fastest horses, one raced north toward Fairplay and the other south toward Salida in search of a physician. Dr. DeLamater was eventually found in Alma, but by the time he arrived at the Mulock Ranch Jacob Radcliff had died.

The bear that killed Radcliff left tracks that measured ten inches across. Most likely it was a grizzly, and some thought it was the same bear that had recently killed a three-year-old heifer at the Mulock Ranch. This bear was eventually given the name Old Mose, perhaps because, in typical bear fashion, it moseyed along at leisure in a shuffling, aimless manner, even when being shot at by angry ranchers. In reality, Old Mose may have been more than one South Park grizzly that had an appetite for livestock and a grudge against people.

And a young man named Wharton Pigg had a grudge against Old Mose. At the time of Radcliff's untimely demise, Pigg was a restless sixteen-year-old bored with life on the family ranch near Current Creek. To make matters worse, the "ranch" had no cattle, only potatoes. Pigg had a passion for hunting and a dislike for potatoes, so he traipsed off to the mountains with his rifle every chance he had. Radcliff had been killed in the Black Mountain area, not far from where the young man lived. Old Mose was Pigg's bear and he was determined to kill it.

But bears are elusive creatures, especially when one is singled out for special treatment. During the next thirteen years Pigg did a lot of hunting and looking for Old Mose, yet never had a clear shot at the bear. His efforts were frustrated by a lack of time. He had to help his parents on the potato ranch, go to school and then college, prospect for gold, discover gold near Cripple Creek, get married, raise a family, sell the gold mine, and buy the Stirrup Ranch near Black Mountain.

Meantime, Old Mose still lunched on livestock and killed anyone, such as James Asher and Pap Rudolph, who got in his way. Pigg never forgot about his bear, and now that he was a wealthy man, he could do something about the notorious bruin. He bought a pack of hounds and a new rifle. Throughout the spring, summer, and fall from 1896 to 1900 the rancher hunted Old Mose without getting close to the beast that roamed in his backyard.

In 1901 Pigg changed tactics and bought a fifty-pound bear trap. Others had tried to trap Old Ephraim by using bait, but Old Mose knew when a trap lurked in the neighborhood and how to eat the bait without pinching his toes. Pigg was determined to outsmart the bear by placing the trap in water. Old Mose was fond of bathing, so Pigg found one of the bear's favorite ponds and placed the trap about one foot below the surface.

Pigg then hired a young boy, John Douglas, to check the trap every morning. Two weeks passed with no sign of a bathing bear. Then one morning, as Douglas approached the pond, he saw a huge bear thrashing around in the pond and roaring in fury. He spurred his horse back to the Stirrup Ranch and blurted out the news. Pigg grabbed his rifle and the nearest horse. When he arrived at the pond, Old Mose was gone and the trap dragged into a meadow. Yet the trapping effort was not a complete loss, for two toes remained in the jaws. Old Mose was now marked and would be easier to track.

Pigg resumed the hunt with new enthusiasm, only to experience two more years of frustration. Old Mose seemed to be enjoying himself. He rambled far and wide, yet he was never too far from his home ground around Black Mountain in the southern end of South Park. The bear paid several visits to the Stirrup Ranch, often selecting a full-grown bull for dinner. Through outdoor magazines and newspapers, Old Mose grew famous, and hunters from as far as Texas and Idaho tried their luck in South Park. A five-hundred-dollar reward was offered for his carcass. Yet the wily old bear was unaware of his notoriety and continued his peaceful, easy life.

When James Anthony arrived, the situation changed. He was a noted bear hunter who had killed sixteen bears in 1903 and had over forty bears to his credit. Unlike Pigg's dogs that had little interest in bears, Anthony had a pack of fifteen enthusiastic hounds, and he invariably hunted bears with these howling canines.

Pigg invited Anthony to the Stirrup Ranch to try his luck at Old Mose, and the hunter readily accepted. In early April of 1904, Anthony arrived at the ranch with eleven of his dogs. The two men hunted almost daily for a month without seeing so much as a track from Old Mose. Pigg wasn't disappointed, for he correctly surmised that Old Mose was still in hibernation. When the bear did emerge, Pigg wanted to be there. A bear just out of hibernation is weak from lack of food and does not travel far. That would make hunting a bit easier, concluded Pigg; but he was wrong.

In late April, Pigg found Old Mose's hibernation den and his distinctive tracks leading away. They followed the tracks for five days, often losing them in the dry grass. As usual, Old Mose was not making things easy for the hunters.

Their luck changed on April 30. They stumbled across fresh tracks from Old Mose. Anthony released the dogs and the hunt was on. The howling pack led them down a forested slope and into an aspen grove. There the hounds milled for a few minutes, then separated into two groups. One group headed along a ridge and down into an aspen thicket. Pigg spurred his horse up the ridge and positioned himself to meet Old Mose when the dogs flushed him from the trees.

The other hounds headed into dense timber, and from the sound of his dogs, Anthony knew they had found Old Mose. The hunter dismounted and cautiously moved into the thicket. There was the huge grizzly, standing broadside to him. Old Mose was confused by the dogs and paid no attention to Anthony. The hunter fired, wounding it in the throat. The bear angled down the slope, ignoring both the wound and the dogs. Old Mose then changed directions and headed up the slope. Anthony blazed away, and a few minutes later Old Mose was dying.

Hearing the shots, Pigg came running and arrived to see the creature that had been his hunting nemesis for twenty years gasp its last breath. He sadly stared at the huge bear for several minutes, then gently lifted the left hind foot; two toes were missing.

Anthony wanted to skin the bear on the spot, but Pigg said no. His old antagonist would arrive in town in one piece. The broken hunter left for his ranch and soon returned with a wagon and crew. The next day, as Old Mose was being hauled to Canon City, Pigg returned to the spot where the bear had been killed. On an aspen tree he carved, among other notations, the following tribute:

Ole Mose's Last Bed
April 30, 1904

Pigg probably never returned to that spot, and he never got over the death of Old Mose. After all, Old Mose was "his" bear.

39
Downhillers

The novice on a pair of 12 foot Norwegian snow-shoes is about as awkward and unmanageable a cuss as a locoed steer. His first break generally causes him to step on himself in such a graceful manner that he up-ends in a snow bank after fifteen seconds of manoeuvering.

Fairplay Flume, January 8, 1885

The newspaper went on to note that winter mountaineering was becoming more popular in Colorado, and many miners were as much at home on the ungainly skis (also called snow-shoes) as a child becomes on roller skates. "An expert snow-shoer will ascend or descend the steepest mountain sides, cross gullies a hundred feet deep with snow and scale ridges almost impassable in summer, and do it all with seeming ease and with startling rapidity."

South Park skiing was born of necessity. When gold was discovered on the Western Slope in 1859, the best route to the Breckenridge mining camp was through South Park to Tarryall, then over the Continental Divide. During that winter, as many as fifty miners a week crossed the Divide, all of them using skis.

A newspaper concluded that skis were the "only practicable mode of traveling in this region of the country at present."

Determined to experience winter gold mining firsthand, William Byers, editor of the *Rocky Mountain News*, set out for South Park and Breckenridge in February 1860. When he arrived at Tarryall he was confronted with skis for the first time. He described them as made from a board, likely pine, about nine feet long, five inches wide, and an inch thick in the middle, tapering to half an inch or less at either end. The front of the ski was "steamed and turned like a sleigh shoe." The foot binding was a simple leather strap fastened to the ski and buckled or tied around the toe, leaving the heel free to move. Only one accessory was needed – a balancing pole seven to eight feet long.

The technique of skiing was theoretically simple. According to Charles Gardiner, a mountain physician forced into skiing, "What we did [when going uphill] was to make long zigzags like a railroad." To prevent the skis from slipping backward, a piece of deerskin was attached to the underside of the ski, with the hair pointing back. If the ski slipped, the "hair would be turned the wrong way and stick out so as to hold the shoe." When traveling downhill, the balancing pole came in handy. "We rode this pole as would a boy, playing horse," remembered Gardiner. "It acted as a brake." When on level ground, the pole was used "on one side as in poling a boat through the water."

It sounded simple, but those untutored in the art of skiing found that this mode of travel consisted of a succession of miscalculations. After many dives into the snow, Editor Byers concluded that if the snow were hard, he would have been rubbing a sore head. Father Dyer, the traveling preacher for South Park and the vicinity, had his share of mishaps when learning how to ski. His most serious problem was getting the skis crossed while zipping down a hill. On one such occasion, he found that a tree was "right in my course, and I could not turn, and dare not encounter the tree with the shoes crossed; and so threw myself into the snow, and went in out of sight."

A reporter for the *Fairplay Flume* also noted that the novice skier spent more time in the snow than on it. On the rare occasions when the skier regained a perpendicular position, one ski often pointed east and the other west. The result, according to the newspaper, was

> another dive at the center of the earth, and increased profanity. After several more hair-breadth escapes he finds that by throwing his legs slightly apart and keeping perfectly quiet he can maintain a natural position for half a minute at a time. Then he cautiously pushes one foot ahead six inches, and in his nervous haste to bring up the other one he finds that it has escaped his control and is going down hill with tremendous velocity. Something has to give, and amid a grand flourish of snowshoes, legs and flying snow he again sinks with a groan into the fleecy bank.

But with infinite patience, the skier can get the upper hand on the skis and "in the end becomes skillful in his evolutions upon them." Father Dyer had to do just that. Desperate for money to support himself and unable to find reasonable employment, Dyer accepted a job carrying the mail from Buckskin Joe to California Gulch once a week. The distance was only thirty-seven miles, but the Continental Divide separated the two points.

The preacher had mastered the art of skiing the previous winter, so using his Norway-style skis he made the weekly trip carrying about twenty-five pounds of mail and five pounds of express. The reluctant mailman soon found that the best time to travel was at night when the snow crusted and the winds often died down. Still, storms represented a constant menace, and more than once he lost his way and spent most of the trip falling down the mountains rather than skiing down them. On one occasion when he was lost, he found himself on the edge of a precipice. Unable to go back, Father Dyer concluded that his "only chance for life was to let myself go over. I took my long snow-shoes, one under each arm and holding the crooked end in each hand for rudders, and believed that if I could thus keep my feet foremost, I could go down alive." The traveling preacher made it, but one winter of mail carrying was enough.

Although getting lost during a storm was a worry, the greatest fear was losing a ski. Because the skis were attached to the boot by only a leather strap, any unexpected stress could snap the leather and leave the skier stranded. That happened to John Jebb in the 1860s as he skied from one mining claim to another. He "was traveling almost at top speed, when suddenly he found himself in the air." When Jebb arrived back at earth, the jolt broke both ski straps. Jebb instinctively grabbed at them and was lucky enough to catch one. But watching the other ski disappear down the mountain made him sick.

The miner was five miles from the nearest shelter and the snow was from ten to twenty feet deep. Jebb considered a number of disagreeable options before he thought of following the errant ski that had disappeared without leaving a trace on the crusted snow. He reasoned that the remaining ski might follow the same path of the lost one. "Accordingly, he carefully found the place where the accident had happened, put the remaining shoe on the track, and then lay down along it, rounding his chest as much as possible and steering with his elbows." It was a fast trip down the mountain, and when Jebb turned into a gully, he "could scarcely believe in his good fortune when he caught sight of the lost shoe."

Other skiers had similar problems. As reported by the *Fairplay Flume*, a miner found himself in Kokomo the day before Christmas and decided he wanted to spend the holiday in Alma. So he packed a lunch, strapped on his skis, and trudged up the Continental Divide. "I was squatting on my snow-shoes, munching my lunch and thinkin' how I'd like to have that view in a frame . . . when zip! one of those blamed shoes went out from under me like a flash, and before I could grab it, it went a-flying down the mountain I had just climbed up." The miner had two options: freeze to death or go after the ski. So he sat down on the one ski and used it as a sled. He cautiously slid down the mountain until, two hours later, he came to a cabin.

There he hunted around and found a barrel stave. A little bit of work turned it into a passable ski. "When I had got that fixed onto my foot I felt more confidence and was making great time down the mountain, when I caught the front end of the stave in a hard bit of snow." He went "a-flying" again. Four hundred feet later he piled up against a rock and broke his ankle. He just wasn't having a good day on the Colorado slopes. There was no use stopping to lament his injuries, so he continued down the mountain and managed to find the other ski. He tied both skis together and made a fairly decent sled.

The frazzled miner arrived at the railroad tracks just as the sun set. "I tell you, I was in a terrible fix, and if that section gang hadn't a come along and took me back to Kokomo I'd a-died before morning sure." The newspaper concluded that "adventures of all kinds are met with by the hardy mountaineer who practices this means of locomotion."

Although skiing in Colorado started as a serious and strictly utilitarian activity, it soon turned into a sport. As early as 1878 those who lived in isolated mining towns found that skiing helped pass the long winters. The *Rocky Mountain News* noted that "the population of Silverton during the dull season drive dull cares away by social contrivances, one of the most popular of which is snow-shoe exercise in moonlight, which is joined in by big and little of both sexes." A favorite event was for parties of three to six to start down a hill abreast, all holding to one balancing pole and traveling at an "astonishing" speed. Of course the participants shared a common fate; the skiers usually plowed up a long furrow of snow when their skis went one way and they another.

The skis themselves were soon transformed from crude homemade planks of bent wood to finely crafted masterpieces usually made by Norwegian carpenters. The best skis came from straight-grained ash that had just enough spring. "They were very strong; their lines and curves were so nicely adjusted that they were works of art," remembered a physician when skiing in 1878. Each pair was made to order and varied according to the height and weight of the skier, shoe size, and use of the skis. Some had a "single groove running along the underside to prevent sideslips. The sliding surface was rubbed down as smooth as silk; then wax was applied by a hot iron and polished until it shone like a mirror."

It wasn't long before ski clubs formed in mining towns and racing soon followed. In 1887 Crested Butte challenged Gunnison to a downhill race. "While there was some grand and lofty tumbling, the boys showed great skill in the great mid-winter sport of snowshoeing." Of course, betting was lively during the January meet. The *Denver Republican* reported that the town was painted that night by the Crested Butte "boys," wild with enthusiasm over their victory.

The passion for skiing grew, and just after the turn of the century the *Denver Times* concluded that "ski-running is one of the most exhilarating outdoor sports that can be imagined, besides the spice of danger which adds zest to the sport." This time, the newspaper had it right.

40
In the Twinkling of an Eye

The shrill cry of the alarm whistle had already summoned the village people, and the wives, mothers, fathers and children stood about . . . the slope with agonized faces, anxious yet fearful to learn the truth.

Fairplay Flume, January 12, 1893

At 11:35 a.m. on Tuesday, January 10, 1893, the ground shook beneath the town of King, home to about three hundred people and just a few miles east of Como. The shock of the explosion reverberated throughout the King Coal Mine, and the miners knew that it was not the usual noon blast to break out the coal. They swarmed out of the mine like ants from a poked anthill.

The crew of about one hundred and twenty miners frantically looked for friends and asked questions, ignoring the bright light that hurt their eyes and the frigid cold that penetrated their coarse mining garb. Few had any information, except for the pit boss, James Lee, and two other miners from the vicinity of Level Six.

While working near a water pump in the main entry, they had heard a heavy, deafening boom followed by a rush of air that had knocked them flat. Stunned, the men had lain for a moment in the silent darkness, then had scrambled up and run in the direction of the explosion. Thick smoke coming from a crosscut vein had driven the men back and out of the mine. A twenty-five man crew, mostly Italians, worked in that part of the mine known as the south side of Level Six, nearly one thousand feet from the surface. No one from that crew was among the miners milling about the smoking mine entrance.

The men marked time, hoping that the miners from Level Six would emerge, but none did. Although volunteers quickly prepared to enter the mine, the dense smoke drove them back. It wasn't until two hours after the explosion that Superintendents William Berry and Elmer Rogers plus six other volunteers disappeared into the mine.

Men and families waited in agony for the rescue workers to return. In hushed voices the men wondered what might have happened. Speculation focused on coal gas. Air in the mine was fair at best, but a huge Murphy fan constantly rotated and did a reasonable job at venting the workings. The fan had worked before the blast, the men realized. Besides, if gas was the culprit, the explosion would have been much bigger, and few men would have survived. If not coal gas, then dust must have been responsible. Fine coal dust covering the mine floor often filled the air when miners scrambled out of the workings just before a shot was fired. An improperly placed shot could have blown outward and could easily have ignited the dust, speculated the miners.

Hushed voices changed to audible groans when the rescuers emerged with the mangled remains of Charley Derock. The *Denver Republican* recorded that "Italian women came running, bareheaded, crying loudly in their unfamiliar tongue, and rushing frantically upon the corpse that lay in awful death at the mouth of the shaft."

More bodies were recovered and brought to the surface. A cry of anguish went up from the miners when the body of Charley Antonolli was brought up. He was young and a favorite among the Italians. "His two brothers are down there, too," announced one of the rescue workers. Something between a curse and a groan arose from the sullen miners.

The row of corpses grew longer and longer as the cold winter afternoon wore on and a light snow fell. Joseph James was the first married man brought up. When his wife recognized him, she threw her arms around his neck, heedless that his flesh and hair fell away at the touch. Even the curious turned away.

Bodies continued to arrive, but suddenly a cry of hope went up from the crowd. One of the supposedly dead miners moved slightly and seemed alive. His face was quickly bathed with water; the miner's feeble breathing became stronger and his eyes slowly opened. Word went out that James Carmosini was alive. Immediately, a small lady with long, dark hair darted out of the crowd. Mrs. Carmosini knelt beside her husband, smoothing his hair as low moans escaped from her lips. The miner was gently carried up the hillside to a row of shanties that paralleled the railroad track. His wife and Dr. Mayne, the company physician, followed.

The work of removing the victims continued as night descended on the town of King. Lanterns and torches provided quivering light that was reflected by the packed snow smudged with coal dust. By midnight all twenty-four bodies had been removed and placed in the carpenter's shed. "The dead lay side by side, as closely as they could be placed on the floor, and reaching from end to end of the shed." Worn black boots peeped out from beneath the coarse wool blankets placed over the dead men.

When Wednesday morning arrived, the ghastly task of preparing the dead miners for burial began. Grim miners dressed in overalls and dirty blouses and sympathetic women dressed in black gently placed each miner on a table in the center of the shed. There they washed away the dirt and soot as best they could, but the force of the blast had driven coal dust into the flesh and much of the black could not be removed. They dressed each body in clothing provided by friends and relatives. Preserved by the January cold, the corpses formed a row at the end of the carpenter's shed; the coffins had yet to arrive from Denver. Here and there a bright ribbon was tied about a victim's neck as a token from some bereaved relative. A slip of torn paper pinned on the breast of each man gave his name.

Meanwhile, anxious miners surrounded Carmosini's house. His sealed lips might hold the explanation of what really happened at Level Six. The company physician thought there was a reasonable chance that the injured miner might survive. "It was feared that the flames had reached his lungs, but this happily proved not to have been the case, and the care he is receiving will doubtless pull him through," printed the *Rocky Mountain News*.

As state and company officials investigated the explosion on Thursday, preparations were made for the mass funeral. A "large force" of men started digging two trenches, each eight by twenty feet, at the Como cemetery that overlooks South Park. Because the ground was frozen, the men used dynamite to make the excavations. Father Fogerty of Breckenridge began preparing the small Catholic church for Saturday services.

An inquest convened in Como on Friday. State Coal Mine Inspector John McNell concluded that the explosion was caused by Stephen Conti, a miner inexperienced in the art of blasting, and perhaps his partner, Joseph James. "It was just the same as an explosion of mill dust," said the inspector. "I think there were altogether too many shots placed within so small a space as 300 feet. There can be no doubt that the explosion was caused by a shot blowing out into the atmosphere already inflammable, and made more so by the escape of the gases from the freshly uncovered coal." So instead of expending energy in breaking the coal, Conti's clustered shots had flashed back and out of the hole. This had ignited a small pocket of coal gas that in turn had ignited the coal dust, and in the "twinkling of an eye every man but one employed in that entry lay a blackened and disfigured corpse."

According to the *Denver Republican*, placing shots close together violated an iron-clad company rule. The miners knew of this rule and accepted the inquest's findings without complaint, although some thought the company could have done more to improve the ventilation. More important, the company should have done something to cut down on the coal dust. The dust could have been removed or kept wet using the ample water found in some portions of the mine.

Pinpointing the blame did little to comfort the mourners gathered for the mass funeral. At ten o'clock Saturday morning a special funeral train consisting of two coaches for the living and two box cars for the dead pulled out of King and soon arrived in Como. No sooner had the train stopped when a hundred men jumped from the cars and formed a column. Every man wore a black suit, and pinned on each lapel was a black and orange ribbon tied in the form of a cross. Two men opened the doors of the first boxcar and reverently lifted a coffin into the waiting hands of six men. This coffin was chosen at random to represent all the deceased, for the small Catholic church where the services would be held could only accommodate one victim.

A somber and melancholy procession slowly trudged up the snow-covered hill and into the church where the priest celebrated Requiem Mass. "The words spoken by Father Fogerty were able, distinct and full of tender sympathy, and moved the hearts of all of those present." Then the congregation filed out of the church, carried the coffin down the hill, and boarded the train where the other coffins waited.

As Father Fogerty spoke of everlasting life, Carmosini rallied and appeared to be winning his fight against death. Dr. Mayne said Carmosini would survive, minus one eye. As his condition improved, the miner mumbled a few disconnected words. "Fire, quick fire!" repeatedly escaped from his burned lips. Those few words summarized the terrible event that put twenty-four of his comrades on the train to the cemetery.

Once the black-clad mourners had reboarded the train, it slowly pulled away from Como and within a few minutes arrived at the desolate cemetery on a windswept hill west of town. Confusion reigned as the men unloaded the coffins and reverently lowered them into two long trenches. The mournful wailing of the women subsided long enough to allow Father Fogerty to bless a shovelful of dirt and drop it upon a coffin. Without any further ceremony, the men filled the graves. With their dead properly buried, bereaved friends and relatives walked to the train and returned to King where their shattered lives demanded attention.

The final reverberation of the King Coal Mine disaster was felt later that day. According to a short article in the *Fairplay Flume*, the "twenty-fifth victim was added to the roll of the King mine disaster. James Carmosini, who was the only survivor of that fatal Tuesday, died after enduring great suffering."

41
My First Roundup

Although I had been to a good number of round-ups, it was in the summer of 1893 that I was to go and stay a week.
Harry A. Epperson, on his first roundup, 1893

After all, at age thirteen Harry had considerable holdings. He owned a "large string of horses, consisting of two little Indian ponies, weighing about 650 pounds each." His cattle holdings were likewise impressive and were made up of a heifer purchased two years earlier from a trail herd, a cream-colored Texas cow, and several offspring from this breeding stock. Harry thought that a man of his standing should have his own brand, so he duly recorded a "H7V" in the state records. His next step was to rebrand his cattle, which required attending a portion of the early summer roundup where the stock was branded. However, he encountered strong opposition from his mother.

Harry was much too young for a roundup, argued his mother. She supported her argument by mentioning young Cameron who, while roping a horse, got caught in the loop, was thrown off his horse, and killed. Dick Wilmoth next came to mind. A rope caught around his hand, and he was dragged until his hand came off. Then Wilmoth's brother had a horse fall on him and lay there for a day before someone found him. Many other cases followed and it became obvious that Harry's mother thought that most of the young men in South Park were doomed to be killed at roundups. "But after an all night session, with my promising to keep my horse out of prairie dog holes, and promising to keep away from all ropes, horses, and cattle, she said I could go."

Harry rolled his blankets and left that morning. He found the roundup crew working about thirty miles from his home and in the southern portion of South Park. As he rode into camp he noticed that men had bunched the horses and were roping their afternoon mounts. A short distance from camp stood the day herd of almost two thousand cattle. These cattle had been rounded up that morning and now waited for sorting, branding, and castrating as appropriate. Two cowboys, going in opposite directions, rode around the herd, keeping it in a compact circle while the crew changed horses.

Silas Pollock was roundup captain that year. The well-respected cowman had worked his way up to become foreman of the VVN outfit, one of the largest ranches in the Park. Long after the roundup, Harry remembered that Pollock was a man who displayed plenty of humor and was a good conversationalist on topics of the day but silent about his own affairs.

Pollock had the rare ability to "take the conceit out of the young cowboys and quiet the strife and trying moments of the older ones" with his good judgment and quick humor. As Harry rode into camp, he quickly realized he was in for a siege of quick humor, much to his discomfort.

The captain took one look at Harry and asked, "Where are you going with those burros, prospecting?" Harry was crestfallen, for the captain implied that his horses looked like burros and he looked like a prospector. Yet his hopes rose when the captain asked if he was any relation to William Epperson, a VVN ranch hand for many years. Harry proudly answered yes, Epp was his older brother. Pollock looked off into the distance and drolled, "Like begets like, old Epp never was worth a darn and so you might as well go home."

Silence followed as young and old looked at each other. Then Pollock took the pipe from his mouth and said, "Wait a minute. There are five wagons down there." He pointed his pipe at one that Harry was to use; it had the VVN brand painted on the canvas top.

As Harry started off, the captain renamed him "Little Epp," a name that stuck through many roundups. Pollock also delivered a word of warning, explaining that he had just picked up the cook from the Pueblo insane asylum and that the poor man was not playing with a full deck. Don't ever lie to him, admonished the captain. "Why," he said, "there was a man this morning told him he wasn't hungry and then ate all of the potatoes, and the cook took a butcher knife and cut his throat."

Little Epp rode down to the man with the sharp knife and short temper. To his surprise, the cook was George Weller. "If there ever was a good-natured cook that enjoyed feeding hungry men," it was Weller. He worked as a ranch cook for many years in South Park, then moved to Montana. Weller cheerfully gave Little Epp a late dinner, complete with blueberry pie.

As Little Epp ate his dinner, Weller became both nurse and doctor. Nest Giraud had been chasing a horse that had broken away from the remuda. Just as he was about to turn the horse back, his horse found a badger hole and turned end over end. The horse scrambled up and started off, keeping its head to one side to avoid stepping on the reins. But Giraud didn't get up, and he appeared to be another cowboy Little Epp's mother could add to her list of roundup casualties. Several men ran to the fallen rider and one yelled back, "He's all right, his heart is beating." They hauled him back to camp.

It was now up to Weller to keep Giraud's heart beating. As the cook worked on the cowboy, who showed signs of stirring, Pollock rode up. He quickly dismounted and then started rummaging around the camp, looking under everything.

"What are you looking for?" asked Weller.

"I'm looking for my gun. I guess Nest Giraud will never be any good any more, so I might as well shoot him."

Little Epp's account of the roundup didn't mention any

funerals, so it's safe to assume that Pollock didn't find his gun and that Giraud made a complete recovery.

Although the VVN foreman was roundup captain, Little Epp found that Pollock's authority ended about fifty feet from the chuck wagon, where the cook reigned as monarch and his word was law. This arrangement worked well, for the chuck wagon formed the social hub of the roundup where the men found bed and board, a change of clothes, care for the sick, and a place to talk, sing, and smoke with friends. But as reigning monarch, Weller did not allow any gambling within his domain.

Some South Park cooks were professional gamblers wearing aprons as a disguise. As soon as a gambler-cook had all the money in camp, sometimes as much as two thousand dollars, he quickly left. Others stayed on, insisting that they were cooks first and gambled only to keep the cowboys company. On a later roundup, Little Epp remembered one such cook who quietly sat around the campfire playing poker when the stakes weren't too high. Once the money in the pot got interesting, the cook became concerned about his biscuits. Just at the right time, he left to look into his pots. The cook had a winning hand every time he returned from one of his biscuit trips. After a few nights, a cowboy was assigned to keep an eye on the biscuits and the cook lost his monopoly on winning the large pots.

Little Epp didn't miss gambling during his first roundup. He had no money to lose and little knowledge of how to keep it in a card game. Best of all, he could roll into his blankets whenever he had a chance and sleep without the disturbing remarks of "I'll raise you another bat hide," or "Seven come eleven, the baby needs shoes."

Weller had other rules. He didn't like the men to arrive late for breakfast, and he didn't have time to kick them out of their blankets. So every night he wound and set a large alarm clock and inverted a tin bucket over the timepiece. The reverberating noise woke half of South Park.

Much to the disgust of the cowboys, it was a matter of pride among roundup cooks to serve breakfast early. Whenever there was more than one outfit in the roundup, breakfast competition among the cooks was sure to arise. Several years after his first roundup, Little Epp recalled one such event where Forrest Dill, cook for the VVN outfit, decided that he had to outdo Goody, cook for the IM outfit. Early one morning, Dill "had twenty-five of us cowhands seated in a circle, all of us trying to guide the food to our mouths with the aid of a lone candle placed in the neck of a beer bottle."

Just as they got started, the cook from the IM wagon cannoned into camp, waving a long steak knife and shouting that he was "tired of this dirty competition and was going to quarter Dill and throw him to the dogs." Dill calmly picked up his rifle and told Goody that he had five seconds to get back to his own wagon. After a few more threats, the irate cook left. Little Epp and the rest of the VVN roundup crew then silently sat by the cook wagon for the next two hours, waiting for daylight. But on Little Epp's first roundup, there was only one outfit and one cook, so the men enjoyed a civilized breakfast at daybreak.

During Little Epp's second day at the roundup, Pollock ordered the men to cut Epperson's cattle out of the day herd and brand them. The young cowboy, determined to show his prowess as a cowhand, roped one of his big steers that was milling at the edge of the day herd. Just as the rope settled around its head, the steer headed for open country. When the burly beast hit the end of the rope, Little Epp's small horse wasn't able to hold it. Both horse and rider flew into the air. "When my little horse came down, he came down as a cat, about thirty feet from where he had gone up," remembered the young cowboy. The steer made another run and this time the horse was jerked from under Little Epp. Standing, Epperson watched the war. The steer ran first one way and then another. Each time it came to the end of the rope, the little horse was propelled into the air. But the horse knew what he was doing, for he kept his head pointed at the steer and finally threw the critter. Some of the men immediately jumped on the animal and hog-tied it for branding.

When the dust settled, Pollock ambled up and peevishly stated that he gave the orders when he wanted cattle roped. Then he assumed his droll manner and said, "We only put on shows on Sundays and holidays." Yet Little Epp had some consolation; all of the men agreed that his pony was the best little roping horse they had ever seen.

After a week, it was time for Little Epp to leave the roundup. It was customary for outfits to charge a dollar a day for food, so Little Epp went to Pollock to pay his bill. Much to his surprise, Pollock had doubled the price and Little Epp didn't have enough money. He promised to send the rest, but the captain refused to accept credit. Instead, Pollock said he would take Little Epp's saddle as payment. The young cowboy thought he was serious and pleaded with the unreasonable boss. Finally, Pollock agreed to consider the debt paid in full if the youngster would write his name in the captain's roundup book and promise never to return to another roundup.

Two years later Little Epp arrived at another roundup. He unpacked his bed by the IM wagon just as Pollock rode by. With some effort, the captain promptly picked up Little Epp's blankets and rode off as the confused cowboy followed. He threw the blankets next to the VVN wagon, making it clear that his friend wasn't going to stay with another outfit. Then he added, "That IM outfit has ruined more young fellows than any other cow outfit in Colorado. Take a dumb kid like you, and in thirty days you'd be a red-flagger with no other future than looking for sundown and pay day."

Using his own brand of humor that often disguised his caring nature, Silas Pollock took care of his friends, both young and old. Little Epp never forgot that cowman who later became county sheriff, and he never forgot his first roundup in South Park.

42
Backfire

Mr. Tom Borden . . . states that nothing has as yet developed to throw light upon the mysterious disappearance of his neighbor, Mr. Fluhmann. It has been found that a surveying instrument belonging to the latter is gone, so that there is a bare possibility that he has gone off to some of the new camps with it.

Fairplay Flume, January 12, 1893

The carefully laid plans of Gottlieb Fluhmann, a small-time rancher in South Park, backfired. Born in Switzerland, Fluhmann came to the United States in the 1860s and eventually made his way to South Park. Although he was an expert gunsmith, a carpenter of merit, a surveyor, and casual prospector, he preferred the occupation of a rancher.

In the early 1880s, Fluhmann built a beautiful log cabin at the edge of a lush, spring-fed meadow near Tarryall Creek. The logs that formed the walls had been hewed squared and fitted to preclude the need for much chinking. Large windows, five in all, overlooked the surrounding meadows in all directions except the west. Four huge logs formed the ridge poles for the roof that ran at a low pitch. Inside, thick planks covered the floor and sanded boards lined the interior walls. Attention to detail was found everywhere, and perhaps best exemplified by the built-in cabinets and the molding around the plank ceiling. Sheds and corrals stood not far from the cabin, but Fluhmann's artisan touch did not extend to these purely functional structures.

Few visitors ever enjoyed the beauties of Fluhmann's cabin, for he was a suspicious, argumentative, and flighty old man with almost no friends and no relatives closer than St. Louis. The focus of his lonely life was a herd of about one hundred and fifty well-bred cattle that grazed the meadows and open ponderosa pine forests of his ranch. With his faithful dog, he carefully checked his cattle every day, armed with an 1886 model .38-caliber Marlin rifle strapped to his saddle and a .45-caliber pistol under his coat. Fluhmann was convinced that someone was stealing his beloved cattle, but he was at a loss to stop the rustling.

It was probably sometime in 1892 that Fluhmann came up with a plan to trap the rustlers. Less than a mile southwest of his cabin stood an immense rock outcrop that towered above his small ranch. Fluhmann climbed the rock face of the outcrop and eventually found a small cave near the north end and several hundred feet below the summit. Actually, it was more of a crevice than a cave. This crevice, almost twenty-five feet deep, was five feet wide at its mouth and narrowed as it extended back into the outcrop. The ceiling sloped gradually to the back of the crevice, but even at its highest point, Fluhmann, who was only five feet and four inches tall, was unable to stand fully upright.

The entrance to the crevice could not be seen unless an intruder negotiated a steep climb over solid rock to a sloping ledge about four-hundred feet above the valley floor. Even at that, a huge rock blocked the approach, and any intruder would be forced to crawl under the boulder to enter the crevice. Approach from any other direction was impossible. The entrance to the crevice faced east and gave Fluhmann an unobstructed view of his cabin and hay-covered meadows. It was just what the old rancher wanted.

Fluhmann built a snug hideout in the crevice. He hauled lumber up the outcrop and fit the boards carefully to make a floor, walls, and a ceiling. A small stove was placed in one corner; shelves and racks were installed along the walls. The front of the hideout supported a hinged door and a glass window that could be opened by sliding it to the left. The only comfort lacking was room. Fluhmann's hideout was barely fifteen feet long and six feet wide; the ceiling missed the floor by just five feet.

Yet the lack of room did not prevent Fluhmann from bringing most of his possessions from his spacious cabin into the cramped hideout. Rifles, reloading equipment, ammunition, rattraps, wood-working tools that included a fancy spirit level, a Dutch oven, a brown jug, dishes, food, a two-gallon crock, kerosene, bottles of wine, clothing, letters, and blankets survived the precarious trip up the rock outcrop.

The rancher organized his household goods with his usual attention to detail. He cleaned, oiled, and loaded his two double-barrel flintlock shotguns and suspended them from a ceiling beam. Fluhmann had made these gold inlaid guns; both were models of gunsmithing and his name was engraved on the barrels.

Into a large dishpan Fluhmann placed his Swiss passport and letters from relatives. One letter was from his niece, Alice, who lived in St. Louis. She had scrolled a poem that eulogized him and the mountains; then she inquired as to why he did not answer her letters. A State of Colorado notice that his payment of sixteen dollars for leased land was overdue, mining papers, a circular about land in Idaho, a thermometer from W. H. Schieffelin & Co., a .45-caliber pistol, and a pair of expensive smoking pipes completed the dishpan items. Fluhmann hoisted the pan to the ceiling and there suspended it by wire; he was determined that no rodents would get his treasures.

Finally, a brass surveyor's transit and tripod were placed directly in front of the sliding glass window. Following a few adjustments, Fluhmann had a clear, magnified view of his cabin, hayfields, and more importantly, his cattle. Now the only task was to deal with the rustlers once they showed up.

How long the old rancher waited is unknown. There was some concern about his absence and Tom Borden, a distant neighbor, thought that Fluhmann might have gone off to the new mining towns in South Park. His transit was missing, and Borden speculated that Fluhmann was surveying. As time went on, others occasionally asked questions about the peculiar rancher, but no trace of Fluhmann was found. In the spring of 1894, Henry Krebill was appointed administrator of Fluhmann's estate. He disposed of the cattle at $13.50 per head and sold Fluhmann's land.

South Park forgot about Fluhmann, until fifty-one years later. In the fall of 1944 a hiker on military leave decided to tackle the rock outcrop overlooking the remains of a long-forgotten cabin. He climbed a tall ponderosa pine, then scrambled over the massive rocks to the summit. Finding himself stranded, he started down the northeast face of the outcrop. Part way down he encountered a crevice, then noticed a window sitting upright in a frame. He slid the window to one side and peered into Fluhmann's hideout.

Subsequently, Sheriff Sylvester Law investigated the scene. Fluhmann's possessions were found undisturbed and in excellent condition. The old rancher's body was near the center of the hideout. Beside Fluhmann was his Marlin rifle, loaded and cocked, and the remains of his faithful dog.

The mystery of Fluhmann's disappearance was finally solved but not that of how he died. Fluhmann was more than fifty years old when he disappeared, and he may have simply died of natural causes while waiting for the rustlers. Suffocation from a fire in his small, tight hideout may have brought the end. Perhaps the lonely old rancher committed suicide.

Murder could not be ruled out, however. The rancher had exchanged angry words with others and was hunting rustlers; both situations could have led to a shooting. Supporting the murder theory was the ugly scar of a bullet that had plowed through the stock of Fluhmann's Marlin rifle. The bullet had entered high on one side of the stock and had continued across it and down at a forty-five-degree angle. According to Sheriff Law, "a right-handed man holding the gun in readiness or at his shoulder to fire would have been killed." Fluhmann was right-handed. In addition, he was an accomplished gunsmith, and it was likely that he would have repaired the stock had he been alive. Yet no attempt had been made to fix the hole.

If Fluhmann was murdered, who was responsible? Some blamed Benjamin Ratcliff who was executed in 1893 for the murder of three school board members. The *Rocky Mountain News* stated that Ratcliff tried to buy Fluhmann's cattle, but the two men had failed to agree on a price. "Ratcliff went away, but in a few days returned and was the last man seen with Fluhmann and the last man who saw Fluhmann." This was enough information to feed rumors. A story surfaced that Ratcliff enjoyed taunting the rancher about stealing his cattle and that the Ratcliff children had a habit of trespassing on Fluhmann's land. The old rancher finally drove the children off his land and sent a few bullets into the air as a reminder to stay out. Those who told the embellished story claimed that Benjamin Ratcliff then promised to kill the rancher at some convenient time. This threat drove Fluhmann into building the hideout; Ratcliff eventually found it and then shot the old man. The story was good, but there was no supporting evidence; additionally, more than fifteen miles of rugged mountains separated the two ranches, and it was unlikely that Fluhmann and Ratcliff had sufficient contact for a bloody feud.

So the mystery remains. Rustlers may have done the dastardly deed; but evidence is lacking. All that can be said is that Fluhmann built an elaborate hideout, and his plans to protect himself and his cattle from rustlers backfired.

43
South Park Races

Friday, the second day of the races, was set apart as Park County day, and drew the largest crowd, partly on this account, and more especially to witness the cowboy race.

Fairplay Flume, September 21, 1893

The South Park cowboys had raced ten years earlier, but that time they ran afoot. The race wasn't the cowboys' idea. The railroad crew working near the Slater Ranch came up with the scheme. With fall roundup in full swing, about fifty men were employed by the ranch located near Como. Roadmaster Bradley and his railroad cronies thought it would be a good idea to turn the roundup into a profit-making venture by promoting a footrace. A cowboy on the ground was about as fast as a fish out of water, so the railroad men were sure to win.

The railroaders boldly issued their challenge and named their runner, a railroad man named Lake. The cowboys immediately accepted the challenge and found a willing runner, a ranch hand "traveling under the euphonious title of Broncho Slush." Betting was heavy and soon one hundred and sixty dollars a side was up. At that point the cowboys ran out of cash, so they "offered to back their man with ponies, saddles, stock on the hoof, or any personal property they had." But the railroaders had reached their limit and declined the offer.

A distance of one hundred yards was marked off in the dust and the two runners lined up. At the sound of the starting gun both contestants bolted forward, but it wasn't much of a race. Broncho Slush, otherwise known as Pete Clark, easily won the race. "The railroad crowd took their chastisement meekly and returned to Como, wiser, if poorer, men."

On horse or afoot, cowboys knew how to win a race. So these men took note when the *Fairplay Flume* announced the fall races of 1893. Of particular interest was the cowboy race and its unusual rules as explained by the newspaper:

> Three mile cowboy race; each rider to have three horses, saddles and bridles to be changed at the end of each mile; first money $75, second money $25. Riders will be required to use regular cow outfits and will not be allowed to receive any assistance.

This race was scheduled as the fourth, and last, event for Friday, September 15. So the cowboys had to wait for the pony race, the quarter-mile horse race, and the half-mile trotting race before their event came up. Unfortunately, these races took longer than expected, so the cowboy race was rescheduled for the next day.

Saturday morning a large crowd arrived in Fairplay to witness the odd race. The weather was clear and warm, the track dry and dusty. The three entrants – John Rogers, Henry Pasco, and William Amalong – waited impatiently for the race to begin. At last, the starting shot rang out and the three cowboys disappeared down the track. The changeover at the end of the first mile apparently came off without a problem, for the newspaper made no mention of it. Not so at the end of the second mile where chaos reigned.

The third set of horses had been tied to a rail. When the cowboys arrived at full bore, the horses became excited. Pasco's and Amalong's third horses broke away from the rail. After a chase and with the help of a friend, Pasco finally caught his. Amalong was not so fortunate, and the cowboy never caught his horse. So he "removed his saddle, at once replaced it, and started on the third mile with the same horse." Roger had no trouble with his horse, so he was in the lead but not for long. His horse spotted greener pastures in the distance and took off in the wrong direction. By the time Rogers got the cayuse back on the track, Amalong had taken the lead. It was a scramble to the finish line, and Amalong came in first with Rogers second and Pasco bringing up the rear.

The judges went into a huddle and discussed every detail of the race. They concluded that Rogers was the only one who followed all the rules, and they awarded him first money of seventy-five dollars. Second money was divided evenly between Pasco and Amalong. The ruling seemed fair, and the crowd soon reassembled for the half-mile race.

But not all South Park horse races were fair, and a rancher by the name of William James George Hardy Epperson (Hardy for short) likely agreed. A few years after the cowboy race, Hardy decided to enter a horse named Little Henry in the Fourth of July races at Fairplay. Hardy's son was confused, for he knew that other horses, particularly Snip, could outrun Little Henry. His father merely said, "I never enter Snip in any of the races." Instead, Hardy fitted Snip with the oldest harness he could find and hitched her to the spring wagon. She couldn't pull a wagon worth a darn, but for some reason the rancher didn't care. After all, this horse was a family heirloom and had earned her right to go on outings. She also served as the family calendar and time was marked by her birth. When a question of age arose, Hardy might settle it by saying, "I know just how old that girl is, because Snip was seven years old when she was born."

A nag in an old harness, a slow race horse decked out in a new halter and blanket, and the Epperson family headed for the Fairplay races. Once at the racetrack, Hardy scrutinized the horses entered for the various events, selected one of the least challenging races, and entered Little Henry. Despite some overly enthusiastic girls throwing their hats at the horse and scaring it half to death, Little Henry won his race. So far events were running according to plan.

The Eppersons then went down to a cottonwood grove for their lunch. Just as they started eating, some city men appeared with handsful of cash and challenged Hardy to a rematch. The rancher looked at the men and their horse and then did something foolish. According to his son, "he bet them two hands full of money that his old work mare could beat anything they had. They took him up so quick it looked as though my dad was scared."

A starting line was scratched in the dust, the racing distance (usually one hundred yards) stepped off, and the finish line marked. One of the men agreed to start the horses, probably by waving his hat. The details completed, Hardy removed the worn harness from Snip. She perked up just a bit. When his older son climbed aboard the nag, she bowed her neck and started prancing. The city folks watched in amazement as Snip easily won the race. They paid up and joined the ranks of the railroad crew as "wiser, if poorer, men."

44
Last Meeting of the School Board

Ratcliff entered the building and engaged in a discussion with the board over school matters. The discussion was becoming very excited, when Ratcliff accused the members of the board of making slanderous statements concerning himself and his family.

Rocky Mountain News, May 7, 1895

Benjamin Ratcliff had problems with the school board, the only political organization in the settlement known as Bordenville. Located along Tarryall Creek, this small settlement consisted of a store, post office, school, blacksmith shop, sawmill, cemetery, and a few houses. Probably the least likely place for trouble in South Park, Bordenville became the scene of "one of the most sensational [events] that ever occurred in the county," according to the *Rocky Mountain News*.

Ratcliff owned a secluded ranch about seven miles from Bordenville. Considered wealthy by one newspaper and impoverished by another, the rancher had a sallow and care-worn face, prominent nose, and somewhat sunken eyes. His bushy hair and chest-length beard were white. He walked with stooped shoulders and a halting gait. Ratcliff was fifty-two years old at the time of the trouble, but he looked much older.

In his younger years, Ratcliff had fought in the Civil War. He took great pride in telling of his exploits as a Union soldier from Ohio. Following the war he had worked in Missouri as a special agent for the government. He and his wife, Elizabeth, arrived in South Park in about 1870, staked out a ranch in the scattered timber at the northern edge of the Park, and led a relatively secluded life. They had three children: a boy named Howel and two girls, Elizabeth and Lavinia. His wife died in 1882. She was "about forty years of age and a model wife and mother," according to the *Fairplay Flume*.

Without his wife, Ratcliff became eccentric, crotchety, and ill-tempered, according to some of his neighbors. A family friend, Susan Crockett, described Ratcliff as "somewhat peculiar in his nature, rather high tempered and set in his ways, but a moral man and a gentleman." The *Denver Republican* claimed that "in some circles he was termed cranky, but for all that, he was deemed to be honest and a good citizen of the community." He lived a quiet life with his family and took no interest in community affairs and politics, except the school board.

His interest in the school board was made even more unusual by the fact that his children did not attend school. "The school board gave Ratcliff notice that he must obey the law and send his children to school." Ratcliff refused. Now twenty years old and working at neighboring ranches, his son was obviously too old for school. Perhaps Ratcliff thought that his daughters – Elizabeth was seventeen and Lavinia fifteen – were needed at home. Apparently the school board disagreed.

Another argument centered around the proposed location of the school. Ratcliff didn't want the school built in Bordenville; he wanted it closer to his home. Ratcliff's neighbors supported this idea, but the log school was constructed at the Dunbar Ranch at Bordenville. The issue of free books for the school children also rankled the eccentric rancher. Apparently he did not think much of the idea of handing out books or giving anything away for that matter.

These matters were not considered serious by most citizens, but another issue developed into a deadly exchange. According to one newspaper, about a year earlier the "eldest girl [Elizabeth] was seen by a group of ranchmen driving near the house and they saw, or possibly imagined, certain things which reflected strongly upon the father." A rumor started circulating in South Park that "accused Ratcliff of incest with his daughter." The juicy gossip was embellished by the suggestion that Elizabeth was pregnant; people began "making a broad intimation as to the author of her ruin."

Susan Crockett, who had become "guardian" of the Ratcliff children, heard the rumor when she visited her former home in Jefferson. She traced the rumor back to the school board in general and one of its members, Lincoln McCurdy, in particular. Concerned, Mrs. Crockett rode to the Ratcliff ranch. "I visited the Ratcliff home and saw the girls, and I certainly found no evidence of the truth of the story," she explained during an interview with the *Rocky Mountain News*.

Mrs. Crockett returned to Denver, but she could not forget the sordid affair. She decided that "Mr. Ratcliff ought to know what was being said so that he could call the authors of the slander to account for it." So she wrote Ratcliff a letter giving all the details of the rumor. Although the story had been circulating freely in South Park for a year, this was apparently the first time the rancher had heard it. Ratcliff, a prideful man who took family matters very seriously, felt he and his daughter had been grievously wronged by the school board.

The school board consisted of prosperous ranchers considered to be the "best known and most highly respected citizens of the north end of the Park." McCurdy, still in his twenties, served as chairman; George Wyatt, about thirty-five, was the secretary; and Samuel Taylor, almost sixty, often spoke for the group.

On May 6, 1895, Ratcliff set out for Bordenville. This was the day of the annual school board election, and he knew that the three board members would be in the schoolhouse, supervising the voting. As usual, Ratcliff carried a gun. He had been robbed several times, so he wore his pistol conspicuously as a warning. But on this day he carried both a pistol and a Winchester repeating rifle.

He seemed to be in no hurry as he rode to Bordenville, and he even dismounted and spent time talking with men working on a ditch near the school. When one of the men asked him why he was armed with two guns, Ratcliff said that coyote scalps were worth money and that he wanted to be ready if he sighted one of the critters. The rancher seemed nervous and asked for the time more than once, the men later recalled. He acted as if an important event was going to happen and he didn't want to miss it. When 9:55 A.M. arrived, he immediately mounted his horse and rode to the school. He hitched the horse to a fence post near the school. It was now ten o'clock and the schoolhouse was open for the annual school board election. Still armed, Ratcliff walked in.

Ratcliff was not interested in voting but apparently had come to set the record straight with the school board and to demand an apology. He immediately broached the subject of the slanderous remarks and charged McCurdy with starting the rumor and the others of circulating it. The school board denied the accusation and the discussion soon became heated, with Taylor apparently taking his usual position of speaking for the board.

Taylor, with his hand in his pockets, started toward Ratcliff. The rancher knew that Taylor usually carried a gun in the pocket of his overalls, so he told Taylor to stop. The man kept coming, so Ratcliff fired a warning shot. The bullet penetrated the floor at Taylor's feet.

Wise men would have stopped the argument then and there, but wisdom was absent on that fateful day. The argument became more heated as shouting commenced across several rows of desks that separated the school board from Ratcliff. Taylor again started for Ratcliff. Convinced that Taylor was about to pull a gun, Ratcliff fired. The bullet hit Taylor in the face and killed him instantly.

What happened next is uncertain. Perhaps McCurdy and Wyatt attempted to assist Taylor or flee from the schoolhouse.

And perhaps, just for a moment, Ratcliff thought he was back in the Civil War and surrounded by enemies. He shot several times from the hip, and then the schoolhouse was quiet.

Fifteen minutes after he entered the school, Ratcliff left, closing the door on the carnage. Taylor and McCurdy lay dead and Wyatt was mortally wounded. Showing no sign of haste, Ratcliff mounted his horse and rode off.

When the hoofbeats faded, Wyatt crawled to the door, opened it, and waved his hat to attract the attention of passing men. One of the men immediately headed for Como to find Dr. Scott while the others made Wyatt comfortable. When the physician arrived there was nothing he could do. Wyatt made a "rather incoherent and disconnected" statement. He said that none of the school board members had been carrying guns and that no threatening gestures were made by the murdered men. No one had been drinking. None of the school board members had assaulted or attempted to assault Ratcliff. Shortly after giving the statement, the third and last member of the Park County school board died.

By this time Ratcliff had arrived in Como and surrendered to Deputy Sheriff Link. The deputy immediately hauled him to the Fairplay jail. News of the killings spread quickly and reporters soon arrived at the Fairplay jail to interview Ratcliff. But he had little to say. He said that he had not gone to the schoolhouse with the intent of killing anyone but had intended to discuss the insulting rumor. Ratcliff freely admitted shooting the men but "felt that he was justified in doing so under the circumstances." He claimed that "it was not murder," and stated that he felt his life was threatened by the men on the school board.

Everyone in South Park called it murder, and lynching was in the wind. Knowing that the Fairplay jail had previously been breached by a determined mob, Sheriff Wilson decided to get Ratcliff out of town. Leaving quietly at midnight, the sheriff took Ratcliff to the Buena Vista jail.

The day after the shooting, South Park stood aghast at the horrible tragedy. "All day long there was a constant stream of all sorts of vehicles on all the roads leading to the scene of the tragedy." Two of the bodies were still in the schoolhouse. The curious peered through the broken windowpanes or the half-open door at the remains of "the most brutal and unprovoked murder ever known in Park County."

A coroner's jury was needed and a dozen men immediately volunteered to serve. The inquest quickly concluded that the three school board members died of "gunshot wounds from a gun in the hands of Benjamin Ratcliff and that the shooting was done with felonious intent."

Three funerals were held on May 9, 1895. It was one of the saddest days in South Park. Business was suspended as people came from every direction to attend the services. They formed the largest funeral procession ever seen in the county.

Meanwhile, Sheriff Wilson was still concerned about Ratcliff. Rumors circulated that a mob of one hundred men was trying to make up a train at Como for a visit to the Buena Vista jail. When Colorado Governor McIntire was wired, he replied that "for the sake of the state, keep Ratcliff for legal punishment." So Ratcliff was transferred to the Pueblo County Jail.

Reporters were waiting for the prisoner when he arrived in Pueblo. Their questions went unanswered. "I will tell my troubles to the judge myself," insisted Ratcliff. He did add that he felt justified in protecting his own life and "in preserving the honor" of his daughter. With obvious feeling, Ratcliff told one reporter: "I gave up part of my life in the service of my country and I am willing to give up the rest of it for my family."

Benjamin Ratcliff did just that, for he was convicted of murder and executed.

45
My Poor Harry

They peered thru the one small window. There, in semidarkness, stood Harry Beeler–hairy, filthy, a shadow in a shadow, except for the glistening white of his rolling eyes.

Denver Post, August 21, 1928

Harry Beeler was a South Park rustler, or at least some people thought so. The Beelers had arrived in Colorado in 1898 from Kansas. His father, who had been a banker until the bank failed during a financial panic, borrowed some money, bought a twelve-hundred acre ranch in South Park, and moved his family west. Harry was a teenager at the time and "wild to be a cowboy," said his mother; he "took to the life enthusiastically."

The Beelers prospered by combining ranching with a sawmill and post office. But prosperity did not last, and soon the Beelers were struggling to keep their ranch going. They began buying sick or lame cattle, grazing them in their pastures, and butchering the animals for the South Park market. But some cattle were butchered before anyone had gone through the formality of buying them; suspicion centered on Harry. Suspicion changed to "fact" when a neighboring rancher found one of his cows about a mile from the Beeler house. It had been recently butchered, and the tracks in the fresh snow led directly to the Beeler ranch.

During the winter of 1913, Harry was arrested and charged with rustling. After posting bond, he skipped town. That was his first mistake. Harry's second mistake was writing to his mother. Park County Sheriff Obe Spurlock had no difficulty tracing both the letter and Harry to Buffalo, New York. The alleged rustler was brought back to Fairplay and convicted on two counts of grand larceny. He was sentenced to three years in the state penitentiary and sent to Canon City in chains.

Harry was in the penitentiary only a short time when his parents received a letter from the warden stating that their son's mind had "given away" and he had been sent to the Pueblo insane asylum. No sooner had the Beelers received the letter than they hitched up their wagon, drove to Fairplay, and took the first train headed for Pueblo. "When we saw Harry in the asylum we were shocked," said his mother. "He looked awful. And they were treating him cruel. He recognized me the minute he saw me and began to cry." Anna Beeler blamed the prison for her son's insanity, but an uncle in Denver stated that Harry had been struck in the chin by a wagon wheel when he was young and had not been mentally right since.

A struggle with the authorities ensued. Determined to get their son back, the Beelers carried on a relentless campaign that led them to the highest offices in the state. In the fall of 1915 Governor Carlson finally ordered that Harry be turned over to his parents. Meantime, Harry's condition had gone from bad to worse. "We had a terrible time getting Harry home to the ranch," remembered his mother. "We saw that we had to watch him like a wild thing. Harry never recognized father. He'd shy away each time father came near. But he knew me."

The Beelers put Harry in a log cabin near the house. He was fed out of a pan like a kitten. Years later, Harry's mother told a reporter how hard it was to care for her son:

> I tried to take good care of Harry. Of course we couldn't

> wash him. We never dared free him from the chains. He couldn't figure out how to do it himself. At night I would slip out and cover him up and then I would get up early in the morning and remove the clothes before he awoke. He slept soundly and that was the only time he would tolerate anything on him.

The family struggled as the years passed. Eventually Harry's father died of a broken heart, according to his wife. Harry never knew of his death or that his sister, Buelah, had married and was living in Salida.

The neighbors knew for years that all was not right on the Beeler place. As they passed the ranch they often heard the sounds of clanking chains and occasional screams, shrieks, and moans from the building where they assumed Harry was confined. But Anna made sure that no one ever saw Harry, and the neighbors were inclined to mind their own business.

The situation changed when Buelah died in a Salida hospital. Just before her death, she begged the hospital authorities to check on her mother and brother in South Park. The sheriff was notified and together with four deputies, he drove to the Beeler ranch. There they found Anna on the porch of the ranch house. Ignoring both her objections and the dogs that went into a frenzy of barking, the officers hurried to a log cabin set back in the yard. They peered through the one small window and saw Harry, a naked, filthy man with glistening, rolling eyes. The men pried off the padlock on the door and stepped gingerly into the cabin. A *Denver Post* reporter described what happened:

> Beeler sprang at them with a cry that was more like a dog's bark than the utterance of a human's throat. But his spring was abruptly halted as the jingling chains went taut and jerked him off his feet. He got up, growling and grinding his teeth. Then the officers saw that he could move but three or four feet from the iron brackets in the log wall. A makeshift bed was within his reach. The cabin floor was deep in filth and debris.

The odor was sickening. Insects scurried and winged in all directions.

"He was so bad I couldn't get near him, to touch him," sobbed the old mother as she watched the sheriff and his men. "He hasn't had a bath in twelve years, since we got him back from the insane asylum. . . . I did the best I could." Seeing stark tragedy on the aged woman's face, Sheriff Richards nodded kindly.

The sheriff then maneuvered his men into position, and they rushed Harry from three sides. He fought like the caged tiger he was, yet gave up once he was handcuffed. A deputy threw a blanket around Harry as they led him to an automobile. They were forced to walk slowly, for "his legs were small and weak from his long confinement and were out of proportion of the rest of his healthy body."

"He hasn't had a stitch of clothes on him for twelve years," cried Harry's mother, bowing her head as her chin quivered. "But every night I went out, after he went to sleep, and threw a blanket over him." Anna fought to control her voice as tears welled in her eyes. "Only a mother could love Harry the way he is now, the way he has been for the last twelve years. I took the best care of him that I possibly could. . . . Harry is a good boy, Sheriff – and I love him!"

Sheriff Richards handled the difficult situation as best he could. Harry was taken to Fairplay and lodged in a cell. Anna was given a room at the New Fairplay Hotel. She wanted to cover her son with a blanket that night, but the deputies would not let her into the cell. So she stood outside his cell and soothingly called to him. "Harry, be quiet, son – now do as mother says!"

A sanity hearing was held two days later. Despite numerous interruptions by Anna as she attempted to defend her son, the court ruled that Harry Beeler was insane and committed him to the state hospital.

Anna was shattered and tearfully protested "against the cruel fate that was depriving her of her son after twelve years of heroism in caring for him," wrote the *Denver Post*. "They won't treat Harry right in the insane asylum," she told whoever would listen to her sobbing exclamations. "They won't feed him what he likes. They won't cover him at night." Fresh tears rolled down her wrinkled face.

But the court had decided what was best for Harry, and his mother's tears would not stand in the way. The next day when the deputies tried to dress Harry for the trip, he tore the denim overalls and shirt to shreds. He fought the deputies as they led him to the automobile but was soon under control when handcuffed. Seeing her son for the last time, Harry's mother threw up her arms in despair. "Goodby, son, they are taking you away from me," she cried as the car started forward.

"I'm all alone now," she sobbed to the curious crowd that had assembled to witness Harry's departure. "I'm going back to the ranch to die." The old broken-hearted mother was right, for Anna Beeler soon died at her lonely ranch.

Sources

Following are the complete bibliographical citations for the materials that formed the basis of this book. Throughout the preparation of this book, original sources of information, particularly newspapers, were used. However, reporters sometimes thought it necessary to embellish their stories. I have tried to eliminate such inaccuracies by comparing different accounts of the same event, such as court records with newspaper articles. Every effort has been made to eliminate embellishments and to present factual information.

Introduction

Bowles, Samuel, *The Switzerland of America*, Springfield, Mass.: Bowles & Co., 1869, pp. 67-69.

Chapter 1 – Peg-Leg Smith

Hobbs, James, *Wild Life in the Far West: Personal Adventures of a Border Mountain Man*, Hartford, Connecticut: Wiley, Waterman, & Eaton, 1875, pp. 46-59. Lavender, David, *Bent's Fort*, New York: Doubleday & Company, Inc., 1954, pp. 66-77. Lyman, George D., "The Scalpel Under Three Flags in California," *California Historical Society Quarterly*, Vol. IV, 1925, p. 157. "Peg Leg Smith – A Short Sketch of His Life," (San Francisco) *Daily Alta California*, March 8, 1858, p. 1, col. 3-4. "Sketches from the Life of Peg-leg Smith," *Hutchings' California Magazine*, Vol. V, October 1860, pp. 420-421. "The Siege of Fort Atkinson," *Harpers New Monthly Magazine*, Vol. 15, October 1857, pp. 638-648. "The Story of an Old Trapper," *San Francisco Bulletin*, Vol. XXIII, October 26, 1866, p. 1, col. 1-2. "Will Try Again to Find the Lost Pegleg Mine," *Denver Times*, February 5, 1904, p. 8, col. 1-5.

Chapter 2 – Massacre

Rocky Mountain News, July 9, 1870, p. 2, col. 1; July 19, 1870, p. 4, col. 3; August 15, 1870, p. 4, col. 1. (Laramie) *Daily Sentinel*, July 7, 1870, p. 3, col. 1; July 9, 1870, p. 3, col. 2. "Startling News from the North Park," *Rocky Mountain News*, July 8, 1870, p. 1, col. 3. "The Last Tragedy," *Rocky Mountain News*, July 10, 1870, p. 4, col. 3. "Ute or Arapahoe, the Official History of the Affair," *Rocky Mountain News*, August 9, 1870, p. 4, col. 2-3.

Chapter 3 – The Footrace

Cairns, Mary L., *Grand Lake: The Pioneers*, Frederick, Colorado: Renaissance Publishers, 1971, pp. 159-160. *Fairplay Flume*, July 5, 1883, p. 4, col. 3. "Georgetown," *Rocky Mountain News*, November 25, 1880, p. 3, col. 1. "Great Scores," *Rocky Mountain News*, June 5, 1882, p. 2, col. 4. "Idaho Springs," *Rocky Mountain News*, December 22, 1880, p. 3, col. 1. "Mountain Matters," *Rocky Mountain News*, May 24, 1882, p. 3, col. 1. "Mountain Men," *Rocky Mountain News*, January 25, 1882, p. 2, col. 3. *Rocky Mountain News*, April 24, 1882, p. 2, col. 3. Wolle, Muriel S., *Stampede to Timberline*, Denver: Sage Books, 1949, pp. 270-272.

Chapter 4 – A Pot of Tea

"Another Shooting Affair," (Teller) *North Park Miner*, August 9, 1883, p. 1, col. 5-6. *Grand Lake Prospector*, November 15, 1883, p. 3, col. 2. Gresham, Hazel, *North Park*, Cheyenne, Wyoming: Pioneer Printing, 1975, pp. 37-38. *North Park Miner*, August 30, 1883, p. 4, col. 2.

Chapter 5 – The Scoundrel

Grand Lake Prospector, December 23, 1882, p. 3, col. 2. Grand County Court House, Judge's Docket, August 1883. Grand County Court House, *Grand County Record*, "The People vs John W. Farquhar," August 21, 1882, p. 91. "He Bolted," *Grand Lake Prospector*, September 27, 1883, p. 3, col. 2. "If We Don't See You Any More, Hello!" (Teller) *North Park Miner*, November 8, 1883, p. 4, col. 1-2. *North Park Miner*, August 23, 1883, p. 4, col. 3. *Rocky Mountain News*, September 10, 1881, p. 7, col. 2. West, Elliot, *The Saloon on the Rocky Mountain Mining Frontier*, Lincoln: University of Nebraska Press, 1979, p. 12.

Chapter 6 – Mosquito Meals

"A Red Hot Welcome to Bill Nye," *Cheyenne Daily Leader*, May 12, 1876, p. 1. Nye, Bill, "Catching Mountain Trout at an Elevation of 8000 Feet," *Bill Nye and the Boomerang*, Chicago: Belford, Clarke, & Co., 1881, pp. 233-234. "Our Trip to Lost Lake," (Teller) *North Park Miner*, July 26, 1883, p. 4, col. 1.

Chapter 7 – The Newspaper War

"Fiendish Journalism," *Grand Lake Prospector*, November 18, 1882, p. 1, col. 5. *Grand Lake Prospector*, April 12, 1883, p. 2, col. 1; November 15, 1883, p. 3, col. 1; March 27, 1884, p. 2, col. 1. *North Park Miner*, July 26, 1883, p. 1, col. 2 and 5; August 2, 1883, p. 1, col. 2; August 23, 1883, p. 1, col. 4; August 30, 1883, p. 4, col. 2; September 6, 1883, p. 4, col. 3 and 4; September 13, 1883, p. 1, col. 3; September 20, 1883, p. 1, col. 3 and 6; October 25, 1883, p. 1, col. 3 and 5; November 1, 1883, p. 1, col. 3 and 4; November 8, 1883, p. 1, col. 6; November 22, 1883, p. 1, col. 3. (Teller) *Grand County Times*, May 12, 1881, p. 1.

Chapter 8 – Anything But School

Payne, Stephen, *Where the Rockies Ride Herd*, Denver: Sage Books, 1965, pp. 85-111. Payne, Stephen, "Recollections of North Park," *The 1967 Denver Westerners Brand Book*, Boulder, Colorado: Johnson Publishing Company, 1968, pp. 145-173.

Chapter 9 – Grandma Martin

Bailey, Adah B., *History of Jackson County, Colorado, Volume on North Park Church History*, Walden, Colorado: *Jackson County Star*, 1946, pp. 17-19, 62-73. Gresham, Hazel, *North Park*, Cheyenne, Wyoming: Pioneer Printing, 1975, pp. 68-72, 234, 250. Payne, Stephen, *Where the Rockies Ride Herd*, Denver: Sage Books, 1965, pp. 24, 45, 331.

Chapter 10 – Winter

Payne, Stephen, *Where the Rockies Ride Herd*, Denver: Sage Books, 1965, pp. 132-144, 326-353. "The Great Storm," *Fairplay Flume*, March 8, 1899, p. 4, col. 2. (Walden) *North Park Union*, January 27, 1899, p. 4, col. 1.

Chapter 11 – Woollies

"Again the Sheep Question," *Craig Courier*, August 17, 1895, p. 1, col. 2. "Another Fight Is Reported," *Denver Republican*, May 28, 1895, p. 1, col. 6-7. "Clash Between Sheep and Cattlemen," *Denver Times*, November 17, 1902, p. 9, col. 3. *North Park Union*, October 12, 1900, p. 4, col. 3. O'Neal, Bill, *Cattlemen vs Sheepherders*, Austin, Texas: Eakin Press, 1989, pp. 2-16, 35-42, 98. "Settlers Killing Sheep," *Denver Times*, October 25, 1900, p. 7, col. 1. "Sheep in California Park," *Craig Courier*, September 14, 1895, p. 4, col. 3. "Stockmen Buying," *Denver Times*, February 18, 1901, p. 11, col. 1. "The Routt County Sheep War," *Denver Republican*, May 30, 1895, p. 1, col. 5. Towne, Charles W., and Edward N. Wentworth, *Shepherd's Empire*, Norman: University of Oklahoma Press, 1945, pp. 182-203.

Chapter 12 – Rattlesnake Jack

"Annual Meeting of the North Park Stock Growers' Association," (Walden) *North Park Union*, March 9, 1900, p. 1, col. 2-3. Colorado Historical Society, newspaper clipping entitled "Famous Old Trapper Suicide," February 27, 1911, CWA Biographical Files. Condit, Thelma G., "The Hole-in-the-Wall, Part III–The Wolfers," *Annals of Wyoming*, October 1956, Vol. 28, p. 160. Gresham, Hazel, *North Park*, Cheyenne, Wyoming: Pioneer Printing, 1975, pp. 307-308. Harding, A. R., *Wolf and Coyote Trapping*, Columbus, Ohio: A. R. Harding Publishing Co., 1909, pp. 124-132. Payne, Stephen, *Where the Rockies Ride Herd*, Denver: Sage Books, 1965, pp. 309-316. (Walden) *North Park News*, January 6, 1899, p. 4, col. 1; January 13, 1899, p. 4, col. 4. (Walden) *North Park Union*, January 5, 1900, p. 1, col. 2; February 2, 1900, p. 4, col. 3.

Chapter 13 – Lead with the Mail

"A Sensational Shooting," (Walden) *North Park Union*, March 22, 1901, p. 1, col. 2-3. "Coroner's Inquest over the Body of John Price," *North Park Union*, March 29, 1901, p. 1, col. 2-4. "Death on the Divide," (Laramie) *Daily Boomerang*, March 21, 1901, p. 3, col. 3-5. Gresham, Hazel, *North Park*, Cheyenne, Wyoming: Pioneer Printing, 1975, pp. 203, 233.

Chapter 14 – Willow Creek Pass

Gresham, Hazel, *North Park*, Cheyenne, Wyoming,Pioneer Printing, 1975, pp. 222, 229, 296, 327-329. (Teller) *North Park Miner*, August 1, 1883, p. 1, col 3. Quinn, Elizabeth, "Perilous Adventure of a North Park Pioneer Woman, Mrs. L. A. Gresham," *Colorado Magazine*, July 1939, Vol. 16, pp. 143-144.

Chapter 15 – Rustler Arvean

Jackson County Court House, District Court Record, Case No. 187, June 1, 1926; Warrant, Complaint by Frank Coykendall against Arvean Marsh, November 2, 1925. Sarchet, Fancher, *Murder and Mirth: The Story of a Colorado Trial Lawyer*, Denver: Sage Books, 1956, pp. 49-50, 157-160.

Chapter 16 – Standing Bear

"A Haunted Lake," *Rocky Mountain News*, July 9, 1883, p. 4, col. 3. Harmon, E. M., "The Story of the Indian Fort near Granby, Colorado," *Colorado Magazine*, July 1945, pp. 167-171. Marsh, Charles S., *People of the Shining Mountains,* Boulder, Colorado: Pruett Publishing Company, 1982, pp. 143-148, 181. McQueary, Lela, *Widening Trails*, Denver: The World Press. Inc., 1962, pp. 4-11. Pettit, Jan, *Utes, The Mountain People*, Boulder, Colorado: Johnson Books, 1990, pp. 4-15. "The Legend of Grand Lake," *Grand Lake Prospector*, August 22, 1885, p. 1, col. 4-7. Wier, James, "Tales of Indian Forts and Fights," *Grand County Historical Association Journal*, June 1987, Vol. 7, pp. 82-88.

Chapter 17 – Expeditions

Brackett, William S., "Bonneville and Bridger," *Contributions to the Historical Society of Montana*, 1900, Vol. 3, pp. 175-200. Bradley, Lieut. James H., "Sir George Gore's Expedition (1854-1856)," *Contributions to the Historical Society of Montana*, 1923, Vol. 9, pp. 246-251. Byers, William N., *Encyclopedia of Biography of Colorado*, Vol. 1, Chicago: Century Publishing and Engraving Company, 1901, pp. 26-27. (Columbus) *Daily Ohio State Journal*, June 20, 1854, p. 2, col. 3. "Crossing the Range," *Rocky Mountain News*, August 30, 1874, p. 2, col. 2-3. Dodge, Grenville M., *Biographical Sketch of James Bridger*, New York: Unz & Company, 1905, pp. 24-25. Heldt, F. George, "Sir George Gore's Expedition," *Contributions to the Historical Society of Montana*, 1876, Vol. 1, pp. 144-148. "Middle Park Road," *Rocky Mountain News*, May 3, 1861, p. 2, col. 1. "Report of the Recent Explorations for a Road over the Snowy Range, at the Head of Vasquez River," *Rocky Mountain News*, June 4, 1861, p. 2, col. 4-5; May 8, 1861, p. 2, col. 1; May 9, 1861, p. 3, col. 1; August 21, 1866, p. 4, col. 1. "The C. O. C. & P. P. Express Company's Road Expedition," *Rocky Mountain News,* September 19, 1861, p. 2, col. 1. "The Overland Expedition," *Rocky Mountain News,* July 17, 1861, p. 2, col. 4. "The Overland Exploring Expedition," *Rocky Mountain News*, August 10, 1861, p. 2, col. 2. "The Salt Lake Expedition," *Rocky Mountain News* (weekly), September 18, 1861, p. 2, col. 2. Stansbury, Howard, *An Expedition to the Valley of the Great Salt Lake of Utah*, Philadelphia: Lippincott, Grambo & Co., 1852, p. 74.

Chapter 18 – The Utes of Middle Park

Black, R. C., III, *Island in the Rockies*, Boulder, Colorado: Pruett Publishing Company, 1969, pp. 43-47, 121-123, 129-131. Bowles, Samuel, *The Switzerland of America: A Summer Vacation in the Parks and Mountains of Colorado*, Springfield, Massachusetts.: Samuel Bowles & Co., 1869, pp. 69-79. (Central City) *Daily Miner's Register*, August 8, 1865, p. 3, col. 3. Clough, M. L., "The Parks of Colorado, Visit to Middle Park," *Ladies' Repository*, Vol. 30, May 1870, pp.

373-377. Hampton, H. D. (editor), "With Grinnell in North Park," *Colorado Magazine*, Fall 1971, Vol. 48, p. 291. Miller, Jean, "Buckskin and Berries, Tipis and Tomahawks," *Grand County Historical Association Journal*, June 1987, Vol. 7, pp. 13-35. "The Powell Expedition," *Rocky Mountain News*, August 20, 1868, p. 1, col. 2. Thompson, James. G., "A Big Injun Pow-Wow," *The Frontier, A Magazine of the West*, February 1906, Vol. 4, pp. 12-13. Wier, James, "Ute-White Relationships in Middle Park, Governmental and Semi-Official," *Grand County Historical Association Journal*, June 1987, Vol. 7, p. 73.

Chapter 19 – Damn Bruin

Bird, Isabella I., *Life in the Rocky Mountains,* New York: G. P. Putnam's Sons, 1886, pp. 90-104. (Central City) *Caribou Post*, August 12, 1871, p. 2, col. 2. *Daily Central City Register*, August 5, 1871, p. 6, col. 2. (Denver) *Field and Farm*, May 1, 1891, p. 6, col. 2. *Rocky Mountain News*, July 11, 1871, p. 1, col. 3-4; August 5, 1871, p. 1, col. 4; March 12, 1874, p. 4, col. 1; September 15, 1874, p. 4, col. 2. Tice, John H., *Over the Plains, on the Mountains; or, Kansas, Colorado, and the Rocky Mountains*, St. Louis: Industrial Age Printing Co., 1872, pp. 214-215.

Chapter 20 – Maggie and Jimmy

"Grand County," *Rocky Mountain News,* February 21, 1874, p. 2, col. 2. *Harper's Weekly*, September 3, 1887, p. 635, col. 3. "Notes from Middle Park," *Rocky Mountain News*, July 27, 1875, p. 4, col. 3. Pritchett, Lulita Crawford, *Maggie by My Side*, Grand County Historical Association, Hot Sulphur Springs, Colorado, 1983, pp. 1-43. *Rocky Mountain News*, January 27, 1866, p. 2, col. 2; July 25, 1869, p. 4, col. 2; January 17, 1875, p. 2, col. 7; July 19, 1876, p. 4, col. 1. "Save the Settlers," *Rocky Mountain News*, May 9, 1883, p. 1, col. 3.

Chapter 21 – The Great Fishing Caper

Grand Lake Prospector, July 12, 1883, p. 3, col. 1-2. Hale, Irving, "A Tramp Through Middle Park," *Sons of Colorado*, July 1906, Vol. 1, No. 3, pp. 30-35; September 1906, Vol. 1, No. 4, pp. 3-10. *Rocky Mountain News*, April 15, 1880, p. 8, col. 1.

Chapter 22 – The Buffalo Soldier

Davis, Theodore R., "A Summer on the Plains," *Harper's New Monthly Magazine*, February 1868, Vol. 36, p. 305. Dawson, Thomas F. and F. J. V. Skiff, *The Ute War*, Denver: Tribune Publishing House, 1879, pp. 8-14, 26-47. Dodge, F. S., *Report to the Assistant Adjunct General, Department of the Missouri*, Fort Leavenworth, Kansas, October 27, 1879, Colorado Historical Society. Grand County Court House, *Grand County Record,* Book 19, p. 59, and Book 17, p. 27. Mayhouffer, David, Parshall, Colorado, Interview, May 20, 1994. Meeker, N. C., Letters to L. A. Hayt, Commissioner, Washington, D. C., and Governor Pitkin, Denver, Colorado, September 10, 1879, Colorado Historical Society. Miller, Jean, "A Way of Life," *Grand County Historical Association Journal*, February 1985, Vol. 5, p. 61. Pharo, Glenn, Granby, Colorado, Interview, May 20, 1994. "The Indians," (Central City) *Daily Register-Call*, October 3, 1879, p. 4, col. 2-4. "The Indians," *Daily Register-Call*, October 4, 1879, p. 4, col. 2-3; October 7, 1879, p. 4, col. 2-3. "The Milk Creek Massacre," *Rocky Mountain News*, October 2, 1879, p. 4, col. 3-6. "The Red Devils," *Daily Register-Call*, October 8, 1879, p. 4, col. 2-3. "The Savage Scourge," *Rocky Mountain News,* October 3, 1879, p. 4, col. 3. "They Fought Nobly," *Rocky Mountain News*, October 22, 1879, p. 8, col. 5. Wood, Allyn H., Kremmling, Colorado, Interview, May 20, 1994.

Chapter 23 – Waldron Walks

Black, Robert C., *Island in the Rockies,* Boulder, Colorado: Pruett Publishing Co., 1969, p. 157. Cairns, Mary L., *Grand Lake: The Pioneers*, Frederick Colorado: Renaissance House Publishers, 1971, pp. 107, 109-113. *Grand Lake Prospector*, December 23, 1882, p. 3, col. 1; September 27, 1883, p. 2, col. 2. Hale, General Irving, "A Tramp Through Middle Park," *Sons of Colorado*, September 1906, Vol. 1, No. 4, p. 7. (Teller) *North Park Miner*, September 27, 1883, p. 4, col. 2-3. "Walden [sic] Gets Tired Loafing Around Grand Lake, So He Gets up and Walks Off," *North Park Miner*, September 20, 1883, p. 4, col. 5-6.

Chapter 24 – County Cauldron

"An Episode," *Grand Lake Prospector*, July 12, 1883, p. 2, col. 4. Black, Robert C., *Island in the Rockies*, Boulder, Colorado: Pruett Publishing Co., 1969, pp. 167-234. "Bullets and Blood," Rocky Mountain News, July 6, 1883, p. 1, col. 1-7. "Grand County's Gore," (Georgetown) *Colorado Miner*, July 7, 1883, p. 2, col. 2. "Grand Lake Butchery," *Denver Republican*, July 9, 1883, p. 1, col. 2-3. *Grand Lake Prospector*, July 12, 1883, p. 2, col. 3. "Grand Lake Vendetta," *Denver Republican*, July 8, 1883, p. 1, col. 2-3. "In Justice of Royer," *Colorado Miner*, July 28, 1883, p. 2, col. 3. "Mad Murderers," *Rocky Mountain News*, July 7, 1883, p. 1, col. 1-5. "Middle Park," *Colorado Miner*, May 7, 1881, p. 3, col. 6. "More Blood," *Colorado Miner*, July 21, 1883, p. 2, col. 2-3. "Murdered by a Mob," *Rocky Mountain News*, July 5, 1883, p. 1, col. 1-3. "Our Grand County Letter," *Colorado Miner*, September 15, 1883, p. 2, col. 3. "Painful Suspense," *Denver Republican*, July 6, 1883, p. 1, col. 1-6. Pauly, Nell, *Ghosts of the Shootin'*, Published by Nell Pauly, 1961, p. 167. "Redmon's [sic] Death," *Colorado Miner*, October 6, 1883, p. 3, col. 8. *Rocky Mountain News*, November 16, 1883, p. 4, col. 1. "The Grand County Horror," *Grand Lake Prospector*, July 12, 1883, p. 3, col. 3-4. "The Wars of the Roses," *Colorado Miner*, July 14, 1883, p. 3, col. 7-8.

Chapter 25 – Texas Charlie

Byers, Frank S.; David Gardner, John Gardner, Calvin Kinney, George C. Lee, E. Marker, Walker McQueary, W. L. Pattison, M. Smith and W. L. Veatch, Proceedings, Coroner's Inquest, December 9, 1884, Grand County Historical Society, Hot Sulphur Springs, Colorado. "Died with His Boots On," *Georgetown Courier*, December 18, 1884, p. 2, col. 2-3. Grand County Court House, 1886 *Deed Book*, p. 77, Hot Sulphur Springs, Colorado. "Texas Charlie, the Terror of Middle Park, Dies in Broad Daylight with His Boots On," *Rocky Mountain News*, December 14, 1884, p. 6, col. 2. *Wilson, Charles W., papers taken from his remains*, Grand County Historical Society, Hot Sulphur Springs, Colorado.

Chapter 26 – A Year with Mary

Cozens, Mary Elizabeth, Diary, September 25, 1887 to July 16, 1888, Cozens Ranch House, Grand County Historical Association, Fraser, Colorado. "Dropped Dead," *Denver Republican*, May 6, 1888, p. 1, col. 4. "Miss Mary Cozens," *Middle Park Times*, December 13, 1928, p. 12, col. 3. Murray, Bernard J., "An Historical Account of the Cozens Family and the Relations Between the Cozens Family and Regis," Regis Jesuit History Library, Denver, 1953, pp. 1-6. Reich, Alice and Thomas J. Steele, *Fraser Haps and Mishaps, the Diary of Mary E. Cozens*, Denver: Regis College Press, 1990, pp. 25-77.

Chapter 27 – Chew Pie, the Avenger

Black, Robert, *Island in the Rockies,* Boulder, Colorado: Pruett Publishing Co., 1969, pp. 158, 159, 366. Cairns, Mary L., *Grand Lake: The Pioneers*, Frederick, Colorado: Renaissance House Publishers, pp. 109, 182, 281, 297. "Dramatic Entertainment," *Grand Lake Prospector,* March 27, 1884, p. 2, col. 4. "Dramatic Society," *Grand Lake Prospector*, November 18, 1882, p. 2, col. 2. *Grand Lake Prospector*, January 18, 1883, p. 3, col. 2. Lower, Charence L., "Jack Pettingell's Star Appearance, a True Story," *Sons of Colorado*, September 1907, Vol. 2, pp. 10-13. Pauly, Nell, *Ghosts of the Shootin',* Published by Nell Pauly, 1961, p. 88.

Chapter 28 – The Old Sheriff

"Arrested for Cattle Stealing," (Central City) *Tri-Weekly Miner's Register*, August 18, 1862, p. 3, col. 1. (Central City) *Daily Miner's Register*, August 8, 1865, p. 3, col. 1. (Central City) *Weekly Register Call,* July 4, 1913, p. 5, col. 4-6. *Daily Central City Register*, September 5, 1869, p. 1, col. 2. *Field and Farm*, August 19, 1893, p. 6, col. 1. Grand County Court House Civil Docket, Richard McQuary vs. Frank Vulgamott, June 23, 1898, p 21. Hall, Frank, "How Sheriff Cozens Maintained the Law," *Denver Post*, February 2, 1900, p. 17, col. 1-3. Hanchett, Lafayette, *The Old Sheriff and Other True Tales*, New York: Margent Press, 1937, pp. 1-32. Murray, Bernard J., "An Historical Account of the Cozens Family and the Relations Between the Cozens Family and Regis," Regis Jesuit History Library, Denver, 1953, pp. 1-6. Reich, Alice, and Thomas J. Steele, *Fraser Haps and Mishaps, the Diary of Mary E.* Cozens, Denver: Regis College Press, 1990, pp. 25-77. *Rocky Mountain News*, March 8, 1867, p. 4, col. 1. Strum, Mayme G., "Mary York (Cozens), Pioneer Woman in Gregory Diggings," *Colorado Magazine*, May 1945, pp. 107-113. "The Law Vindicated," *Miner's Register*, December 22, 1863, p. 2, col. 1. "The Middle Park," (Georgetown) *Colorado Miner*, September 8, 1877, p. 3, col. 4. "The Old Building Was Erected in 1862," *Denver Times*, February 25, 1900, p. 19, col. 2.

Chapter 29 – Doc Susie

Bollinger, Edward T., *Rails that Climb*, Santa Fe: Rydal Press, 1950, pp. 297-305. "Death Comes to 'Doc Susie,'" *Denver Post*, April 21, 1960, p. 29, col. 1-2. "Dr. Susan Anderson Is Fraser's Only Physician," *Rocky Mountain News*, December 14, 1951, p. 1, col. 1-5. Frank, Margery, "Doc Susie," *PIC Magazine*, May 11, 1943, pp. 42-44 (Grand County Historical Association Document File). "Fraser's Pioneer Doc Susie Dies at 90," *Rocky Mountain News*, April 21, 1960, p. 34, col. 1-4. (Hot Sulphur Springs) *Middle Park Times*, April 24, 1908, p. 4, col. 3. Kenney, Cale, "Dr. Susan Anderson," *Alpenglow*, December 1980, Vol. 3, pp. 51-55 (Grand County Historical Association Document File). McLain, Ruth G., "Little and Mighty," *Colorado Crosscut*, Arvada, Colorado: We Write of Colorado Publishers, 1975, pp. 7-8. Shikes, Robert H., *Rocky Mountain Medicine*, Boulder, Colorado: Johnson Books, 1986, p. 96.

Chapter 30 – Pipe Dreams

Almirall, Leon V., *From College to Cow Country*. Caldwell, Idaho: Caxton Press, 1956, pp. 17-381. Grand County Court House Miscellaneous Records, Book 46, p. 597; Warranty Deed Book 50, p. 9. (Hot Sulphur Springs) *Middle Park Times*, May 23, 1913, p. 1 col. 3.

Chapter 31 – Trappers' Reunion

Brewerton, G. D., A Ride with Kit Carson Through the Great Desert and the Rocky Mountains, *Harper's New Monthly Magazine*, Vol. VIII, August, 1853, pp. 307-345. Carter, Harvey L., *Dear Old Kit, The Historical Christopher Carson*, Norman: University of Oklahoma Press, 1968, pp. 53-58, 131-132, 179-187. *The Life and Times of Christopher Carson*, New York: Beadle and Adams Publishers, 1861, pp. 85-86. Grant, Blanche C., *Kit Carson's Own Story of His Life*, Taos, New Mexico, 1926, pp. 104-105. Peters, DeWitt C., *The Life and Adventures of Kit Carson*, New York: W. R. C. Clark & Co., 1859, pp. 389-399. Quaife, Milo M., *Kit Carson's Autobiography*, Chicago: R. R. Donnelley & Sons Co., 1935, pp. 146-147.

Chapter 32 – A Lesson in Claim Jumping

Byers, William N., *The Centennial State*, Published by William N. Byers, 1884, p. 24. Hedges, William H., "Buying and Jumping a Claim in Tarryall Gulch," *Colorado Magazine*, October 1952, Vol. 29, pp. 265-273. "History of the Tarryall Mines," (Tarryall) *Miner's Record*, July 27, 1861, p. 2, col. 1-2. Howbert, Irving, *Memories of a Lifetime in the Pike's Peak Region*, New York: G. P. Putman's Sons, 1925, pp. 21-26. *Inter-Ocean*, June 6, 1880, Vol. 1, p. 258. "Pioneers of Park," *Rocky Mountain News*, January 30, 1880, p. 5, col. 1-2. "The Mines, Big Pay on the Bayou Salade," *Rocky Mountain News* (Weekly), September 10, 1859, p. 2, col. 3.

Chapter 33 – Reign of Terror

"Beheading an Outlaw," *Rocky Mountain News*, January 22, 1884, p. 5, col. 1. "Chronicles of Frontier Days," *Inter-Ocean*, June 3, 1883, pp. 376-377. Dyer, J. L., *Snow-Shoe Itinerant*, Cincinnati: Cranston & Stowe, 1890, pp. 151-155. "Espinosa's Head Is Now Being Asked For," *Denver Times*, November 10, 1899, p. 1, col. 3. Hall, Frank, *History of the State of Colorado, Volume I*, Chicago: Blakely Printing Company, 1889, pp. 378-381. "He Killed Thirty-Two Men," *Denver Republican*, February 28, 1886, p. 9, col. 3-4. "Hope It Is True," *Rocky Mountain News*, May 21, 1863, p. 1, col. 1. "Killing of the Espinosas," *Denver Republican*, February 24, 1897, p. 8, col. 5-7. "Montgomery Correspondence," *Rocky Mountain News*, May 16, 1893, p. 2, col. 2. "More Espinosa History," *Rocky Mountain News*, March 28, 1894, p. 24, col. 2. *Rocky Mountain*

News, July 1, 1863, p. 2, col. 1. "Slayer of the Espinosas," *Rocky Mountain News*, March 10, 1897, p. 2, col. 2. "The Bloody Record," *Rocky Mountain News*, May 7, 1863, p. 1, col. 2. "The Murders in Park County," *Rocky Mountain News*, May 7, 1863, p. 2, col. 1-2. (Central City) *Tri-Weekly Miner's Register*, May 21, 1863, p. 3, col. 1.

Chapter 34 – Sojourners

"Cheap Washee," *Fairplay Flume*, September 28, 1882, p. 3, col. 4. "Chinese Cheap Labor," *Rocky Mountain News*, November 27, 1879, p. 8, col. 4. "Chinese vs. Whites," (Aspen) *Rocky Mountain Sun*, October 1, 1881, p. 4, col. 2. *Fairplay Flume*, April 10, 1879, p. 3, col. 1 and 2; December 4, 1879, p. 3, col. 2; April 6, 1882, p. 3, col. 1; September 28, 1882, p. 4, col. 4; October 5, 1882, p. 4, col. 3; September 27, 1883, p. 3, col. 4; February 12, 1885, p. 4, col. 1; February 23, 1888, p. 4, col. 3; March 29, 1888, p. 4, col. 3. Ourada, Patricia D., "The Chinese in Colorado," *Colorado Magazine*, October 1952, pp. 273-284. Rudolph, Gerald E., *The Chinese in Colorado*, 1869-1911, Thesis, University of Denver, 1964, pp. 46-76. "Social Pests," *Rocky Mountain News*, October 29, 1880, p. 8, col. 2-4. Storti, Craig, *Incident at Bitter Creek*, Ames: Iowa State University Press, 1991, pp. 3-7. "The Battle of Como," *Rocky Mountain News*, November 22, 1879, p. 5, col. 1-2. "The Chinese Conquest," *Rocky Mountain News*, November 25, 1879, p. 3, col. 3-4. "The Como War," *Fairplay Flume*, November 13, 1879, p. 2, col. 3-4.

Chapter 35 – Horrible Hoover

"A Warning That Was Heeded," *Fairplay Flume*, May 6, 1880, p. 3, col. 4. "Judge Lynch," *Rocky Mountain News*, April 29, 1880, p. 8, col. 3-4. "Horrible Homicide," *Fairplay Flume*, April 3, 1879, p. 2, col. 2-3. *Rocky Mountain News*, January 15, 1868, p. 4, col. 4; May 31, 1870, p. 4, col. 1. "Sentence and Execution," *Fairplay Flume*, April 29, 1880, p. 3, col. 2-4. "The Dance of Death," *Denver Republican*, April 29, 1880, p. 1, col. 1-2. "They Lacked Nerve," *Fairplay Flume*, May 6, 1880, p. 3, col. 3. Wallis, Mather C., "The Court That Never Adjourned," *Westerners Brand Book*, Boulder, Colorado: Johnson Printing Co., 1967, pp. 257-276. "Wind-up of the Murder Examinations," *Fairplay Flume*, April 10, 1879, p. 3, col. 3.

Chapter 36 – The American Game

Fairplay Flume, July 8, 1880, p. 3, col. 1; July 15, 1880, p. 3, col. 1; July 29, 1880, p. 1, col. 6. "How to Celebrate," *Fairplay Flume*, July 1, 1880, p. 2, col. 4. "The American Game," *Fairplay Flume*, July 8, 1880, p. 2, col. 3. Frommer, Harvey, *Primitive Baseball*, New York: Atheneum, 1988, pp. 61-67, 124-131.

Chapter 37 – The Lost Head

"Diving into the Past," *Fairplay Flume*, February 16, 1882, p. 2, col. 3. *Fairplay Flume*, February 23, 1882, p. 2, col. 3. "Guerrillas at Work," *Rocky Mountain News*, July 26, 1864, p. 2, col. 1. Hall, Frank, *History of the State of Colorado*, Chicago: Blakely Printing Co., 1889, pp. 313-317. Hill, Alice P., *Tales of the Colorado Pioneers*, Denver: Pierson & Gardner, 1884, pp. 169-173. "History of Reynolds' Rebel Band," *Rocky Mountain News*, August 13, 1864, p. 2, col. 2-3. "John Smith Redivivus," *Fairplay Flume*, February 23, 1882, p. 3, col. 4. "Letter from the Park," *Rocky Mountain News*, August 8, 1864, p. 2, col. 1-2. "More About the Raid," *Rocky Mountain News*, July 28, 1864, p. 2, col. 1-2. "The Guerillas," *Rocky Mountain News*, August 1, 1864, p. 2, col. 1-2. "The Guerillas," *Rocky Mountain News*, August 3, 1864, p. 2, col. 1. "The Guerillas," *Rocky Mountain News*, August 8, 1864, p. 2, col. 1. "The Guerilla Raid," *Rocky Mountain News*, July 17, 1864, p. 2, col. 1-3. "The Guerillas Routed," *Rocky Mountain News*, August 2, 1864, p. 2, col. 1. "The Reynolds Band," *Rocky Mountain News*, September 9, 1864, p. 2, col. 2.

Chapter 38 – Old Mose

"A Bear Story," *Canon City Times*, May 5, 1904, p. 1, col. 1. Bell, Jack, "Conquest of the King of Grizzlies," *Outdoor Magazine*, July 1904, pp. 409-417. Epperson, Harry A., *Colorado As I Saw It*, Kaysville, Utah: Inland Printing Co., 1943, pp. 26-29. Hubbard, W. P., *Notorious*

Grizzly Bears, Chicago: Swallow Press, 1960, pp. 114-119. Huntly, Paul L., "Old Mose," *Black Mountain Cowboys*, privately published, 1976, pp. 109-110. "Killing of Old Mose," *Denver Post*, May 15, 1904. "Old Mose at Last," *Canon City Record*, May 5, 1904, p. 1, col. 1-4. "Old Mose Dead," *Canon City Clipper*, May 3, 1904, p. 1, col. 3-6. Perkins, James E., *Old Mose*, Manitou Springs, Colorado: Herodotus Press, 1991, pp. 106. Pigg, Wharton, "My First Grizzly," *Outdoor Life*, April 1904, pp. 211-212. "The Fate of a Pioneer," *Fairplay Flume*, November 29, 1883, p. 4, col. 2. Tinsley, Henry G., "Grizzly Bear Lore," *Outdoor Magazine*, November 1902, pp. 154-162.

Chapter 39 – Downhillers

Dyer, John L., *Snow-Shoe Itinerant*, Cincinnati: Cranston & Stowe, 1890, pp. 144-145, 164-176. Fiester, Mark, *Blasted Beloved Breckenridge*, Boulder, Colorado: Pruett Publishing Co., 1973, p. 69. "From Blue River," *Rocky Mountain News,* March 21, 1860, p. 1, col. 2. Fuller, Z., "Rocky Mountain Snow-Shoeing," *Midland Monthly*, Vol. 9, March 1898, pp. 204-208. Gardiner, Charles F., *Doctor at Timberline*, Caldwell, Idaho: Caxton Printers, 1938, pp. 29-32. "Gunnison Miners Form a Snowshoe Club," *Denver Times*, March 11, 1901, p. 9, col. 2. Jebb, Mrs. John G., *A Strange Career, Life and Adventures of John Gladwyn Jebb*, Boston: Roberts Brothers, 1895, pp. 120-125. "San Juan Notes, How the Mails Are Carried over the Snowy Mountains," Rocky *Mountain News*, March 8, 1878, p. 4, col. 5. "Snow-Shoe Locomotion," *Fairplay Flume*, January 8, 1885, p. 1, col. 4. "Snow Shoe Races," *Denver Republican*, March 8, 1887, p. 1, col. 4.

Chapter 40 – In the Twinkling of an Eye

"A Calamity," *Rocky Mountain News*, January 11, 1893, p. 1, col. 7. "A Coal Mine Horror," *Denver Republican*, January 11, 1893, p. 1, col. 1-2. "Buried the Dead," *Rocky Mountain News*, January 15, 1893, p. 2, col. 7. "Buried Their Dead," *Denver Republican*, January 15, 1893, p. 2, col. 6-7. "Coal Dust and Gas," *Denver Republican*, January 20, 1893, p. 3, col. 6. "Como Mine Disaster," *Denver Republican*, January 12, 1893, p. 1, col. 1-2. "Conti Was at Fault," *Denver Republican*, January 14, 1893, p. 1, col. 6. "Destitute," *Rocky Mountain News*, January 13, 1893, p. 1, col. 1-2. *Fairplay Flume*, January 26, 1893, p. 4, col. 3. "Fixed the Blame," *Denver Republican*, January 13, 1893, p. 1, col. 3. "Most Horrible Disaster," *Fairplay Flume*, January 12, 1893, p. 4, col. 2. "The Horror," *Rocky Mountain News,* January 12, 1893, p. 1, col. 1-2. "The Verdict," *Rocky Mountain News*, January 14, 1893, p. 1, col. 1-2.

Chapter 41 – My First Roundup

Epperson, Harry A., *Colorado As I Saw It*, Kaysville, Utah: Inland Printing Co., 1943, pp. 63-73. Everett, George G., and Wendell F. Hutchinson, *Under the Angel of Shavano*, Denver, Colorado: Golden Bell Press, 1963, pp. 243-250. Witcher, James T., "The Cattle Business in Park County During My Lifetime," in *Cattle Cavalcade in Central Colorado*, edited by George G. Everett, Denver: Golden Bell Press, 1966, pp. 343-366.

Chapter 42 – Backfire

"Did He Murder Fluman?[sic]," *Rocky Mountain News*, May 14, 1895, p. 2, col. 3. *Fairplay Flume*, January 12, 1893, p. 4, col. 4; April 6, 1893, p. 4, col 2. "Old Mystery Nears Answer," *Colorado Springs Gazette*, November 2, 1944 (Denver Public Library, Western History Collection, Fluhmann Clipping File). "Puzzle Persists After 60 Years," *Gazette Telegraph*, February 25, 1973, p. 1B, col. 1-6.

Chapter 43 – South Park Races

Epperson, Harry A., *Colorado As I Saw It*, Kaysville, Utah: Inland Printing Co., 1944, pp. 12-13. *Fairplay Flume*, July 5, 1883, p. 4, col. 3; September 14, 1893, p. 4, col. 1. "South Park Track Fall Races," *Fairplay Flume*, September 7, 1893, p. 1, col. 3. "South Park Track Races," *Fairplay Flume*, September 21, 1893, p. 1, col. 3.

Chapter 44 – Last Meeting of the School Board

"Benjamin Radcliff's [sic] Terrible Crime," *Rocky Mountain News*, May 8, 1895, p. 1, col. 1-4. "Death of Mrs. Ratcliffe [sic]," *Fairplay Flume*, October 19, 1882, p. 4, col. 3. "He Shot Three Dead," *Denver Republican*, May 7, 1895, p. 1, col. 1-2. "Killed Three Men," *Rocky Mountain News*, May 7, 1895, p. 1, col. 1. "Ratcliffe [sic] Goes to Pueblo," *Denver Republican*, May 9, 1895, p. 1, col. 3-4. "Radcliff [sic] Removed," *Rocky Mountain News*, May 9, 1895, p. 1, col. 1-2. "Radcliff's [sic] Story," *Rocky Mountain News*, May 10, 1895, p. 1, col. 8. Tenth United States Census, 1880, Colorado Historical Society, Denver, p. 217. "The Park County Murders," *Denver Republican*, May 8, 1895, p. 1, col. 3-4.

Chapter 45 – My Poor Harry

"Apeman Is Calmed in Insane Hospital," *Denver Post*, August 22, 1928, p. 1, col. 8. "Chained Apeman Rescued from Cabin," *Denver Post*, August 21, 1928, p. 1, col. 7-8, p. 5, col. 1. Epperson, Harry A., *Colorado As I Saw It*, Kaysville, Utah: Inland Printing Co., 1943, pp. 105-113. *Fairplay Flume and Park County Bulletin*, October 24, 1913, p. 1, col. 3. "Mother Fears Apeman Will Die," *Denver Post*, August 22, 1928, p. 3, col. 1. "Mother of Apeman Tells Pitiful Story," *Denver Post*, August 21, 1928, p. 1, col. 7-8, p. 5, col. 2. *Park County Republican and Fairplay Flume*, August 24, 1928, p. 1, col. 2. "Seven Men Finally Conquer Wild Man of Black Mountain," *Rocky Mountain News*, August 22, 1928, p. 1, col. 1-3, p. 4, col. 5. "Worry over Arrest Wrecked Beeler's Mind, Says Ex-Sheriff," *Denver Post*, August 22, 1928, p. 3, col. 4-5.

Index

About the Author

Moving to a small town adjacent to South Park in the early 1980s, Dr. Richard C. Barth quickly gained an appreciation for the beauty and history of this mountain park. Following a two-year study of South Park history, he focused his attention on the historical characters that settled in Middle and North Parks. These characters formed the basis of this book.

Rick is an ecologist who teaches environmental science courses at Front Range Community College and Denver University. He has authored three technical books and numerous articles based on environmental research conducted in the United States and in third world countries. Rick and his family live in Bailey, Colorado, and operate a family ranch in Utah.

Dr. Richard C. Barth

Other Caxton Colorado Books

Books by Robert L. Brown

Colorado Ghost Towns Past and Present
ISBN 0-87004-218-1
$14.95

Central City and Gilpin County: Then and Now
ISBN 0-87004-363-3
$8.95

Jeep Trails to Colorado Ghost Towns
ISBN 0-87004-021-9
$10.95

Colorado on Foot
ISBN 0-87004-336-6
$10.95

Ghost Towns of the Colorado Rockies
ISBN 0-87004-342-0
$14.95

Uphill Both Ways: Hiking Colorado's High Country
ISBN 0-87004-249-1
$7.95

Telluride: From Pick to Powder
by Richard L. and Suzanne Fetter
ISBN 0-87004-265-3
$9.95

Blood at Sand Creek: The Massacre Revisited
by Bob Scott
ISBN 0-87004-361-7
$8.95

For a complete list of Caxton books
visit our Internet Website:
www.caxtonprinters.com

or request a free catalog from:

The Caxton Printers, Ltd.
312 Main Street
Caldwell, ID 83605

Telephone: 1-800-657-6465